Other Times, Other Places

Growing up in Peace and War

Other Times, Other Places

Growing up in Peace and War

TICIAN PAPACHRISTOU

The Troy Book Makers
Troy, New York
www.thetroybookmakers.com

Printed in the United States of America

ISBN: 978-1-61468-1373

For my Judy

FAREWELL

"**YOU HAVE TO** come over," my cousin Tsanos said calling from Athens.

"Your father is ill. It looks bad."

The doctors had diagnosed pancreatic cancer but my father had been told the pain was a symptom of infectious hepatitis. The doctors and Tsanos, himself a doctor in the Greek navy, had followed old custom keeping unwelcome truth from their patient. Niko, who always expected the worst in matters of human hygiene, had probably guessed that something more serious was eating at his innards but, again according to custom, chose to play along. It was a few days before Christmas, 1968. I packed hurriedly, kissed my wife and kids and took the next Olympic flight from JFK.

In those days my parents lived in a spacious rental apartment on Mavromataion Street overlooking Green Park, their ninth dwelling in a period of four decades. My mother's unmarried sister Margarete, my *Tante* Grete, had moved from Berlin to live with them after my grandmother Emma's death some years before. In a cozy, innocent *ménage a trois*, the two women doted over my father - ironing his shirts, cooking his favorite meals, calming his nerves. The year before, Niko and Lotte, my mother, had come to see us in New York, in what would be his only trip to America.

What with the cold February winds and our crowded apartment, the visit had not been a success. My father would stand morosely at the window dressed in his overcoat, looking at the gloomy brick houses across Ninth Street and its scraggly, leafless trees; city buses shook the floor as they passed by, spewing acrid air under leaden skies.

"Everything is so dark," he would say. "And all this brown brick."

"The city looks much better in the spring when everything turns green, Pappi," I countered, eager for him to embrace my adopted country. To make things worse he managed to contract pneumonia and to spend much of his stay in bed, wheezing, hacking, grumpy. I learned later that he had been consulting a doctor in Athens about some digestive discomfort and been following a dietary regimen. In a notebook I found among his papers was a record written in his meticulous architect's script listing each item of food he had been consuming each day for breakfast, lunch, dinner and in-between snacks. But weight was not his problem.

I found him lying under a tufted quilt looking gaunt and more frail than usual. Lotte and Grete, who knew, bustled about puffy eyed.

"I came to help you get well," I said with forced cheer. "These women must be getting on your nerves, ha, ha."

A thin smile parted his lips, his eyes shone with pleasure.

"Echis pachini ligho apo perisi," (you've gained some weight since last year) he whispered approvingly.

"And you look a little thinner," I replied. "We'll have to fix that."

"Sure we will. They've given me some cortisone, it feels better."

I told him every one was well at home and showed him a drawing the boys had made wishing him quick recovery.

"That's good. Can you do me a favor?"

"Of course Pappi."

"Rub my feet a little… they're so tired."

"Turn on the radio," he said the next day. "Papadopoulos is giving an important speech."

The year before, after Niko and Lotte had returned from New York, a group of junior officers had overthrown the elected government and set up the seven-year dictatorship known as the "Junta." In his speech that afternoon, Colonel Papadopoulos, the current top man, praised the military rule as necessary to thwart the enemies of the nation who were ready to hand the country over to godless international Communism. At the same time, he said, it was essential, given the recent decline in morals and public order, to impose on the citizenry certain disciplines of conduct required to run a civilized society and regain the glory that was Greece.

"Bravo," said Niko when Papadopoulos finished and the national anthem was playing. That was too much for me.

"Bravo?" I exclaimed. "How can you take this drivel seriously, Pappi? And from a second-rate dictator at that!"

"My boy, you've been away too long, you don't understand what's going on in this country. Those dreadful people – Papandreou and his wise-ass son, those self proclaimed Socialists," the last word disgorged like some bad food, "they were ready to turn us over to the Bolsheviks." He paused to catch his breath. "If it were not for our army- these people you ridicule- the Russians would be here today turning our farms into cooperatives, opening tractor factories, forcing our children to learn their despicable language and salute the red flag. It would have been the triumph of the Kou-kou-eh that riff raff - you remember them – those mobs parading and screaming with their flags and banners right below the house, up and down Septemvriou, as far as the eye could see... Or have you forgotten?"

By then I was sorry to have provoked this tirade and upset him.

And yet... after all these years, I still could not reconcile this man – an intellectual, a cultured, humane, affectionate man – with one who repeatedly and enthusiastically approved of what to me now were noxious, even criminal views. But wait. While I was still living under his wing, hadn't I too embraced such crude expediencies? Hadn't I joined him in cheering the monarchists, the Fascists? Why, I even cheered Adolf Hitler in Berlin, one memorable morning when I was only eight years old. And hadn't I participated in one or two drills in the Marasleion schoolyard dressed in the bright blue uniform of EON, the Fascist organization that tried to ape the Hitler Youth? I still remember the ridiculous white spats we had to wear over our dusty shoes. On the other hand, sitting on the balcony after the noon heat had abated, or in the *saloni* in winter, our breaths before us, my father and I would converse congenially about any number of subjects for which he, an amateur polymath, had usually set the agenda. I say 'on the other hand,' because most of his interests, and there were many, seemed to discount, to deny, even contradict, his political values. Niko professed to believe in social responsibility; in justice, equality and order; in the peaceful pursuit of knowledge and beauty – noble words, part of today's liberal vocabulary. He admired the French Revolution with its calls for *Egalité* and *Fraternité*. In our bookshelves you could find works by the wise men of the Enlightenment – Montesquieu's *L'Esprit des Lois*, for example, Rousseau's *Contrat Social*. But then, significantly, Niko's approval came to include Napoleon, whose conversion from defender of Democracy to Roman style autocrat he not only accepted but admired and approved with enthusiasm. Books about the little Corsican's exploits in conquest and battle held a prominent position on our shelves. My father could recite the name of every one of Napoleon's generals. The Social Contract was, it seemed, less important.

Still, Niko did feel sympathy for the oppressed and I thought at times that he even saw himself as one of them, although he would never openly say so, being tacitly content with his social status. He could actually be described as a bit of a snob, an elitist. He disapproved of the commercial class and its behavior. Having to make money seemed demeaning – a distasteful necessity, not a primary goal. In later years, my mother complained. "He was above such things," she would say. "He was an artist, a brilliant man, a dreamer," ironically at first, almost sarcastically toward the end.

So, my father and I, his only child, would sit and talk. He was my teacher, and I loved him. After early childhood, my emotional and intellectual center shifted from my mother to him. Like a cat that worships the master who feeds it, I loved him in large part because I was the apple of his eye, because his full attention was trained on me and made me feel supremely important. And he fed me and cared for me and worried about me - in every possible way – sometimes too much. For a long time I thought that it was he, more than anyone else, who made me what I am today. So, after having had him impress on me, day after day, the wonder and beauty of life, the need to be curious, to value, to learn - how could I not, at least for a while, follow him without hesitation down the faulty path to his quick-fix ideologies, eschewing reasoned, consensual answers to maddeningly complex problems?

Outside, the weak December sun was setting behind the rooftops turning long winter shadows into early, cold darkness. Stretched out on the bed facing him, I was rubbing his feet while his mind was ruminating, recalling his youth. With effort, on the edge of delirium, words came slowly. We had been talking of his early days in Berlin before he met my mother.

"How glorious it was, how different from here," he said. "I just couldn't believe my good fortune. There I was, a young fellow from a Balkan backwater, one of a select group of international students in a world-famous institution of learning – the *Technische Hochschule*, Berlin! I had little money but I was so happy, so proud." He stopped, turned to me. "I'm so tired," he whispered, "don't stop, keep rubbing." His black eyes had brightened deep in their sockets. The large nose seemed more prominent under the high forehead. Strands of thin gray hair lay over a pale skull but his little mustache was still black. A wan smile came back. "How new it all was – people, buildings, nature, food, the weather – another world. I couldn't get enough of it." He reached for the glass of water. I held it for him while he took a few sips. "And of course I was very different for them too," he continued. "*Exotischer Juengling* your mother's boss would call me. Others, less friendly, would hiss "*Jude!*" as they passed me in the street. Still others would shout "*Zirkulieren!*" when they bumped into me as I walked on the left rather than the prescribed right side of a crowded sidewalk. Try that in *this* country." He hacked out a feeble laugh. "But the women my boy, the women! Friendlier, prettier than our breed here – and with a depleted male population, so forthcoming, especially to us exotic foreigners."

Again a memory lit up his face. "Listen to this Titsian. When I first came, I lived in a garret off Kurfuerstendamm, near the Zoo station. Other young people had rooms along the same corridor, among them an actress – she couldn't have been more than twenty-gorgeous figure, flashing green eyes, smiling at me as we passed on the way to the bathroom. One evening I hear a knock, open the door and there she stands in some flimsy bathrobe, hair loose on her shoulders. 'Can I come in?' she asks. I forget what she asked for. The image of Mimi entering Rodolfo's room flashed mercilessly into my mind. So… I ask her in, we sit down, I offer some wine, she stays the night." He managed a short, hesitant laugh. "You know, since my army injury I had been in poor health and was careful not to strain myself too much – bad for the liver. But she wouldn't give up. All night long we tumbled around, she wanted more and wouldn't let me rest. What stamina. I was a wreck and had to miss classes next day. But oh, was it worth it!"

I had to chuckle at a memory of my own. Before I left for America as a nineteen year old, my father gave me a letter in which he had written "Not to be opened until arrival." Among a variety of mostly predictable parental admonitions were warnings about women and sexual hygiene concluding with the untranslated adage – *une fois par fois, une fois par semaine.* Did he adopt that motto after the night with the little actress? And was Lotte happy with that regimen, if indeed it was enacted?

I left him three days before Christmas. I held his frail body tightly against mine as we kissed and wept. We both knew that this was the final goodbye.

He was only 72 when he died two weeks later.

A TALE OF TWO CITIES

NIKO

NIKO'S FATHER, MY grandfather George, had joined the lower rungs of a rising new class even though he was only a modest civil servant, the son of a village priest from southwestern Peloponnisos. Niko, like other young men of such striving families, was expected to enter one of the schools of higher education in Athens. George, committed to upward mobility, would have it no other way. The fact that my father ended up in Berlin as a student at the prestigious Technische Hochschule was beyond anybody's dreams and can be credited to an almost unbelievable turn of fate.

Niko was a precocious teenager attending the Greek secondary school known as the *Gymnasion* when he and my grandfather were discussing his future one afternoon. George was suggesting that Niko attend the University in Athens and study law. He became alarmed when his son instead declared that he might want to become an artist. The thought was simply too distasteful. He deftly managed to deflect it however with another idea.

"Here's another choice. You could go to the Military Academy, the *Skholi ton Evelpidhon*, and become an officer. How about that?"

Niko looked up, and George continued.

"You would wear a nice uniform, ride horseback, carry a sword."

George began to caress his moustache sensing a breakthrough.

"And you could serve under the Crown Prince to fight the Turks. Eh?"

Nikolaos, (known by the diminutive Niko by his friends and relatives; also affectionately called Nienchen by his wife and Pappi by his son,) was born in Athens in 1896, the year his favorite opera *La Boheme* was first performed in Italy and not too long after the bloody 1821 revolution that freed Greece from the 400-year Turkish yoke.

Soon after their independence — exhausted, destitute, largely illiterate, barely able to govern themselves - Greeks began to think of enlarging their newly acquired land beyond its narrow borders. Obsessed by nostalgia for their glorious past, they dreamt of a country that would encompass — if not the entire Byzantine empire, at least the still Greek-speaking parts of Asia Minor and, above all, its resplendent capital Konstantinoupolis, that almost mythical center of Greek Christendom, the Polis as it was known during its dark centuries and down to this day. Ever since Constantinople fell to the Ottomans in 1453, this happy fantasy came to be known as I Meghali Idhea, the Grand Idea. It functioned as a balm on the soul of a once dominant but now oppressed people and, after independence, as a distraction from the ills of a small, impoverished nation.

Niko was just entering his teens when one of many endemic military coups brought to power one Eleftherios Venizelos, a man of wily intelligence and political acumen, who, by tenaciously challenging the monarchy, split the country into two warring factions. He is credited today with opening the gates to what is a more or less functioning republic. Once he became Prime Minister, Venizelos shrewdly exploited the Grand Idea and began to spend lavishly, building up the army and navy and coaxing hungry Balkan neighbors into alliances to challenge the imploding Ottoman Empire. Greeks, Albanians,

Montenegrins, Serbs, Croats, Bulgarians, Rumanians – once the vassals of the Sublime Porte – were now eager to consolidate their ethnic sovereignties, jostling to get a bigger piece of the imperial carcass. The opportunity was irresistible.

King George and his son Constantine, (appropriately named after the legendary last Byzantine Emperor, Konstantinos Paleologhos, who died at the ramparts of Constantinople, fighting the Sultan's heathen hordes, thus securing a permanent position in the pantheon of Greek folk heroes,) led the Greek armies north in a giddy race for territory before other nation builders got to it. Their success was beyond imagination. By 1913, Greece had doubled its land area and Constantine was immortalized as tou aitou o yos, *("the eagle's son",) who "goes forward and leads us to glory" in a song that became the royalist paean.*

In 1912, my father entered the Evelpidhon Military Academy as a cadet to be commissioned an officer in the victorious army. Good in math and able to recite every battle from Alexander to Napoleon, he was eager to serve his King. But his enthusiasm waned when masculine prowess meant uncomfortable trudges in cold weather or mock charges on rough terrain with drawn bayonets. He was eagerly looking forward to a horse. After four years he finally graduated, a second lieutenant in the artillery. George was very proud of his only son. A brilliant career lay ahead of him.

But there were problems.

A year or two after Nikos entered Evelpidhon, the Austrian Archduke was shot in Bosnia, erupting the Great War. What followed was theater in the best tradition of Greek politics. King George was assassinated by a fanatic, and his son Constantine became King. As the war progressed, the Allies tempted Venizelos to join them and open another front against the Central Powers in Northern Greece, promising great territorial gains including parts of Asia Minor, maybe even Constantinople, dangling the Meghali Idhea phantasmagoria before the Greeks. Constantine, who was married to the Kaiser's sister, wanted Greece to stay neutral. In this he was supported by the Army Chief of Staff, General Metaxas, (who would later rule the country as its first Fascist dictator). Following heated disputes, Venizelos submitted his resignation. When, a year later, he was reelected, he made his move and invited the allied troops to land up north at Salonika. The disgruntled King dissolved Parliament and fired Venizelos. The Allies, furious at Constantine, helped Venizelos set up a separate government in the north, landed troops in Peireas and forced the King to flee the country. Venizelos returned to the capital, purged the monarchists from the army, joined the war in full force, and eventually became a star at the Versailles Peace Conference hobnobbing with the likes of Clemenceau and Lloyd George.

Instead of celebrating his new commission, my unfortunate father was thrown in jail as an ardent royalist, a victim of the Venizelian purge. He spent his time with like-minded prisoners cursing Venizelos and the Republicans. At other times he wrote morose poetry describing the pain of Love and the inevitable end of Life. Eventually he was released and discovered that the life of an officer had a definite éclat after all. He loved his uniforms and began to cultivate a mustache. Most of all he loved Pericles, his elegant Arabian steed whose charcoal buttocks, black mane and long slender legs shone in the sun as he pranced on the parade ground, ahead of the horse-drawn howitzers and ammunition wagons of his company. "And would you believe it," he would tell in later years, "I had an orderly, a kind of man servant, a private from Karpenissi, a real country bumpkin, Papoutsis; he did everything for me; groomed and fed the horse, polished my boots, kept my room neat, even woke me up at four in the morning with a cup of tea when we bivouacked during maneuvers. I felt like a lord, and I had barely turned twenty." In one of the cardboard mounted pictures from that time my father stands in full military regalia – brass buttoned, epauletted tunic, stiff high collar, saber clutched tightly in left hand, boots freshly shined by Papoutsis, fuzzy shadow under prominent nose - the posture and costume of a young warrior. But the photographer couldn't hide the boy inside. The beautiful, dark, melancholy eyes betrayed uncertainty. "Is this really me?" he seemed to say. That question was soon to be answered quite unexpectedly.

One day, mounted on Pericles, my father found himself in the midst of an Arcadian landscape. All around him, scenes from some Napoleonic battle seemed to unfold. Rows of heavy guns faced an invisible enemy. Each gun, tended by a group of soldiers, was periodically fired on an officer's command, raising puffs of smoke, filling the air with the acrid smell of gunpowder. After each firing, soldiers would run back to the munitions wagons lined up behind the guns to fetch the shells for the next round. Meantime, a cavalry contingent on the left was getting ready to simulate a charge, while clusters of infantry marched this way and that, brandishing bayoneted rifles. My young father, behind the munitions wagons, spurs shimmering on the heels of his knee-high boots, tried to calm Pericles while shouting orders from time to time. Around them nature seemed to ignore the pandemonium. Rows of grape-laden vines, groves of olive trees spreading their silvery boughs above ancient gnarled trunks, grassy fields gently rising up to purple slopes – a peaceful landscape basking under a warm September sun, embraced by an immense azure sky. Suddenly, all consciousness expired and the scene went dark.

Much more time must have passed before he heard the whole story. No one seemed to know what caused the explosion. After all, they were on maneuvers, not at war. One of the wagons blew up, they said. The boys at the nearest gun were killed along with poor Papoutsis.

Niko was barely 23 when he was released from the army as a wounded veteran with a deep red dent in his belly. For the rest of his life he remained a sickly person, tormented by various ailments, some real, some imagined. Inevitably, he embraced the prevailing attitude toward sickness and health to become a devout hypochondriac pressing on my mother and me his unflagging dread of some impending iatric disaster. But not all was misfortune. My father's brief military career produced an unexpected, significant benefit. At his young age he was retired with a handsome pension that only seasoned soldiers acquired when they reached the end of their service.

I imagine that all along there must have been whispers inside Niko's head that drew him in a different direction than the one he had chosen when, too young to know better, he had been attracted by the glamour of plumed hats, swords, horses and parades. But he had also told his father of his artistic inclination, and now, after his accident, his mind was returning in that direction. He had grown up in close proximity to classical architecture, aware that it was part of his proud heritage. Once again, Athens, following the example of elegant European cities, was embracing a classic revival with arched loggias, balustraded marble staircases, Doric and Ionic colonnades and imitation clay statuary perched on heavy baroque cornices. Architecture with a capital A was in the air. Niko made his fateful decision at this critical time.

"Architecture?"

"Yes, Baba. And I've decided to study in Berlin."

George was aghast. He didn't know any architects. And Germany? My God! What will I tell his mother? Her only son, so far away… so long… And how are we going to pay for this?

But my father was prepared. He had already been admitted by the Technische Hochschule, he told George, one of the best schools in the world. His pension would cover all costs. And it was only three days by train, and he would be back every summer. It was only for six years.

Miranda and Achileas on their engagement flanked by my grandparents Aspasia and George. Athens, 1920's.

Eleftherios Venizelos, the dominant politician in the early 1900's. The Athens airport is now named after him.

Niko with sisters Miranda (Toula) and Stella. Athens, 1920's

Second Lieutenant Niko, 1915

LOTTE

IN A BIG CITY, far to the north of Athens, a young woman was talking with her mother.

"Anne has two tickets to the Staatsoper!" Said my excited mother. "Aida is playing tonight."

"Just the two of you?" my grandmother Emma asked suspiciously.

"Oh Muttchen! Just the two of us unfortunately."

"Make sure you don't stay out too late – terrible things are going on in the streets."

"We may just go to Kranzler's for a coffee. Is that permitted?"

"*Sei nicht so frech!* Be like your sister. Stay at home. Don't run around all the time."

"Mutti, I'm twenty two years old. I can take care of myself. Don't worry."

A few minutes later she had her coat on and was walking to the door.

"Pretty girl," thought Emma looking after her. "All that lipstick and rouge is going to get her into trouble."

Charlotte (known by most people as Lotte, Lotta or the affectionate Lottchen and by me as Mutti) was born in Berlin in

1899. Her father Max, a handsome man with mild brown eyes, brown hair and a well-kept mustache, was born in Pommern, along the gray shores of the Baltic, north of Berlin. His wife Emma came from the opposite direction, from Leipzig in Saxony. They met half way, in Berlin. An old photograph mounted on cardboard with the photographer's name printed prominently on the bottom shows them standing stiffly side by side, he in a frock coat, she in a dark, tight fitting, high-collared dress, hair pulled back with little curls on top, her face pinched, bland, unsmiling, Victorian. Several photographs of their two daughters show them at various ages. In one, Lotte as a toddler wears a flounced baby dress and beams at the camera. In another the two girls stand side by side some years later. Margarete (Grete), three or four years older, is tall and thin, tight-lipped, destined to become a spinster. Lotte, cute as a button, looks ready to go out and conquer the world.

My grandfather Max, a businessman, could afford a large apartment in the fashionable western district of Charlottenburg not too far from the charming baroque *Schloss* built by the King of Prussia Friedrich the First for his wife Sophie Charlotte. In later years Lotte spoke with nostalgia about her parents' house before the Great War when the Kaiser still reigned and the Reich was all-powerful. *"Weihnachten bei uns, damals…das ist fuer mich unvergesslich,"* she would say. "For me, Christmas back then, in our house…it's unforgettable." The huge *Weinachtsbaum*, she went on, *eine wirkliche Tanne*, a real spruce, reached the ceiling and was decorated with tinsel and silver balls, real burning wax candles, thick as broom sticks, propped up in brass holders, their long wire arms screwed all the way back into the thick trunk. Glittering, wondrous presents were piled high at its base – a magic she tried to recreate in her Greek exile, for me and for herself, every year until she died.

Mutti adored her father. They did boy things together – roller-skating, ice skating, ball playing. "He loved me more than Grete," she would boast to me. "I was like a son to him, the boy he wanted. Grete was too timid, too serious. She was so jealous. She would secretly pinch me. Sometimes she would slap my face for no reason at all. Pappi and I went all over Berlin together. What a wonderful city it was then. Palaces, tree-lined avenues, parades, music, elegant shops, restaurants filled with happy well dressed people." A deep sigh. "Not like here. *He* took me away from all that. I told my mother that I'd go to the end of the world with him. And now…"

When the Great War came, fifteen-year-old Lotte cheered the soldiers on as they left for the front. They would soon be back triumphant. The air was filled with the rousing beat of martial sounds. "I remember one of the songs," she said, "listen."

> *Wenn die soldaten durch die Stadt marschieren*
> *Oefnen die Maedchen die Fenster und die Tueren*
> *Tarah, tarah …*

(When the soldiers march through the city the girls open doors and windows …)

But the war went on and on. More and more young men were killed and wounded, many of those who did return were maimed or blinded or crazed. Those who stayed behind became used to the word *Ersatz* – ersatz food, ersatz coffee, ersatz sugar, ersatz clothing; many had to work in the war industries. Grete and my mother put on nurses' uniforms and helped out in the hospitals.

Worse was to come. My grandfather, who escaped the draft, died of diabetes as the war was coming to an end. The armistice brought no joy. Left behind, like so many others, the three women had to fend for themselves. The Charlottenburg apartment became a luxury and they moved to a small third-floor walk-up in a dour gray block of a building on Swinemuenderstrasse in the northern petit bourgeois neighborhood of Gesundbrunnen near a freight train depot. The girls managed to get jobs. "You can't imagine how bad it was," my mother would tell. "We lost the war and all those poor soldiers came back – to what? No jobs, no money, no food, no future. And men were scarce of course. One reason Grete never married – besides not being pretty. I thought I was luckier." And before things got better, they got even worse. "The war was barely over when the Communists tried to take over," she continued. "That horrible little Jew Liebknecht and that woman Luxemburg were behind it. We were terrified. There was shooting everywhere. What a time that was. During the four years of war the fighting was elsewhere — now it was all around us."

I picture my mother and Anne moving slowly along the row to their seats, heads up, gaping at the tiered horseshoe of the great opera hall. The enormous chandeliers cast their glitter on the loges rich with plaster ornament, on the heavy, brocaded stage curtain, on the faces, bejeweled bosoms and starched white shirts of the festive crowd. Fans were wagging. The warm air buzzed with chatter. In the pit, under the curtain, the orchestra, tuning up, contributed its own polyphony. Still looking up, Lotte felt a movement - somebody had taken the seat beside her. A quick glance sideways revealed the presence of a dark young man, wrapped in his overcoat, sallow, bony features, absorbed in the program — interesting.

The tune-up sounds from the pit died out as the conductor approached the podium and Anne put her finger to her lips. Lotte sneaked another look to the right and started. He was looking straight at her! What a lovely smile! His dark eyes shone under a high forehead crowned by a sheaf of straight black hair. Between dominant nose and sensuous mouth was planted a smudge that reminded her of that little Austrian rabble-rouser in Munich she had read about.

Soon Radames was declaring his love for Aida. A quick glance to the right told Lotte that her neighbor also was captivated. As the first act came to an end in a burst of applause, he leaned over and whispered *"hat es Ihnen gefallen?"* (did you like it?) Startled, she looked to her left for help, but Anne, busy with clapping and bravoing, ignored her, so she blurted *"Ja"* and lest the opportunity was lost, added daringly, *"und Ihnen?"* (and you?) He looked into her eyes, serious. *"Fuer mich war es ein Traum"* and added, *"Ich liebe die Oper sehr.*" (It was a dream for me. I love the opera.) "He rolls his r's and misses the umlaut," she thought. "Adorable."

She had never met anyone like him before. There had been boys and men, youthful friendships, flirtations. A pretty, cheerful, fun loving girl, she always had good times with them and her female pals. But they were neither profound nor lasting. Many of the foreign men she saw looked interesting to her and her girlfriends. They giggled when approached in the street by swarthy youths whispering endearments. German boys didn't do that. And right after the war many were either too young or frequently damaged – crippled, depressed, bitter. Lotte had noticed that foreigners were having a good time in Berlin. Their money was worth more, and Berlin was there for their enjoyment. At her young age and with a taste for fun and adventure, Lotte longed for excitement. There was a beautiful, big world out there and she wanted a share of it.

"Fast work there, old girl," said Anne on the way home.

"Jealous?"

"Don't be ridiculous. You know that Berlin is full of foreigners like him."

Anne was referring to the many students, entertainers, artists, business people, hustlers who had crowded the city looking for pleasure, opportunity and excitement. Berlin was a sexual paradise for them. Prostitution was rampant and young girls would do "almost anything" for a meal or a pair of stockings.

"What's his name by the way?" asked Anne trying to sound bored. Lotte giggled trying to pronounce it.

"My god, Lotte, how will you introduce him to people? What will your mother say?" Silence.

"Where is he from? He looks Arab or Indian."

"He is from Greece, a student at the Technische Hochschule. Wants to become an architect." She felt better now.

"Sounds very impressive. Make sure he's not putting you on, though. He could be one of those dark types from god knows where, washing dishes in some restaurant on Kurfuerstendamm pretending to be a prince," Anne said with a mean smile and added, "Watch out, he may just be after you know what."

"What?"

"Oh Lotte! You're impossible! Twenty two years old and you still don't know what's going on in this city."

As they walked on Anne turned to her. "But I like his first name, at least it's familiar. Reminds me of the little fat man with the white beard and the red suit."

Lotte pouted.

"That's not funny, Anne."

Inside though, she could barely contain her excitement.

My grandfather Max Krause.

My grandmother Emma and my two year old mother.

My mother (left) with her sister Margarete (Grete) about 1909.

Teenage Lotte.

Grete and Lotte in 1920's Berlin.

BERLIN

MY FATHER WAS no hero. As I try to imagine his first trip to Berlin, I see him in a state of feverish excitement subverted by creeping apprehension. What lay ahead? He had scoured libraries and bookstores in Athens, found magazines, newspapers, an outdated Baedecker. Meantime he was struggling with that language searching for the verb in endless sentences only to find it casually dangling at the end. He had pushed on and felt that he would be able to communicate somehow. He forced himself to construct a vision of what the Greeks knew as *Verolino*. He would close his eyes to behold what looked like an expanded misty Athens with taller buildings, wider streets lined with leafy trees where traffic moved in stately pace. In this city lived beautiful people, Siegfrieds and Brunhildas with flowing blond hair, wearing sandals and togas, walking in the patrician strides of Homeric heroes. He would shake his head to dispel the fantasy but it came back and drifted into his dreams.

Of course, Berlin was not the Walhalla he had imagined. In vain he looked for some evidence of Wagnerian heroes and heroines. Men tended to have short-cropped hair, a ramrod posture and strident walk; they spoke in angry, authoritarian tones. Except for some of the young, most women shuffled about in shapeless overcoats, little felt hats and manly brogues, carrying fishnet shopping bags, looking disgruntled. He was made to feel like a foreigner because he clearly looked like one and frequently behaved like one. Loud rebukes would greet his inborn aversion to queuing when he was caught cutting the line onto a bus. Some would bellow "Go back where you came from!" provoked by his dark complexion and prominent nose.

At the Technische Hochschule he was most comfortable in the company of other expatriates – Asians and southern Europeans. They enjoyed Berlin together, feeling rich. Their drachmas, pesetas and yen appreciated miraculously against a mark battered by huge war reparations. After four years of slaughter, German men were scarce, largely unemployed and bad tempered. Girls were much friendlier - attracted to the foreigners for their carefree youth, their exotic looks, their solvency. There were no virgins in Berlin, went the saying. "Prostitutes!" one of Niko's fellow students liked to say. "Who needs them when you can get it for a *Kuchen mit Kaffee* at Kranzler's?"

As a student of architecture and a native of what until recently was a Balkan village, now valiantly trying to raise itself to the status of a western capital, my father must have been overwhelmed by Berlin even as his early fantasies were disappointed.

"Unter den Linden," he told me as we were both reminiscing years later, "That marvelous tree-lined avenue, Berlin's Champs Elysees, guarded at one end by its own Arc de Triomphe." Inspired by Roman triumphal arches, the Brandenburg Gate, he explained, was merely an update of the true original - the Propylea on our own Acropolis.

"Aren't they very different?" I asked.

"That's exactly my point. The Propylea is a simple, elegant introduction to a holy precinct in a more or less egalitarian society."

"Even if they had slaves."

"Well…yes."

These later "updates" were built to symbolize royal or imperial authority, he said, and cited the sculptures crowding the top of the gate - the horses pulling the chariot with the goddess of victory holding the reins and the staff with the Prussian eagle and the iron cross - mixed allegories from imperial Rome. He saw the avenue as a ready-made parade ground - victorious Prussian armies and Hitler's mighty Wehrmacht beating their jackboots on it in wide phalanxes.

"Periclean Athens was quite something else of course," he added.

"Didn't they put horses, young maidens, Gods and Goddesses on the friezes and pediments of the Parthenon?"

"Touché," said my father with a smile. "Not quite the same though, is it?"

He much preferred the other end of the avenue. In those days the *Museumsinsel* was the pride of Berlin. The *Schloss* stood prominently on axis with the avenue, an image of imperial power, its recent occupant now living in Holland, disgraced. Niko stood on the bridge crossing the Spree and took in the panorama: the magnificent palace, the domed Cathedral, and to the left, down a leafy *allee*, Schinkel's colonnaded *Altes Museum*.

"Another affront," said my father, "although quite impressive – after all, Schinkel was one of the best revivalists. But look, he took the classic temple, its proportions fine tuned over centuries by the Greeks and stretched it out like a bratwurst, and even worse, he put the entrance on the side! Compare that with the clarity and power of that group of stones on the Acropolis. Something our miserable little country can be proud of, my boy."

Niko's perambulations were seriously tested by German weather. The fall had been bad, with rain and more rain followed by periods of drizzle and chilly winds. But winter was a totally new experience, with snow and ice and numbing, lachrymose blasts from the Baltic. He defended himself with layers of wool scarves and hats and on really bad days bandaged his entire head provoking snickers as he entered the TH wrapped like an Egyptian mummy. Such measures notwithstanding, he suffered the same sniffles, coughs and sore throats he remembered having in Athens. He seemed to invite affliction on himself, (and as I learned through the years, on others too). But he was young and tried to enjoy his new life.

A letter came from Athens.

> My dear boy,
>
> We have read your letter and are all very happy to learn of your progress at the Polytechnic and your life in Berlin. But we worry over your health. You tell us that it's very cold and humid there. My God, five below zero! You know how delicate your health is. You must dress warmly and not stay out late at night. Are you eating well? Is your room well heated? Money holding out? Your mother is particularly concerned. Toula and Stella are well, as are we, but winter here too is quite cold and, can you believe it, we saw some snow flurries yesterday! In spite of the cold though, the almond trees have begun to bloom.
>
> You no doubt have heard the troubling news from Anatolia. We're still hoping for a reversal. All I can say is we are very happy that you are no longer in the army and safely away from here.
>
> Keep writing and take good care of yourself. Many kisses from all of us.
>
> Your loving father."
>
> PS Toula is seeing a lot of a handsome young man, Achileas. He comes from a good family. Says he wants to be an artist, a painter. God help us.

At about that time a conversation like this probably took place.

"Mutti…I have a friend," my mother told my grandmother as they sat in the kitchen.

"You have too many friends if you ask me." Emma replied.

"This is serious Mutti."

"What do you mean serious? Are you in any kind of trouble?"

"No Mutti, I'm not in trouble, I'm in love."

"Ach mein Gott! Who is it? Does Grete know?"

" Mutti, he's wonderful. A student at the Technische Hochschule, an architect."

"Why didn't you tell me?"

"I wanted to be sure. He…he's a foreigner. A Greek."

Emma wiped her forehead with her wrist.

"Are you saying you want to marry this…this man? Has he asked you?"

"Yes Mutti, yes. We love each other, we want to marry and live in his country after he finishes his studies. I'm so happy, Mutti. I'd go to the end of the world with him."

"What's his name?"

"Say that again?"

Lotte repeated the name slowly and then spelled it.

*"Ach du Lieber…*So many letters. Sounds like father of Christ."

"No, no Mutti. He explained it to me. His grandfather was a priest…"

"A priest? That's horrible. Priests don't marry."

"Please let me finish, Mutti. In Greece priests marry, they're not Roman Catholics, they're Orthodox."

"Like the Jews? With beards and all that?"

"I think they have beards but they're Christians, like us."

"We're *Evangelisch.*"

"Yes, yes, I know. Anyway, Niko's grandfather's name was Christos and the Greek word for priest is Papas. Now put these two together and you have his name."

"People will think it odd, especially with Charlotte tacked on to it."

"It's a common name. Niko tells me that it's like Schulze or Maier here."

Emma's lower lip began to tremble.

"Oh Mutti, don't start crying now. He's a wonderful man. He's going to make me very happy. I'll bring him over. I know you'll like him."

She embraced her mother's small, frail body, held on to her for a while. They were both crying now.

My mother never forgot the trauma of the war and its even worse aftermath. She thought of her parents and, to some extent, her sister, as victims of the disaster that befell Germany. Niko came along and saved her, took her away from the mess. The great inflation brought chaos to Germany. That was the year my parents were engaged. The little nest egg Max had left his family became worthless in just a few days. In 1936, the second and last time I saw my grandmother, she still had stacks of bills with unbelievable numbers – millions, billions, even trillions. All worthless!

"So many zeros," my mother said. "People stopped counting, carried their money in packets stuffed in suitcases. Went shopping immediately after they got paid, otherwise a kilo of cabbage would double or triple within an hour or two."

Poverty was everywhere, she told me. People stood at street corners selling their possessions to get food, thousands slept in tents in camps outside the city. She and her sister were lucky to have jobs and Niko helped with his Greek drachmas.

"Didn't conditions improve later on?"

"You won't like this, Titsian, but the truth is that Germany didn't recover until after Hitler came to power. That's why your father liked him."

Niko and Lotte's happiness was undisturbed by the misery around them, even with worse news coming from the south.

The second act in the King-Venizelos drama was now unfolding. In 1920, after the show at Versailles, the crafty Prime Minister Venizelos negotiated a miraculous deal with the Allies at Sevres, giving Greece large portions of the Ottoman Empire, including a generous slice around Smyrna on the shores of the Aegean, a city inhabited mostly by well-to-do Greeks, Armenians and Jews. Having once again revived the ancient dream of Meghali Idhea, Venizelos rushed an army to Smyrna to take possession of his reward before the treaty was ratified. Events rapidly turned sour. The treaty was never ratified. Venizelos lost the next election and the fickle Greeks brought Konstantine back to the throne. He immediately put himself at the head of the expeditionary force and heedlessly marched deep into Asia Minor. Meantime, a certain Mustaffa Kemal, known to history as Atta Turk, became the head of a new Nationalist government, reawakened the Turks, and staged a counterattack turning the westward retreat of the Greek army into a rout. In September 1922, the Turks entered Smyrna and took their revenge. They sacked the once prosperous jewel of the Aegean and slaughtered thirty thousand Greeks and Armenians. Thousands more took to the sea, many drowned as French, British and American warships in the harbor watched, refusing rescue.

Still worse was to come. After the debacle in Turkey, over a million refugees flooded Greece in a negotiated exchange of populations. They settled in disease-ridden camps and shanty towns, many of them around Athens. Whole families lived in one-room paranghes, shacks hastily built out of odd scraps of wood and tarpaper on muddy hillsides, without heat, water or sanitation. Angry, unemployed men lolled about cursing their fate and their hostile hosts in Greece. Women ferried water from some public outlet downhill for washing and primitive cooking over an open charcoal or wood fire. Bare-foot children, heads shaved to ward off lice, would roam about stealing, picking fights with the host kids, waiting to be accommodated in public schools. Ironically, many of the Mikroasiates, (the people from Asia Minor,) as they were disparagingly called, had enjoyed a higher level of culture and material well being under the Turks than the locals who resented them as dirty, uncouth intruders.

At about that time, and just a few years after the Bolshevik takeover in Russia, the Kommunistiko Komma Elladhas, (the Communist Party of Greece), also known as KKE or Kappa Kappa Epsilon or informally as KuKuEh, was founded. Predictably, the refugee shanty towns became a fertile ground for the Communist cause and the KKE would grow as my father's principal obsession and nightmare, destined to loom large in his, his family's and his compatriots' future.

During those troubled years ('22-'23,) my parents became husband and wife in a simple civil ceremony at the red brick Rotes Rathaus near Alexanderplatz. They celebrated their union with a short holiday on the chilly shores of the Baltic Sea, their *Flitterwoche*. Sepia photos show them posing on what looks like a sandy beach. The glaring contrast between them, I realize, was an uncanny prediction of their future. My father, in a business suit, white shirt, bowtie and street shoes, looks ready for the office. He clearly has no intention to get his feet wet, probably afraid that he might catch a cold. She, on the other hand, is ready for a dip in a 'twenties bathing outfit with short skirt and tight-fitting bloomers down to her knees, a bathing cap and canvass shoes laced above the ankles. With a large beach towel wrapped here and there as an added prop, arms this way and that, she is leaning against my father or reclining seductively at his feet – Theda Bara and Rudolph Valentino, very much in love. Their roles already cast.

In later life my parents had ample opportunity to speak of Berlin between 1921 and 1927. I'm not sure they knew what a remarkable time it was. They must have gone to the theater, as many Berliners did even in the worst of times. My father would mention the Max Reinhardt production of *As You Like It* at the Deutsches Theater, or my mother would exclaim, "*Ach*, Elisabeth Bergner, *die hab ich damals gesehen. Na. Das war eine Schauspielerin!*" (I saw her back then. Now, that was an actress!) But they never spoke of Bertolt Brecht or the productions of Piscator, idols of the avant-garde in those days. If they knew of them my father would probably have dismissed them as "disgusting stuff, communist drivel." And he would have made similar comments, and worse, about difficult new operas like *Wozzeck*. He loved romantic opera, (remember *Aida?*), and I can still hear him whistling bits from *Lucia, La Boheme* and the like. Niko would have pooh-poohed the music of Ravel, Stravinsky and Prokofiev, not to speak of Schoenberg, performed by the Berlin Philharmonic and conducted by luminaries like Klemperer and Bruno Walter while he and my mother were living there.

Many of my father's books, shipped to New York after his death, fill a substantial portion of our shelves today. Among them are fat volumes on art - mostly color reproductions of paintings from the great museums - and of architecture, his, and my, chosen profession. But Niko preferred to spend his reading time, (usually in bed,) with literature, mostly French, although he also liked German poetry, all read in the original language. He liked eighteenth and nineteenth century fiction and non-fiction – from Montesquieu and Rousseau to Stendhal, Sand, Hugo and Daudet and among the Germans, Heine, Storm and, of course, Goethe and many more. While in Berlin, he must have heard of Mann, Stefan Zweig, Brecht and Rilke and even the young Nabokov's Berlin novels. None of these names appears among his books. Neither was he much interested in Greek authors, (although writers like Kazantzakis and the poets Kavafis and Seferis gained international acclaim.) Niko preferred Baudelaire. My mother's reading was limited to a few German novels and illustrated weeklies.

Until Hitler put an end to it, Berlin and Germany were at the forefront of new, exciting, experimental architecture like Eric Mendelsohn's surrealist "Einstein Tower," Mies van der Rohe's prophetic glass skyscraper proposal, and even before the War, young

Gropius' Fagus factory. My father never spoke of them although his own buildings in Athens looked more Bauhaus than neoclassic Schinkel.

"What a time that must have been," I told my father sitting by his sickbed years later.

"You mean all those girls?"

"Yes," I wanted to humor him. "But also the amazing culture that grew like a beautiful flower out of the dung of that horrible war."

"I guess so," he said feebly. "But, it was so bad for so many people."

"Many people did well though, like you. I would have loved to be there. What a waste of talent it turned out to be, what a loss of opportunity."

"Full of communists, profiteers…"

"Was Hitler better? He came and soon chased them all away. Architects, writers, musicians, scientists, artists."

"Quite a few stayed behind."

"But not a single Jew. That huge pool of genius, German genius, was driven out or murdered. Most went and flourished in America, Pappi." I looked at him. "Like me."

Niko (right) with fellow students in Berlin, early twenties.

My parents honeymooning on the Baltic Sea.

ATHENS

THE MARRIED IDYLL in Berlin came to an end in 1927 when my father took my mother to his home country. They must have had some warning of what was to come. She was surprised, however, if not dismayed, that the capital of Greece was more a large village than a metropolis. Before independence in 1830, Athens had been a hill town - a few houses clustered under the Acropolis, its inhabitants largely unaware of its glorious past. The city founded by the virgin goddess Athena (the *Parthenos*) had fallen into obscurity during the Byzantine Christian millennium and the four hundred years of Muslim Ottoman Turkish rule. Athens and other villages lay scattered in a fertile valley encircled by the three mountains –Ymittos, Pendeli and Parnis and on the fourth side by the smallish Mount Aeghaleo and the Saronic Gulf. This basin, along with the rest of the peninsula known as Attiki (Attica) was the bread-basket of ancient Athens. In antiquity, Attiki was divided into several communes called *Dhemoi*. Under ideal circumstances, each *Dhemos* sent representatives to Athens to vote on matters of state in a system that came to be known as *Dhemokratia*. Unfortunately this was not always the case. From time to time power would fall into the hands of one or more rulers, bypassing the *Dhemoi*. A single ruler would then be called a *Tyrannos* and a system of several rulers *Oligharxhia*, resulting in the familiar terms tyrant and oligarch.

By the time my mother arrived, Athens had spread from its origins around the Acropolis to reach Lykavittos, an even taller hill, while other tentacles began to make contact with nearby villages. The population had reached several hundred thousand. Today the *protevousa*, the capital district which includes Peireas (Piraeus) and many erstwhile suburbs, numbers about four million inhabitants, almost half the country's population. Neighborhoods still carry the names of villages which stood here before the urban explosion, reminders of once rural charm, of gentle coexistence with nature – now lost and nearly forgotten.

One of the original villages in the valley was Maroussi, the ancient Amaroussion. In 1927 it was a typical Attiki hamlet surrounded by farmland, less than an hour's distance from the City by horse drawn transport. In the *plateia*, (the village square) a traditional fountain supplied fresh water to the community until a piped network brought it to each house. Early in the morning women would gather there to socialize and fill their *stamnes* (thin-necked terracotta jugs) with cool mountain water. Under the shade of two ancient sycamores, a cluster of small, round iron tables and straw-seat wooden chairs welcomed men to the first coffee of the day served from the *kafeneion* next to the small grocery. Until recently, the *bakaliko* (a Turkish word for grocery) was a familiar sight, usually a small, cozy space crammed with foodstuffs. A few canned goods (sardines, stuffed grape leaves, condensed milk…) were stacked in shelves. Most merchandise was out in the open where customers maneuvered around sacks of dry, colorful legumes and wooden barrels offering layered, salted *bakaliaro* (cod fish) and enormous chunks of feta cheese submerged in pools of milky water. On the counter sat an array of large tin containers of olives – pointed ones from Kalamata, plummy ones from Amfissa and small, shriveled black *throumbes*. An amalgam of pleasantly musty smells permeated the air.

The road north from Athens skirted the little square bringing busloads of people, animals and freight, horse drawn carts and traveling merchants peddling their wares from the backs of donkeys and mules. Maroussi was still a farm community of whitewashed houses. Indoor plumbing was yet to come.

It was here that my father brought his young bride from Berlin. He couldn't afford Athenian rents, and his mother, my grandmother Aspasia, wouldn't let them stay in her house. She would have nothing to do with her son and his wife. Niko had shamed the family by marrying before his older sister Stella did and, even worse, by marrying, not only a foreigner, but also a Protestant. "I never want to see you again," Aspasia had shouted a year earlier when he told her of his wedding and sought her approval. His father and sister Toula had also been upset, but soon relented and reconciled. Aspasia and his sister Stella did not.

When my parents arrived from Germany, Aspasia was bedridden, dying of a broken heart, some said. She wouldn't see her son even when she knew that my mother was pregnant. On her deathbed, pointing a finger to the ceiling, she croaked with Sophoclean wrath, "I want to see him dead!" Her first grandson was born a few days later. She never saw me.

A letter arrived in Berlin.

My dear ones,

I'm still trying to get used to this amazing place. Everything is so different. I thought I had seen poverty in Berlin, but this is much worse. Children run around half naked with shorn heads and runny noses, and so many women wear black! Every time a relative dies, even a distant relative, they change to black. And the streets are so dirty, many are unpaved and dusty. The people often have a strange smell. Niko says that's because they eat a lot of onions and garlic and they don't bathe very often.

Here it is September, and it's still unbearably hot. I sweat even when I am out of the sun and have trouble sleeping at night.

And speaking of sleeping – you'll be amazed – every body sleeps in the middle of the day after they eat a big lunch! Work stops and all the stores close. How do they get anything done? But they do go back to work after their naps, until early evening.

Now the big news. I wrote to you that Niko found a place for us in a village outside the city. We just moved into the second floor of a house, (another family lives downstairs.) You won't believe what it's like. We live among chickens and goats! A rooster wakes us up in the morning. I have to go down to the yard to pump water for drinking and washing! It's a new experience and I laugh about it. Niko says we'll soon move to a nice house in the city. Meantime my belly is getting bigger. I feel a kick now and then and have dizzy spells in the morning. I'm alone here during the day, no one to talk to. I couldn't anyway. I'm excited to be learning Griechisch, even though the pronunciation and those letters are driving me crazy. Did you know that they have some of our German words? (Niko tells me that it's the other way around! I find that hard to believe, but he's usually right.) He wants to rent an office and hang his Diplom Ingenieur sign on the door. He needs clients, of course, but there seems to be a lot of construction.

With much love to you both,
Your, Lotte

PS I hope it's a boy. Thinking of names – how does Julius sound?

The baby's name was becoming an issue. I can imagine the bickering.

"How about Emma for her and Julius for him?"

"I like your mother's name, but Julius?" He thinks a bit. "Actually custom here demands that he be named George after his grandfather."

"Or Max after his other grandfather."

"Either would be acceptable. But I was thinking of something more unusual…unique… unforgettable…inspiring."

"But Niko, it's only a baby. He's not Napoleon for God's sake."

"Napoleon – not a bad choice."

"You must be joking."

"Let's think about it. There are so many possibilities."

By Christmas she was quite impatient. She was very big and Niko was getting on her nerves with his endless admonitions.

"You can't go out in this weather…lie down…you'll catch cold…bad for the baby…you're not eating enough…"

"I can't stand this any more!" she would shout. "When, when?"

Choosing a name became a distraction. They settled on Emma for a girl. After much discussion for a boy, they found fertile ground among the Renaissance artists and architects Niko had admired in his travels. Donatello? Rafaelo? Michelangelo? ("For heavens sake!") Bramante? ("Oh, come on Niko!")

"I think you'll like this one," he finally said, pleased with himself. She eyed him suspiciously.

"One of the greatest…from Venice. Tiziano Veccelio."

"Two names?"

"No, darling. His first name only. Tiziano. It's lovely, don't you think? In German it's Tizian, in French Titien, in Greek Tisianos. It has a beautiful yet authoritative sound to it. No?"

"No."

"Oh come on *Liebchen*. We can call him Titzel when he's still small. But standing behind him will be a formidable presence – a name that speaks of greatness, of genius."

In late January I was born in a private clinic just off Omonia Square in the center of Athens. Until her death sixty-five years later, my mother would describe in lurid detail the ordeal she endured in order to bring me to life. She would raise her skirt and lift her leg to show me, or anyone else, a calf disfigured by swollen varicose veins.

"This happened because of you," was her merciless reminder. "It was the worst experience in my life. I was in agony for hours, thought I'd die."

Looking at me straight in the face she added, "Never again!"

My parents returned to Maroussi with their little bundle. January and February were exceptionally cold that year. They installed a petroleum heater to warm up my room and heat water and milk. Even so, they wore hats, coats and gloves indoors to fend off the chill from moisture-laden stonewalls, the air cold enough to turn breath into cloudlets of vapor. I gave my father the first of many parental fits when I ran a temperature and he saw mucous ooze from my red nose. (Thus started a long tradition: every morning, in all the years I lived with them, Niko would place his palm on my forehead, checking.) That winter, my mother probably wished she were back in her mother's cozy apartment up in the frigid north.

"*Es ist so warm in Griechenland,*" she had told her sister as they were packing. "All those naked people in those statues, I won't need these woolens."

"No, no," Niko, who knew better had cried, "Bring everything!"

Spring finally came. On occasional walks outside their hovel and the impoverished village, my parents found a welcoming countryside. Over the sparse rocky landscape, winter thistles and grass yielded to fields of white and yellow daisies, red poppies and tiny blue-purple wildflowers. Among the pines the land rose gently toward the Pendeli slopes, the white gash from centuries of marble mining still visible on their sides.

Leaning against a pine, holding their baby between them, Niko and Lotte faced an itinerant photographer's camera. A warm, sunny spring day. My mother, who loved to pose, has assumed a Greta

Garbo stance with carefully selected components – medium length darkish hair, well applied makeup, loose fitting blouse with belt and casually draped scarf, white pocketbook held against dark knee length skirt, hefty but shapely calves in white stockings and heels. She is looking away at some distant sight to the left. My father, as if he had just come out of the office, in a serious dark suit, white shirt and necktie, sports a John Gilbert mustache. He smiles looking straight at the camera. I snuggle in his arms, dressed in white, my hair and eyes black as coal.

Eventually my father found a small one-story house on Evzonon Street in an up-and-coming neighborhood near the center of Athens. It stood inside a tiny fenced garden in a new development financed by a retired officers' fund. As a retired officer, my father could eventually build his own house there on favorable terms.

"We finally have rented a nice house," Lotte wrote in a letter to Berlin. "Niko says that someday we'll be able to buy our own. Isn't it wonderful?"

Little did she know how long it would take for that dream to come true.

Niko, Lotte and little me in Maroussi.

Lotte and I in our Maroussi hovel.

EVZONON

HOUSE HOPPING

LIFE BEGAN HERE, on Evzonon Street close to the center of Athens. The street, rather narrow and short, shorter than a soccer field and still unpaved in those days, was named after the Evzones, the elite soldiers dressed in the traditional skirted costume of the War of Independence. The Moni Petraki Monastery took up the entire south side. Bearded monks scurried around a quadrangle of cells, invisible behind high walls, quiet as mice. On a paved courtyard nearby, behind a guard of mournful cypresses, one could catch sight of the Monastery church. Its Byzantine attire of pink brick and orange stone topped by little tiled domes said it had been there for a few centuries. Night and day, on the hour, one of its bells, the tenor, not the baritone, affirmed its presence.

Along the north side of Evzonon, the uphill side if you will – for the terrain sloped quickly up toward the Lykavittos hill – new houses began to rise as the development grew. When it was finished, fewer than a dozen two and three-storey apartment buildings would line up the street, their plastered neoclassical facades, decorated with Baroque cornices, Roman arches, overhanging balconies and black iron railings flaunted a new bourgeois taste that would soon replace the whitewashed village houses that still stood here and there in the new city.

Evzonon was my universe until I was nine. While still unpaved, the street remained the area's unofficial playground – a long, friendly sandbox, a cocoon that still envelops rosy childhood memories. Now and then a policeman (*astynomos* or *polisman*) would stroll by, his hands clasped behind his back, to remind the neighbors that all was well. Cars rarely came by, and when they did, -a long, black Packard or Buick, detached headlights, chrome trim, running board and all - they caused an uproar among the urchins. "*Aftokinito!*" we shouted and gawked at the slow moving vehicle, straining for a glimpse of the fancy people inside. Most of the time, what passed through our street would be a horse-drawn cart or a donkey led by a sunburned hawker heralding his wares with his own particular ditty, loaded with water melons, mountain greens, pottery and firewood or offering to buy old clothes, sharpen knives and scissors, or loosen the packed cotton inside old mattresses. At other times a flock of turkeys or goats would round the corner, filling the street, urged on by a country herder with a long bamboo stick, making Lotte and Niko think they were still living in Maroussi. When the passers-by were gone, the dust settled, and play resumed.

My parents and I lived on Evzonon hopping from house to house for most of the nineteen thirties. The import of those years was revealed to us gradually and only in disconcerting fragments. Endless political turmoil filled the news until later the Metaxas dictatorship gave the illusion of stability. At the same time, totalitarian solutions were being tried elsewhere in Europe, the most dramatic – and most far reaching – befalling Germany, my mother's home country. China and Japan were too remote for my parents to be shocked by the rape of Nanking. And it was only when it was spreading the world over that they learned of the great depression in America. All along, they, and I, as I grew to understand, were missing the wider picture, being entertained by little wars here and there, royal scandals, athletic dramas and military parades - until events coalesced, bringing to our very doorstep the biggest catastrophe history has ever recorded.

We began house hopping at one end of the street, opposite the church and not too far from the British Archeological School and the Ionic colonnade of the Ghenadhian Library. The modest house at the corner would be the only one-family dwelling my parents and I would occupy. The last of its kind in the neighborhood, its fenced garden and white-washed walls, part of the city's vanishing rustic charm, it would soon be demolished to make room for the apartment blocks that would eventually turn Athens into a desert of gray.

I see a toddler digging among the weeds with his toy shovel. A pale, late winter sun warmed the fragrant, moist air. A thick blanket of dandelions, thistles, crabgrass and tiny, tender wild flowers lay across the yard. Winter was kinder here than summer. I stood up and waddled over to the iron gate. Across the way, a cluster of ominous, dark trees pierced a cloudless sky. Children were playing in the street. They were older and used bigger shovels to load a little red wagon with scrapings from the unpaved roadbed. Pappi called the blond boys *Amerikanakia*. Their babas worked at the American Archeological School up there. The neighborhood children admired the fire-engine-red wagon of the *Amerikanakia* - almost as much as the big black car that went by the other day. *"Nein, du darfst nicht!"* came my mother's voice from the window as I rattled the gate, trying to join the fun in the street. Disgusted, I returned to my own earthmoving project among the thistles. My sudden howl brought my mother out of the house. "Silly boy," she fussed, exasperated. "There you go again, little devil, sticking your hands among the *tsouknidhes*. Time to take you in"

I'm watching my mother getting ready to go out. Still in her slip, she put on her makeup sitting before an oval mirror. I loved to see the lipstick turn her mouth bright red. She rubbed some rouge on her cheeks and carefully combed her hair. "Hand me my stockings, *Suesschen*," she said. I walked over to the bed to get them and continued watching as she bunched up one stocking and slowly eased it over her outstretched leg. At the top she fastened it to some clips hanging from a belt. She ran her hands up and down her leg to remove wrinkles and repeated the sequence on the other leg. *"Ach diese Ader,"* she said, vexed, as she caressed her varicose vein, and looked at me. She got up, put on a rose silk blouse, slipped into the skirt and jacket of a brown wool suit and finally stepped into a pair of brown high-heeled pumps. She stood before the mirror, made some adjustments and smiled, pleased with what she saw.

"I'm going out, Titzel. You be a good boy. Sofia will give you milk and some of those biscuits you like."

"Nein, nein, Mutti."

"But I'll be back very soon, sweetie."

"Nein..nein..Mutti..nein!" I sobbed, stuttering.

She put on her belted winter coat with the fur collar and the smart *muetze* she had brought from Berlin, opened the door and quickly walked out into the street. I rushed to the window, desperate, pressed my face on the cold glass as tears ran down my cheeks.

"Meine Mutti," I sobbed, *"meine Mutti."*

She turned and waved, smiling, happy. Young and chic, free for a while, she turned the corner and faded from my sight.

Sofia was cooking lunch, humming. I sat on the floor studying her big backside on top of sturdy legs shuffling back and forth from pot to chopping counter. The fragrance of onions seared in hot olive oil had invaded the air as a little cloud and a sizzle rose from the pot. Nearby the *bamyes* (okra) were marinating in a pool of vinegar and sugar while Sofia cut the tomatoes and the parsley. They would soon join the onions in the pot with a big swoosh and more clouds. I loved the smell of cooking onions but not the slimy *bamyes* – yuk.

Mutti came in all rosy cheeks, smiling, greeted by my shrieks of delight and complaints from Sofia who had suffered the brunt of my fury while cleaning house and cooking. Mutti picked me up, smothered me with kisses. "*Ach mein* baby," she cooed. She adored her chubby little boy, his keen black eyes, his pageboy black hair. She and Niko still called me "baby" unable to let go of my precious infancy, reluctant to recognize me by my grandiose name. As they abandoned "baby", Titsel would become an acceptable variant for a toddler, for a child, even for an adolescent.

2:30 and my father came home from the office for his lunch and siesta. He kissed his wife and quickly walked over and scooped his son off the floor.

"Has he been outside?"

"I had him out for a while, he played nicely."

"In this weather? It's freezing!"

"Oh Niko, it's not. It was sunny. There was no wind."

"I was very cold walking here from the office. Even with my heavy overcoat."

"It's much colder in Berlin, you know that. And yet I would be outside on my skates with just a light jacket and I was never sick."

"It's different here. People get sick very easily, especially children. We've gone over this I don't know how many times. Will you listen to me? The child is not to go out in this weather without his heavy coat, gloves and hat and only for a short time. Is that clear?"

I was startled by the sudden rise of my father's voice and the sides of my mouth began to droop. But as usual after his frequent outbursts, he eventually calmed down. He picked me up and nuzzled me. "Tickle, tickle," he said pressing a finger into my belly, provoking delirious giggles. My mother looked at us. She still had trouble accepting his Mediterranean temper, his *nevra*.

After lunch and the customary siesta my father would go back to work. He had recently rented a space, a walk-up in an old building near Omonia Square, downtown. The sign on the door described him as an Architect and a diplomate of the Superior Technical School Berlin. The Berlin connection he knew gave him a leg up. Only a handful of his colleagues had studied abroad, and anything that came from *Evropi* was considered superior, even a wife. Like every young architect, however, he had to start with small renovations and additions while waiting for the opportunity to get bigger commissions. He dreamt of designing department stores, government ministries, expensive seaside villas for the rich, luxury hotels, movie theaters. He saw such projects published in periodicals and in books he had brought back from Berlin.

"This is the new architecture," he told his wife. "You see it all over Europe – Holland, Germany even in Russia. This Mjelnikov is quite amazing, designed the Russian pavilion at the Paris exposition – and he's a Communist, would you believe it?"

"Can you get projects like these here? This is such a poor country," said Lotte, who by now knew the difference between Munich and Maroussi.

"I need connections ..."

"Ah, yes," said Lotte her eyes turning toward the busy little boy on the floor. Niko had recently upset her when he told her that commissions were still hard to come about. They would not be able to buy a house for a while, he said, and furthermore, she would have to postpone her trip to Berlin. She had been eager to show me off to her mother and sister.

My mother loved to tell this story.

While still living in the little corner house we had a visitor. With me in her arms, she went to open the door and found a dark figure standing outside. Black stovepipe hat, black cassock from head to toe, unforgiving black eyes above a long black beard, a silver cross hanging below it. His baritone greeted her: *"Kalimera sas."* My mouth began to quiver, I didn't like this man. I had seen him come out of the church across the street. He looked like one of those tall dark trees. And you couldn't see his face behind that beard and those bushy eyebrows. Just a big nose and those eyes. No smiles. And the other kids were scared of him. They stopped playing when he walked by. Some walked up to him and kissed his hand.

Mutti, flustered, understood his "good morning" but knew that chances for further conversation were dim. "Sofia!" she cried desperately. As Sofia rushed in from the kitchen it occurred to my mother that their domestic pigeon-language would not suffice. Still, the three of them put together some sort of dialogue. This much Mutti understood: The papas had learned that the family had recently moved here and wanted to welcome them and invite them to attend Holy Liturgy on Sunday. The *psaltis* had a particularly sweet voice. Through Sofia Mutti tried to explain that although she was married in the Orthodox Church…she herself was still a Protestant…although…she does not attend the German Church here, and therefore…

"You mean madam that you have not converted to our Orthodox religion?"

It…it had not occurred to her and her husband…he of course is Orthodox…

"His grandfather was a priest!" she blurted, delighted to remember the connection.

"Has your child here been baptized?"

Yes, yes, he certainly was baptized…and when he was only three months old…the poor thing…he cried so…The priest was exasperated. He struggled to understand her words, her gestures, and that stupid servant was totally useless. The pretty young foreigner didn't seem to take him seriously, she looked amused.

"Madam, we are very disappointed." He was trying to keep his composure. "We fear for the salvation of your soul," he declared and turned to Sofia who cowered under his stare.

"Tell your mistress I will come back to speak with her husband. Good day!"

Mutti had to suppress a giggle as she noticed the little chignon on the back of his head poking out from under the stovepipe. Sofia looked at her reproachfully. "Ha," she grumbled as she turned to go back to the kitchen. I was happy to see him go.

—

Some time that spring, my parents made three decisions. An advance for a renovation project would allow Lotte and me to travel to Berlin in August. Then, when she returned in September, they would move to a better house at the other end of Evzonon. And they decided to hire a full time, sleep-in maid.

"I have already found a maid," said my mother pleased with herself.

"You have?"

"Elsa met her in the hospital when she was having her baby. She was cleaning toilets there and wants to work in a house. She will cost us practically nothing."

"Room and board is not nothing."

"You won't believe this."

"Tell me."

"She's not Greek. She's from somewhere in Africa."

"Africa?"

"Yes Niko, she's *eine Schwartze*. Pitch black, Elsa says, a tiny little person. I don't know how she got here – no friends, no relatives, poor thing."

"What's her name?"

"Rosa. I don't even know if she has a surname."

—

In our next hop, shortly after our return from Germany that fall, we moved to the extreme opposite end of Evzonon. Ilias Papamandelou, a classmate from the military academy, had recently built a lovely three-story house there. The space between the house and the iron fence in front was planted with orange trees and shrubs on one side and paved with cement tiles on the other. A wide marble staircase rose majestically to the second floor portico. Through the vestibule inside, one could enter the second floor apartment we had just rented, or continue up an interior stair to reach the landlord's quarters.

The Ethiopian Ambassador had been renting the middle floor apartment. When my father heard that he was leaving, he grabbed the opportunity. It was a bargain and a great improvement over the other end of Evzonon – bigger, and with its arches, marble and balconies, it made a more respectable impression. For my mother at least, our first house had been too reminiscent of Maroussi squalor. The new place offered a unique feature: the walls in the *saloni* had been surfaced, in thick artist's oil paint, with a floor-to-ceiling mural depicting monkeys frolicking among the palm fronds of a tropical forest – no doubt a contribution of the homesick Ambassador. There was also a dining room, three bedrooms, a maid's cubbyhole, kitchen and bath. Behind black decorative railings outside, extended a recessed terrace under three arches, the recess painted terracotta red in the manner of Schlieman's Minoan palace mansion on Panepistimiou Avenue, much smaller, of course, but still, in those days, a house of some pretension. Mutti must have been pinching herself.

A photo, taken a year later, shows me, my parents and a friend holding on to the garden railing by the street below, the house rising behind us. For reasons that still baffle me, we had moved to the ground floor of the same house. My mother had loved the second floor. What happened? By now we had lived in four dwellings in five years, and it was only the beginning – three more moves were in the offing. Years later my mother blamed my father. "There was always some excuse," she said. "Usually more favorable rent, or a better view, a more commodious layout." But his real reasons were mostly negative. When I was little he was afraid I would fall off the balcony. Or there were too many drafts. Or he didn't get along with the landlord. Always some fear, some controversy. I, on the other hand, remember liking the change - the excitement of entering yet another empty house offering new smells, new spaces to explore, watching our furniture being moved in new positions, different windows opening on familiar views but seen from different angles and heights. My mother didn't share the excitement. On the contrary, in later years the moving became her favorite lament. As a retired wounded officer, my father had many opportunities, she claimed, to buy land, to build a house big enough to earn rental income, or just to own an apartment, all at favorable cost paid out over time. He just couldn't do it, she'd say. Business was not for him, he seemed to feel contempt for such people. He thought of himself as a thinker, an artist, above money, above ownership.

When I was even slightly indisposed my father insisted that my bed be brought into their bedroom. This made eminent sense to me. Why should I sleep alone in another room away from them? After all, they *slept* together. And even though I was the sole possessor of their full, totally devoted attention — cuddled, spoiled, smootched, adored - I was not satisfied. I wanted an in-house playmate.

"Kostakis has a sister," I told my mother, "they play together."

"That's nice."

"Why can't I have a brother or a sister Mutti?"

Lotte was taken by surprise and thought of her varicose vein. She had to do something to counter such subversive thoughts.

"I told you last time that the stork brings us babies. If we do something nice for him he may bring you a baby brother." I had never seen a stork.

"What's a stork?"

"It's a big, big bird with a long *Schnabel* and long legs, like sticks. In Deutschland we have many. They build big nests high up on top of chimneys and roofs."

"So, what can we do?" I asked eagerly.

"Now let's see…how about putting a plate of something on the windowsill, something the stork will like?"

"Yes, yes…what?" I was really excited.

"Maybe a little chocolate, the kind you like, and some grapes?"

An hour later, Mutti came back to the bedroom to find me standing on a chair next to the windowsill the offering still awaiting the stork's arrival. By now the grapes were floating in a brown pool of chocolate.

"Oh Tietzel," she said trying not to laugh. "You're still waiting for the stork, poor darling. He won't come when you're standing there. He's very shy. He'll come at night when we're sleeping. Now go see what Rosa is doing. I have to go out for a while."

Rosa was peeling potatoes in the kitchen. Mutti liked to make a salad with them, German style. I perched on a table near by, watching, spellbound. In my little world there was nothing like Rosa. Her skin was shiny and the color of the Pavlidis bittersweet chocolate I was sharing with the stork, the one with the blue wrapper with pictures of all the international competition medals, my favorite special treat. Her head was covered with tiny, tight little curls, blacker than my own – and those lips!

My friend Tasoula was calling me outside. I joined her in the back garden to resume our excavation project. She was not exactly a brother but she'd have to do for now. The garden was small, but to me it seemed a vast unexplored universe, a landscape of hills and valleys inhabited by wild creatures slithering and crawling in the leafy green shade, among giant columns that rose into a tracery of branches and clouds – an Egyptian temple, a Wagnerian forest. On hands and knees, we dug the moist, warm earth with our toy shovels.

"It's a snake!" screamed Tasoula.

"Just a big worm," I said manfully. "Here, would you like it?"

"No, no, it's yucky, go away!" I had just discovered new powers.

Tasoula walked into the house with me and her pal Athena. We gathered in the kitchen and Rosa gave us each a *kourabie*. We danced and hopped around as the sugar powdered our lips and showered the floor. In a bacchanalian mood, little Athena observed that she and Tasoula wore skirts but that I was wearing pants.

"What's inside your pants?" she giggled.

"What's under you skirts?" I retorted.

"Nothing," they shouted, lifting their hems to show their underpants.

"But I have something," I said and proudly brought out my little instrument, resuming my dance to squeals of merriment from the girls. More laughter and dancing until Rosa turned, looked, screamed and ran out of the room to tattle.

Evening in early spring, 1933. We'd been living in the ground floor of the Papamandelou house for a year. The family had gathered in the living room in uneasy silence. Yet another election was held, the monarchists winning by a small margin. My father was pleased but apprehensive. Gunshots shattered the quiet night.

"It must be Plastiras," he told my grandfather who had recently joined the family. "He's staging a republican putsch, I heard. Afraid the royalists will bring back the King."

"They seem to have won a majority."

"Yes, but that's not enough for that clique. I'm sure Venizelos is behind all this. He just won't give up, even with the mess he's brought on us."

"Still, he's a great statesman, a patriot."

"Come on Baba, this man will do anything to stay in power. He's defaulted on foreign payments, wants to change the voting system, he's muzzling the press for God's sake!"

"Still, he's a great supporter of democracy…"

"Democracy, democracy, it's become a joke. With a new government every six months, nothing gets done."

"We've had hard times since '22. We need patience."

"Nonsense. Look at Germany. After the war, they had exactly the same problems with your democracy. Nothing got done, it was chaos. But they're coming to their senses. Hitler will establish order now that Hindenburg has made him Chancellor. Wait and see. This miserable country can learn something from them."

My father may have read of the burning of the Reichstag building and the March elections that gave the Nazis a majority. He may have seen photographs of Adolf Hitler, appearing before the Reichstag in full Nazi uniform, to obtain dictatorial powers and effectively dissolve the legislature. Feeling as he did about the Greek parliament, Niko must have applauded the speedy outlawing of all opposition in Germany, making the NSDAP the only legal party. But I wonder if he realized that the press was indeed muzzled; that the S.A. went on a rampage, killing and terrorizing the perceived enemies of the State; that concentration camps began to appear along with the persecution of Jews. Had he known, would my father be pleased to learn that an efficient, streamlined, ruthless totalitarian state was put together in record time?

Around that time, my parents staged their fourth and last hop on Evzonon by moving halfway up the street to the top floor of the Andhreou house. We were to live there for four happy years. Two more hops were to occur while I lived with my parents – one, to an apartment on Vasilissis Sofias Avenue not too far from Evzonon and the last to Kodringtonos Street, on the opposite side of Athens. Including the brief stay in Maroussi, we occupied seven different dwellings in a period of eighteen years.

The Monastery Chapel on Evzonon street.

My pretty mother at a roof top party.

*With my Teddy, 1931, and
a rather girlish haircut.*

*My grandfather, my parents and I stand in
front of our first Evzonon house, ca. 1930*

*My hair was curled for this posed
studio photograph.*

*One of many pictures posing
with my mother.*

PAPOUS AND ROSA

"**B**ABA, WHY NOT move in with us?" Niko asked his father who had been living alone since Aspasia died. George, who valued his dignity, resisted, saying that he was just fine in his own house. But my father knew that he was lonely and could no longer manage by himself. Stella and Toula were now married with children and could not help.

"We have a nice house now," said Niko, "and a new maid. You'll be comfortable with us."

George fidgeted in his chair. It was an embarrassing situation.

"Wouldn't Lotte mind?"

"She would love it. And you would be with your grandson every day. He adores you."

Lotte had objected, but I was delighted.

My grandfather George, called Papous (Papou in the vocative and genitive cases) by me and my mother, was an elegant man of the old school. In photographs spanning three decades he appears to be the same age – an older man between sixty and seventy. And this is how I remember him from the decade of our life together: an old man with a shiny bald top rimmed by thin grey hair and a liver-spotted furrowed face between a pair of a large seashell ears. A still vigorous broad-brush mustache under a conspicuous nose completed the composition. He dressed impeccably, wearing a suit and necktie even at home. In winter he lounged about the house in his heavy black overcoat and beret, (houses were notoriously under heated.) Wearing his fedora, he promenaded in the neighborhood at a pace suitable to his social standing and age. He never hurried. Seemingly accustomed to have others do things for him, he was rarely seen carrying an object of any kind – perhaps a carefully rolled newspaper, and if by some chance he had weakened and made a small purchase, he had it well wrapped and held it casually behind his back pretending it did not exist. Now and then he took me for a walk around the neighborhood. He held firmly onto me as we ambled along in his customary pace. I liked the way my hand felt inside his bony fist, although at times it seemed as if I was dragging him along - like a dog on a leash.

Like most of his fellow countrymen, Papous was addicted to sugar and caffeine. He would start his day with a demi-tasse of heavy Turkish coffee he cooked in his room over a tiny brass contraption fueled with alcohol, known as a *kaminetto*. To this brew were added two to three heaping spoonfuls of sugar. "Enough energy there," my father would say, "to guarantee eternal life." Between sips Papous would dunk a piece of bread in the little cup and conclude his breakfast by scooping up the syrupy dregs with a spoon followed by a satisfied smack. Most afternoons, after his nap, he would amble past the Marasleion school down to Kolonaki Square lined by a string of cafes. In those days the *kafeneia* were still Levantine bastions of male prerogative. Men sat around for hours in a haze of smoke, fondling their *komboloi*, loudly expounding on affairs of state. From some distance Papous could hear the lively crackle of dice hitting backgammon boards as he approached his cronies and his third or fourth coffee of the day. "Don't these men have any work?" my mother liked to say as she passed by with me. "Some take up two or even three chairs to hang their feet and arms, like pashas. No wonder nothing gets done in this country!"

Among the photographs in my possession, three stand out. A sepia print with the date 1872 written in the back shows a male trio posing stiffly in a studio shot. A man with fierce eyes and a full grey beard is seated in the center dressed in magnificent priestly regalia. All in black, with his stovepipe hat, long cassock, wide sash around an ample waste, large silver cross on his chest and a wide sleeved robe over his shoulders, he could be Zeus impersonating an Orthodox Patriarch. He is flanked on one side by an unknown young man and on the other by a serious looking boy, maybe fourteen years old, dressed in a suit and stiff collar, longish, neatly combed hair, his left hand resting on the priest's right shoulder. The boy is my grandfather George, the priest is Christos, my great grandfather. In another picture George, older and this time seated, his arms resting on the chair, stares at the camera with the unforgiving glare of El Greco's dreaded grand inquisitor Nino de Guevara. He was probably in his late forties, but he already looks as I remember him - bald head, grey mustache, sagging cheeks. Next to him stands Niko, still a shy teenager trying to look severe in his stiff Army uniform. The third photo has me and my Papous at the bottom of the marble stair outside the Papamandelou house on a balmy winter afternoon. George wears his usual outdoor costume, one hand in his coat pocket, the other over his grandson's shoulder. He poses gazing dreamily at some distant vision. I, about five years old, am also dressed for winter in a kind of buttoned, belted sweater, short woolen pants and high socks exposing vulnerable knees. I hold my arms behind my back leaning against the stair parapet but I might bolt any minute. Three pictures, four generations.

Salt and matches were government monopolies, and Papous entered civil service as manager of sea salt harvesting plants, a job that took him and his family to various coastal locations over the years.

"How did you get the salt?" I asked him.

"Have you ever tasted sea water?"

"Awful."

That's because the sea contains a lot of salt, he explained. Waves leave it on rocks on the shore. Something similar happens in the *alykes*, the salt fields where he worked. Large flat areas were dug close enough to the sea to let it flood them. The sun and air made the water evaporate leaving behind a field full of nice white crystals.

"And then you scoop it up and put it in those boxes we buy in the store."

"You could say that."

Papous lived with us for some dozen years until his death in that horrible first winter of the German occupation. Rosa's tenure in the house coincided with his, and even though my mother frequently grumbled about one or the other, they were part of a tight *ménage a cinque,* surrogate parents in an extended family.

In the five apartments that Papous and Rosa shared with us, I was frequently deprived of a bedroom to call my own. Not that it mattered - especially during the early years when I didn't seem to know the difference. I was tucked away in various rooms designated for other uses and at times of crisis such as illness, revolution or warfare, compelled to share the dubious safety of my parents' bedroom well into my teens On the other hand Rosa, a mere servant, was less underprivileged. In a new custom for housing the up-and-coming bourgeoisie, apartments included a separate room for a servant. More like a prison cell, barely large enough for a narrow bed, a tiny cabinet and possibly a chair, the room was always located above the apartment's bathroom and reached by a steep narrow stair. As a result, both rooms had very low ceilings. Fortunately no one in the house was taller than six feet. Unlike me, Rosa who was tiny, had her own room.

Papous always got the best room — spacious, private and with a good view — but there was nothing luxurious about it, rather monastic I would say, its décor closer to a monk's cell across the street, than a gentleman's quarters. In vain would one look for pictures on the white plaster walls or for carpets on the oak floor or curtains at the window. A narrow, celibate bed filled one corner, an armoire the opposite. A light hung from a cord in the middle over a table and a couple of chairs. Papous still used a washbasin and pitcher for his toilette even though the bathroom down the hall offered a sink with running water. He liked doing his ablutions without leaving his room. Sharing the top of a cabinet in a corner with an assortment of bottles and jars and a glass of water for overnight storage of dentures, was George's miniature shrine - an embossed silver icon of the *Panaghia*, the Virgin Mary holding baby Jesus, their painted faces peering out of two little holes in the silvery surface. A tiny flame from a wick floating in an oil-filled cup illuminated the icon — a traditional Orthodox ensemble. Perhaps Papous said his evening prayers before this miniature iconostasis; I never caught him in the act. Nor did I ever see my parents perform such rites.

Papous was my frequent companion in evenings when my parents were out. My best memories are of our hours together in winter, a time when the apartment was usually under-heated and we wore outdoor clothing indoors. He lay on his bed wrapped in his black overcoat, his beret tilted forward, staring at the blank wall across the room. We exchanged words in idle conversation while I sat next to him, sometimes with a sketch pad on my lap. His profile was of great interest. Faces, in general, attracted my attention. I fancied myself able to read temperament and character from them - had even divided them into generic types to fit attributes like intelligence, beauty, kindness, etc., or their opposites, or their possible combinations. Couldn't evil, I thought, lurk behind "the face of an angel?" I found the imprint left by the passage of time equally surprising, even shocking, sometimes depressing. The ripe cheeks of baby Jesus in a Titian I had seen in one of my father's books would some day turn into leathery furrows on the visage of an old man. Looking at my own grandfather's countenance, I could see a virtual landscape of vertical and horizontal ridges and valleys populated by mini craters and brown spots. On the side, (remember this is a profile,) hung a sizable oyster-shaped appendage. A major promontory dominated the center just above a grey field of thatch growing over a slim pale pink trench. All this resided under a smooth shiny dome, ringed by more grey thatch, hidden, most of the time, by a dark blue cloud.

So, I held a big black pencil over the sketch pad and drew, night after night, versions of my grandfather's profile, stopping from time to time to rub the cold off my fingers. Not great art, but a record of brief obsession and, more importantly, a souvenir of our cozy time together while I drew and he entertained me with stories of old times in the ancestral hamlet where his father, the priest, held sway.

"In those days Kyparissia sat on top of a hill opposite the Frankish castle," went Papous. "Below us, the Ionian Sea stretched out to the sunset, toward Sicily. In between and all around us lay another sea, silver green – the endless olive groves of Messinia, all the way down to Kalamata. What a sight, Titsian, what a place for a boy to grow up in. Now and then we'd hike down in the shade of the olives to gape at the fishing boats in the port, get some fish, splash around in the bay and return uphill. Quite a climb. It's all different today. The town center has moved down to the sea, hardly anyone lives up on top, why should they? No danger from pirates anymore."

"Another world back then," Papous continued. "As the village priest, father was one of the few who could read and write. He was known as Papas Christos, loved and respected, but very severe, people were a little afraid of him. So was I. Mother took me to church so that we could watch him conducting the liturgy. At Easter, during Holy Week, he hardly got any sleep and by Easter Sunday he had almost lost his voice. So many hours, day in and day out – exhausting. He had a good voice, deep and strong, also mellow, like an opera singer's baritone."

Papous went on and on during those nights, long enough sometimes for me to start another profile, encouraged by his approval of the previous one. "Very good my boy, but is my nose really that big?"

His narrative eventually went beyond Kyparisia to encompass a larger world. All through the *Tourkokratia*, the four hundred years of Turkish rule and even before, during the turbulent Byzantine millennium, people from diverse origins, speaking various languages, inhabited the Balkan Peninsula, moving around a lot. A cultural caldron, he called it. Most people were illiterate. Orthodox priests could read and write Greek and could preach from the scriptures. Communities gathered around them, they taught the children at school and conducted the liturgy in church – teachers and holy men. The Jews in the Middle Ages were like that except their priests were Rabbis and their language Hebrew – peoples clinging together in a hostile environment, tenaciously holding on to their culture. "Your great grandfather was among the last in this long tradition," he said. "All through those centuries, people like him kept the faith and, more importantly, salvaged the language. Today we can pick up books written two and a half thousand years ago and connect with men, who, naked or wrapped in sheets, inhabit our ruins and our museums today. Amazing how the language survived even as the population was changing through the ages."

He was approaching his favorite tirade.

"We are a small marginal country today, especially when compared with our antiquity. Greek colonies were spreading across the entire Mediterranean and beyond, when Alexander moved our borders to India and brought the Greek language across the Middle East and Egypt and with it that fabulous Hellenic culture."

By now I knew what was coming.

"And what are we today?" he continued with his customary flourish. "We have the audacity to call ourselves the heirs of that civilization, direct descendants of Perikles, Zenon and Sappho. Look at us, do you see any similarity to the *kouri* or the tender girls on the tombstones of Keramikos? Look at our noses: mine – as you have been drawing it – your father's and, in spite of your German mother, probably yours when you grow up. Not even a trace of that elegant Apollonian profile in Olympia. We belong in the Middle East my boy – among the Semites, the Turks, the Armenians."

How attractive the Greek peninsula must have been to people from the north, he went on, including the original Greeks who came from up there somewhere thousands of years ago. But that was just the beginning. Over the centuries a continuous rush of invaders came down – Persians, Romans, Goths, Albanians, Slavs and later proto-tourists from the West, the so-called Franks, who, disguised as crusaders, loved the climate and the wine dark sea and set themselves up in Mistras, Constantinople, Crete and Rhodes. The Turks were late arrivals and stayed the longest.

"So, who are We?" Papous asked rhetorically. "We are the descendants of all these people who came and settled in this lovely part of the world over the many centuries since that other, older Greece saw its gradual demise. What is amazing, after all that turmoil, is that the present inhabitants of this same peninsula still speak a version of the language brought here by the original invaders four millennia ago. And one of the people who helped preserve it was your great grandfather Christos, the village priest."

Rosa had joined the household about the same time as Papous. In a time of endemic, pervasive poverty, even the less affluent in the middle class could still afford a maid. Girls, some as young as eleven or twelve, came to the city from the refugee neighborhoods or the destitute provinces, probably driven away by parents who couldn't feed them, ready to take a menial job for sustenance and shelter and, if they were lucky, a small allowance.

> *In polite society they were called* ipiretria, *or* paradhouleftra,
> *appropriate words or 'servant' but in street parlance they might be*
> *referred to as* dhoulika, *a word related to* dhoulia, *the demotic word*
> *for work, derived from* dhoulos, *slave. It should be noted that* erghasia
> *is the ancient word for labor and* erghatis *for worker, generally used*
> *today in more formal, printed or broadcast occasions. I know of no other*

language where the purported nobility of labor was debased by linkage to slavery.

Many years later however, in the Architecture School of my American college, I ran into an astonishing parallel – astonishing because I did not expect to hear such an expression uttered in the cultured environment of a University and therefore that much more disturbing. Traditionally, younger students helped graduating seniors with their thesis projects, working through the night, performing minor drafting duties. The verb for such labor was niggering, and the seniors would be asked "do you need a nigger to help out tonight?" I had of course forgotten that slavery had been practiced with commercial alacrity by the very same people who had crafted the Bill of Rights in a country that still enforced racial segregation. But then another memory came back from my school days in Athens. We're studying ancient Greek history. Among the usual praise of Athenian Democracy, ("Greece, the cradle of Democracy") and without a trace of embarrassment, the fact trickled in that Athenians owned slaves! That is, there were citizens who voted and ran the country, there were non-citizens and… there was chattel, human beings who were bought and sold, obeyed their owners and did the dirty work. Unfazed by such details, we pupils kept our sights high and continued our readings of Thukydhidhis, Plato, Herodhotos and all the others.

Rosa was unique in Greece. She was black – not the North African, Arabic speaking black, nor the tall, elegant Ethiopian or Massai black. Rosa was short, sturdy and very black with thick lips and short, tight steel-wooly hair – more Ugandan, although she called herself an Abyssinian. Seemingly illiterate, she spoke Greek with a minimal, heavily accented vocabulary. Mutti, with her own limited and mispronounced Greek, and nearly illiterate in her adopted language, got along famously with Rosa. They held regular kitchen meetings in the morning when the day's menu was planned and household chores were divided – two immigrants from opposite sides of the hemisphere grappling with an impossible language, in a country foreign to both, united by their common predicament.

Things went relatively well as long as Rosa stayed indoors. "We must eggs, butter and flour for *Kuchen*," said Mutti in her inimitable Greek. "Take the boy with you in the pram. He must some air." Rosa just stood there.

"Well?"

"I no go."

This was not new. Rosa dreaded going out. She knew what awaited her. As soon as she came out of the house, opened the garden gate, stepped out into the street and started walking toward the grocery near Vassilisis Sofias Avenue, a small figure in a plain, long sleeved gray smock with a neat white collar out of which protruded a pair of black legs and hands and a black head under a short-brimmed hat, the neighborhood urchins, and some adults, would drop whatever they were doing and run after her. She walked purposefully, her head bent down, her eyes fixed on what lay ahead. She would have preferred plugging her ears and wearing blinders. As the mob grew, shouts and finger pointing multiplied and soon reached a crescendo of loud and cruel taunts. Her tormentors followed Rosa down the street heckling mercilessly, hooting, whistling, laughing, screaming, touching, repeating the same word, the word that for them said it all – *Arapeena!*

> *One who came from Aravia, Arabia, is formally called an* Aravas. *In the vernacular we find the word* Arapis, *meaning Arab but also black African and, not surprisingly, bogeyman, defined in the dictionary as "a monstrous imaginary figure used in threatening children," or "a terrifying or dreaded person or thing." And black of course is also the color of mourning, of death. The feminine noun for* arapis *is* arapina. *From the mouth of the hecklers,* arapina *projected a confusion of biting ridicule, fear and senseless fury, the equal or worse of* nigger. *It was my earliest lesson in the dread and hatred of the Other.*

Rosa was a unique Other in 1930s Greece. There was no "minority" here to call her own as there would be in America for example - no people to cling to for shelter and solace. My parents and I, alas, were not her kind of minority. At times unbearably miserable, she lived like a prisoner in an alien, hostile environment. A slave in a slave culture may find some comfort among other slaves who may be wives, husbands, offspring, relatives, friends or simply bearers of the same misfortune. Here she suffered in naked isolation except for what shelter Niko and Lotte offered with little sympathy and no love.

Rosa never referred to her country of origin, or a village or tribe except to say vaguely that she came from *Avissynia*. She never spoke of her mother or father or siblings. Her age remained a mystery — she could have been sixteen when she came to us or ten years older. Her name was probably given to her when she first came to Greece. Was there a surname?

Whatever her age, Rosa seemed to have the normal hormonal drive of a young woman. From time to time she was seen walking with an unknown man. He hung very close to her, sometimes holding her hand or arm, smirking seductively, whispering into her ear. His presence kept the urchins away, protected her. She was unable to suppress a shy smile and for a brief time she seemed to be happy. "Stay away these men!" My mother shouted with cruel indignation. "They use you. They never marry you!" Rosa, who rarely showed emotion, yielded to despair with a pained moan. There were no tears, no sobs, and no comfort from her employer.

"Does she go to bed with them?" asked Niko.

"She better not," answered his wife. "That's all we need. Raise *einen kleinen Schwarzen* here."

Niko was amused. "Let her have some fun, the poor thing."

"Niko! Don't talk that way. I don't want to hear about it."

"What I'm afraid of," he said, "is that they take money from her. She doesn't seem to be buying anything for herself with her little allowance. Could she be taking money from us?"

"She'd be out on her ears if I found her stealing."

In my childhood I saw African people as performers in 'thirties

Hollywood movies – tap-dancing darkies, obsequious servants *(Yeah massa)*, fat google-eyed Aunt Jemimas. When I was six or seven I had admired a saucy, chocolaty Moroccan girl in provocative pose, one lovely breast exposed, in a leather bound book of North African sepia photographs, one of my father's treasured possessions. One day however, I met what seemed to be the only other black person in Athens – a uniformed chauffeur who regularly stood before a shiny black limousine parked along Vasilissis Sofias Avenue, opposite the Old Palace, probably waiting for some diplomat. An affable, jolly man, he smiled and waved as my mother and I, with Rosa in tow, passed by. We saw him a number of times after this and each time he grinned and waved hallo. Delighted to find a male replica of Rosa, I naturally came to call him by the masculine equivalent – *Rosas*.

As I grew older, the urge to avoid being seen with Rosa in public increased. I was shy and quite self conscious and I saw that the ridicule she invariably attracted rubbed off on me as well. At times however, my father, prompted by his habitual obsession, often insisted that she accompany me on one or another public occasion.

"I want someone to be there with you," he'd say.

"But why Pappi, why? I'm old enough to take care of myself."

"For your safety."

"This is ridiculous," I protested. "The other kids just laugh at me. I'm the only one trailed around by a *dada* (a nanny), like a baby!"

It was the day of our annual spring school outing. I was nine or ten years old, still wearing the short pants of childhood, although I felt old enough to take care of myself, and was allowed to walk unaccompanied in parts of Athens. The outing was anticipated weeks before with great excitement. This year we were visiting the ruins of the palace of the Duchess of Plakendia, in a pine forest at the foot of Mount Pendeli, less than an hour's bus ride from the school.

This was a lady with a certain past. Born in Philadelphia, early in the previous century, she married the Duc de Plaisance, a Frenchman, who had inherited an Italian title. She became a philhellene, spending many years in Greece. An Athenian architect was hired to build her a chateau out of Pendelic marble and, oddly, in the pointed-arch Gothic style, in deference to the Gothic idiom of Piacenza. Legend had it that she chose Pendeli, not because of the proximity to its marble quarries, but to be near her lover, the notorious brigand Davelis who would come to her at night through a secret tunnel.

That morning, my father had to go through the usual medical drill, (forehead, pulse, thermometer,) before I was declared free to go - with Rosa in tow, of course.

"I don't want you to hang around with me," I snapped at her as soon as we left the house, "just stay away, you understand?"

"Yes, Titsian, I understand. But Mr. Niko wants…I try."

A large photo commemorates the day. The entire school, all four grades, is spread out in various poses. Teachers stood formally in the back row – Mr. Sachnikas prominent in his vested suit and generous belly; the two buxom women teachers; assorted functionaries and some Academy disciples. A mob of kids stood in front of them, boys with shaved heads and short pants, girls in knee high skirts, some with bows in their bobbed hair. Those in front were sprawled out on the ground, one boy holding a soccer ball, a girl reclining seductively, her head resting on her arm, barely covered legs lying horizontally. On the far left, next to last, stood none other than Rosa, looking fetching in a dress buttoned from neck to hem, a white collar and a wide brimmed hat. Close by reclined her ward, looking not at all unhappy. No one was yelling *arapina*.

Years later, my mother told me how I had once betrayed Rosa when, still a toddler, in the midst of the usual screaming mob, I stood up in my stroller and, with great gusto, joined the cacophony and yelled *Arapeenaaa*! My mother laughed heartily, thought it was hysterically funny.

My great grandfather, the priest Christos Anagnos-topoulos flanked on the left by my fourteen-year old grandfather George and an unknown man. 1872

My grandfather George with my young officer father, 1916.

George and I in front of the Papamandelou house.

With our new maid Rosa in the National Gardens.

With Rosa on a school excursion, 1938.

Marasleion school excursion to Pendeli, 1937. I sit under Rosa on the left.

THE VILLAGE SQUARE

THE ANDHREOU HOUSE sat at the corner, halfway up
Evzonon Street, directly opposite the Petraki monastery and
only four lots away from the Papamandelou house. The top floor
apartment was available, more spacious, great views, and if I know my
parents, a tempting rental deal. From that corner, and perpendicular
to Evzonon, the street rose rather steeply to the foot of the Lykavittos
hill where it turned into a path through the pine woods, continuing
in a zigzag along the precipitous side of the big barren rock above to
arrive in the forecourt of the little chapel on top of the hill. Once up
there, a bit out of breath, the visitor enjoyed a 360 degree view of the
city and the entire *lekanopedhion* of Athens, the large bowl containing
city, suburbs, villages and farms – a sprawl on the march, framed
by the four mountains – Ymitos, Pendeli, Parnis and Aeghaleo and
- beyond the Peireas harbor and the Phaliro seaside resort to the
south - by a long sliver of the sparkling Saronic Gulf.

"See our house down there?" My father asked, holding me on
the parapet. "It's right there, just below us." I thought I could reach
out and touch it, like a toy.

Here we are at our new house. White marble steps took us
up to an open landing where we were greeted by a pair of heavy
oak doors each equipped with a bulbous brass knob. For the next

four years, my parents, Niko and Lotte; my grandfather, George, known as Papous; our African maid, Rosa and I would step across this threshold to enter the high-ceilinged vestibule and climb the winding oak stair with its massive balustrade to reach our floor.

Through a pair of patterned glass doors at the landing on top we came into a large room. Imagine it as a public space surrounded by a group of houses - an agora. Then imagine that each "house" is a room with a door opening into what we will call the Village Square – not a bad name for a space that must be traversed to get from one room to another, (from one "house" to another,) or where some or all members of the family congregated daily for any number of reasons like villagers, or, in a bit of a stretch, like Athenians in the ancient agora.

At the center of the Village Square stood a large rectangular table. Chairs were casually placed around it, others stood against the wall. Here Rosa served breakfast, lunch and dinner; family and occasional guests lingered after meals, sometimes deep into the night. Stories were told and political discussions turned into passionate argument. Here I did my homework, my mother wrote letters and mended socks, Papous read the newspaper.

Entering from the vestibule at the top of the stair we were confronted by seven doors. We will enter each as we progress from left to right. Through the first door on the left we entered the service area - the kitchen and Rosa's quarters amounting to a tiny toilet and, by way of a ladder, a sleeping cubicle with a ceiling demanding a posture of obeisance for all except Rosa and me. The kitchen was equipped with primordial appliances. The sink, carved out of a block of Pentelic marble, had a single faucet with running cold water, (a step ahead of the water pump in Maroussi.) The stove was still fired by wood, charcoal or anthracite, its round steel burners turning red at peak combustion. Everything was cooked at a rolling boil. A massive wooden table covered with oil cloth provided a work counter and casual dining surface. A door lead out to a rickety iron service landing attached to a spiral stair connecting all three building floors with the flat roof terrace.

In the little wash house up there, a scene of *Walpurgis Nacht* magnitude was staged every month. A beefy woman from the refugee camp nearby came to do the heavy washing. Sheets and pillow cases, towels and napkins, shirts and underwear, even blankets and curtains were submerged in a deep masonry caldron and boiled for hours as clouds of steam escaped and rose to the sky. One by one they were taken to another tub and viciously scrubbed on a wooden washboard before being rinsed, brutally twisted, furiously shaken out and finally hung to dry on parallel rope lines. No bacteria could possibly survive the ordeal. "Marighula alone must lose several pounds in that steam bath," said Niko referring to the laundress. "I hear baths like that are common in Japan. Whole families sit around naked cleansing their pores."

A heavy parapet ringed the roof *taratsa*. Here and there, Paleolithic works of art and 'Runic' inscriptions of recent vintage could be found scratched by me and others into the soft sandstone floor paving. On occasion, the whole family and friends would climb the shaky steps to enjoy the panorama of mountains, hills, trees and neighboring rooftops – a view of a still innocent city checkered with low houses and empty lots, a village on its way to urban explosion. They leaned against the parapet and posed for photographs, squinting into the sun, smiling, laughing, the breeze messing their hair, the little church on top of Lykavittos crowning their heads. They filled their lungs with the pine scented air.

Back in the Village Square we move to the next two doors. One leads to the family bathroom, the other to my parents' bedroom. Two beds were pushed together flanked by two *komodhina*, night tables. My father kept a glass of water and his night reading on his side. A chamber pot, known as the *perla*, sat under his bed. (My parents slept close to each other but not under the same covers. Some mornings though, I would find them squeezed together in the same bed smiling sheepishly.) A large armoire loomed on one side.

A pair of glass doors led from here out to the long balcony stretching across the entire south side, guarded by a black metal railing. An outdoor living room in spring and fall only (too hot in summer, too cold in winter,) the *balkoni* was also a popular vantage point for observing action on Evzonon and the monastery below and more distant sights such as the barren slopes of old Ymitos (Mt. Hymettus) topped by dramatic cloud formations. We stepped out and took deep breaths of fragrant clean air unaware that a few years from now Athens would join other mega-cities in competition for dirtiest air.

It was on this balcony, that Rosa and I first met snow one day. I had seen snow before, but only from far away, beyond the houses, up on the mountain. It made Ymittos look like Mutti's *Kuchen*, sprinkled white with sugar. Today, it covered everything, even the balcony under our feet, leaving a white strip on top of the iron handrail. I stood, open mouthed, well bundled, dazzled by the magical transformation of the familiar view. I recognized Ymittos, its profile lost in a pale sky, its mass fused with the white roofs below. Across the street the little Byzantine domes were hidden under white skull caps, the steep cypresses turning ominously black as the wet snow weighed down their branches. Under my feet I felt the chill of the soft, silent powder. I grabbed a fistful, packed it into a ball and hurled it as far as a boy who had never seen a baseball could. It landed down in the street to join the other snowballs flying back and forth amid a joyous crowd. Rosa stepped out, a blanket on her shoulders and a bath towel wrapped around her head, Ugandan style. "Come see Lykavittos," she shouted, jumping up and down. We slid to the other end of the balcony, two kids holding hands, to see that the hill had turned into a three-layer wedding cake.

The ephemeral wonder soon melted away, leaving mud and puddles behind. Next morning the sun shone as usual. The puddles vanished, the mud caked up and the *tsouknidhes* would again menace little intruders. But Rosa and I would talk of the white miracle for a long time.

On another day Papous and I were idling on the balcony. Well bundled up, eyes closed, George was enjoying the sweet warmth of the late winter sun in his favorite chair. A light breeze wafted down from Lykavittos flavored with the pungent smell of pine sap. Spring should be coming soon. Holding onto the railing, my head resting on the bars, I was studying the quiet street below – the gang had not come out yet. Suddenly a big black car rounded the corner and slowly came to a stop next to one of the Evzonon houses.

"Papou!" I shouted. "Get up Papou, look. It's him!"

Papous rose reluctantly and shuffled over to my side. A uniformed chauffeur came around, opened the door and a little man emerged. White hair and goatee, spectacles, black overcoat and homburg, bent over but determined forward stride.

"My God," said my grandfather, " it's him all right, it's Venizelos!"

For some time now I had been seeing him stop in front of a house in his bulletproof limousine. He was visiting a doctor.

"You better not tell your father," said Papous with a grin.

In 1936, Eleftherios Venizelos died in his bed, having escaped royal wrath, endless parliamentary challenges, accusations of corruption, unconstitutional behavior and the bullets of assassins. The fickle Greeks had just voted to return the King to the throne, and greeted him with parades, martial music and 21 gun salutes from the top of Lykavittos. King George II soon dissolved parliament and limited constitutional freedoms, to usher in the dictatorship of German-trained General Metaxas who had supported the King's father Konstantinos during the World War debacle. Venizelos however had the last word. Decades later the new international airport would carry his name and his image would appear on many statues throughout the land. No such honor was bestowed on the dictator.

Back in the Village Square, centered on the wall opposite the vestibule, a pair of doors glazed with opaque panes, announced the *saloni*, the traditional parlor where guests were received – what Americans would call a living room today, as opposed to a less formal family room. By choice or happenstance however, it was the village square that functioned here as both a parlor and family room. My parents didn't seem to care. It would be difficult if not embarrassing to drag an important guest through the village square with its large, frequently messy table and scattered chairs into a room that lacked the requisite pomp and comfort of a sofa and upholstered chairs, a room into which Rosa, dressed in a white uniform, would have to bring a tea set, a carafe of liqueur and a tray of petit fours to impress some grandee and his plump wife. I have no memory of that sort of entertaining. Usually the Saltiels, Elfriede and her Greek husband, Frau Wark, my aunt Toula and her daughter Bebe, various other friends, colleagues and relatives would gather around the big table, chatter in two or three languages, eat and drink and laugh a lot. Sometimes Papous and I were allowed to join the fun. The *saloni* was almost never used for such occasions. It is difficult to describe its function. There were times when I slept there, that is, times when I was not in the slightest bit indisposed. Otherwise my father would order me to sleep in the little bed in their bedroom kept there for close parental observation.

It was in the *saloni* however that the most important event of the year was staged. A week or two before Christmas the double doors from the village square were locked and the room was declared out of bounds for all except my parents. I knew of course what this lock-out foretold – the step by step, day by day, unbearable wait for the rapturous unveiling on Christmas Eve, when the doors were flung open and I beheld the tree in all its splendor lit with real candles, festooned with glittering baubles, dripping with silver icicles, while the old music box played the familiar syrupy carols and tears came to my mother's eyes as she was transported back to her own childhood. A picture shows me riding on a rocking giraffe, probably on Christmas day. My mother lounges on a chair nearby, glamorous in a short-sleeved dress, (in winter?) long wavy tresses, legs crossed, one arm carelessly slung over the chair, her ironic gaze fixed on the photographer. Rosa in a modest smock, stands primly on the other side. Behind them looms the Tree all aglitter.

Other than those few days in December, the *saloni* functioned as a kind of multi-purpose room – for sorting laundry, ironing, playing on cold days or just sitting around. From here too, a pair of glass doors led out to the long balcony.

Back in the Village Square, we next turn to the third wall where, near the corner, a door takes us into Papous' room. It was a difficult room. Three of its walls and the roof over it were exposed to the elements, rendering it hot in the summer and cold in the winter. To make things worse, two pairs of glass doors and one large window invited the God Aeolos and his icy winds to whistle in through the cracks. Papous could be found frequently in bed, with a cold, complaining. At such times the doctor came to administer a popular treatment known as *venduzes*. The rest of us would gather around to watch like medical students observing a famous professor. Papous was turned over face down and his shirt was removed exposing a bony, wrinkled back. Then the doctor opened a case to bring out six or eight small glass cups, about two inches in diameter. The patient was already moaning, invoking the Virgin in anticipation of what was to come. My mother stroked his head whispering soothing endearments. The doctor dipped a wad of cotton in rubbing alcohol, lit it, inserted the flame into one of the cups, quickly removed the cotton and deftly placed the cup on the naked flesh as Papous gave out a little cry. The procedure was repeated until all cups had found their way on the ailing back, each creating a red circular blister. They were kept there for a while sucking on Papous' skin until the doctor removed them one by one, provoking more moans and whimpers.

"He's lucky we're not giving him *koftes venduzes*," said the doctor as he left. "What are *koftes venduzes*?" I asked. My father took me aside to explain that before putting each suction cup down, a small incision is made on that spot with a blade to draw blood.

"That's horrible," I protested, "why?"

"It's an old cure. They say that bleeding makes a sick person feel better… reduces the pressures of bodily fluids…cleanses the arteries…"

One pair of glass doors in George's room led to the long balcony. The other, on the opposite side, opened onto a large paved terrace, in effect the roof *taratsa* over a portion of the larger apartment below. Here one summer evening Rosa and I staged our *Karanghiozi* shadow show.

In a shadow show, images, cut out of cardboard or hardened animal skin and held on long sticks by performers against a cloth screen, are projected to an audience by means of lights placed between the images and the performers. Shadow shows go back hundreds of years, probably to Byzantine times, if not longer. They were found as far away as Persia but became most popular in the Ottoman Empire. Their hero's name, Karaghioz, means 'black eyes' in Turkish. During the four hundred years of Turkish occupation, Greeks adopted the Karanghiozis tradition, adding Hellenizing modifications - characters like Barba Ghiorgos, a rugged Greek country man, dressed in the traditional fustanella kilt and tsarouxhia clogs; Nionios, who speaks in the Italianate sing song accent of Zakinthos; Omorfonios, the lady- killer dandy with a beauty mark on his cheek; Kolitiri, the leading man's bratty little son; Kolokotronis, the hero of the Greek War of Independence and finally, to show the conquering glory of ancient Greece and stick it to the Turks…Alexander the Great. Karanghiozis and his side kick Xhandzaivatis are ridiculous, cunning, raucous types. Karanghiozis is endowed with a large Middle Eastern nose. His arms are extremely long, with extra joints for vigorous gesturing and beating enemies, mostly nasty Turks. He is earthy and vulgar, but still lovable. He speaks for the little people, the downtrodden

who get along, survive and triumph against the high and mighty
through their grit and wits. When he and his pals are in trouble they call
on Alexander to save them – the deus ex machina of the show. This was
theater for the masses, performed mostly outdoors in makeshift venues for
cheap tickets, beloved by all.

Within the opening between my grandfather's bedroom and the taratsa we stretched a bed sheet. With my mother's help, Rosa and I cut out the cardboard figures of the cast and attached long sticks to moving parts of their anatomy. Then we pinned a cut-out of the evil Bey's seraglio, symbol of the Turkish oppressor, on one corner of the sheet and one of Karanghiozis' wooden shack on the other. Three or four candles were placed in a row just inside the bed sheet. The audience, (Papous, Niko and Lotte,) sat on the other side, on the terrace facing the bed sheet. The show began. Soon Rosa and I ran into trouble coordinating the characters' movements and voices, (there were no women in the cast and Rosa had to fake a baritone – as did I for that matter.) Then we discovered our hands were getting singed by the candles, distracting us from the performance. The show ended abruptly when the sheet got undone and fell on the candles creating brief panic. "That was very good," Niko said valiantly. "I liked the voices. But you two need to practice a bit."

There was a view of the *taratsa* from the dining table in the Village Square through another pair of glass doors. Once, a few days before Easter, just home from school, I looked out that way and gasped. "My God," I croaked, "it's…it's a sheep! What's going on?" My father, as part of a fee, had accepted a baby lamb from a client and not knowing what else to do had it tied out on the terrace next to a bucket of grass and lettuce.

"I think they keep there until Big Friday." Rosa told me in a whisper.

"And then?"

"Then…" and Rosa ran her hand across her throat.

"No!"

"Yes," Rosa said gleefully, "we have big feast Sunday. We cook him out there with *souvla*, turn slowly over coals. A man come and do it."

Her eyes sparkled, probably with fond memories of some tribal cook-out. Predictably, we all became attached to the cute, furry creature. I brought it water, secretly fed it spinach and broccoli, stroked its long, sticky coat, squeezed its snout affectionately, called it Pluto. "They can't do this to you, Pluto," I whispered in its ear, "I won't let them." When the day of execution came on Good Friday, the church bells rang all day in mourning for the Savior's agony and death. Were they also ringing for Pluto's impending suffering and death? Would its martyrdom save the world? The butcher arrived with his tools in a sack, like a hired assassin. Mutti took me into the *saloni*. "We stay here," she commanded. I was sniveling. "I don't want to eat Pluto," I sobbed. Mutti couldn't stand it. She grabbed me and pressed me to her chest.

A large crowd assembled around the big dining table on Easter Sunday. Uncle Achileas, aunt Toula and cousin Bebe were there along with assorted Greek and German friends. Sipping their wine they passed around Toula's pink *taramosalata*, chattering and laughing. Hard-boiled eggs, dyed bright red, were brought out for the annual Easter egg cracking tournament. Holding one egg firmly in their fists, guests went around the room hitting each other's eggs nose to nose. The egg that survived this ordeal without cracking was declared the winner - to great cheer. Bebe and I meantime were crawling under the table tickling various legs, provoking screeches and more guffaws. Outside, greeting the Resurrection, church bells rang joyously, accompanied by the cacophony of firecrackers and booming warlike explosions.

Suddenly the kitchen door was flung open and a festively attired Rosa, all in white, followed by Niko, entered the room holding a huge platter of meat. The platter was ceremoniously put on the table to the applause of the gathering. I stared at the meat apprehensively. It looked like any other meat we had eaten except there was more of it. On other dishes I saw my favorite potatoes, glistening yellow with crispy dark edges; and dark green spinach and flowery broccoli and my father's famous *marouli* salad of thinly shredded lettuce, green onions and dill doused in an oil, vinegar and sugar dressing. Niko had carefully dissected Pluto in the kitchen, and I, the little hypocrite, stuffing myself with the succulent meat like a cannibal, had already forgotten my woolly friend. *"Kali anastasi,"* I said joining the others in the traditional Easter wish. Good Resurrection.

Finally, behind yet another pair of opaque glazed doors, on the fourth wall of the Village Square, a small charming room was tucked away with its own separate balcony hanging over the front entrance below. Whenever the bell rang this is where we ran to look down to see who was there. Before Christmas and New Year's Eve, children from the refugee camps would ring the bell and ask *Na ta poume?* (Shall we tell them?) They offered to sing *ta kalandha*, traditional carols, to the accompaniment of steel triangles and a harmonica.

In this little room with its balcony, my nomadic existence in the house came to a happy end on my eighth birthday. The umbilical chord was severed; my parents finally granted me my own space at the opposite end of the apartment from theirs. I felt grown up here with my own bed, my own chair and desk. The word "privacy" which oddly does not exist in Greek, subliminally acquired a meaning here.

The Marasleion school was less than a ten minute walk from the Village Square. I must have been six when I entered first grade there. Mr. Maraslis who made his fortune in Russia, had financed the construction of a unique public school. Its several buildings housed four elementary grades, a teachers' college, an auditorium and a gymnasium all spread over a large, landscaped campus like a small college. I remember its luxurious open spaces as an urban

Versailles, its pseudo-classical main building as a Petit Trianon – or better, as the terraced gardens of a Palladian villa.

Here I am walking to school that first day – alone. Under a short, regulation smock, a pair of skinny bare legs kept time with the slap-slap of sandals on the pavement. I had to cross only one street. Looking to the right and to the left as instructed, tightly clutching my new book bag, I charged across. On that day the walk seemed endless. I was approaching my doom. At the next corner I came face to face with an ominous sight. The hulking grey mass of Evanghelismos, the main city hospital, had always been frightening. Sinister humming sounds mixed with strange antiseptic smells exuded from it. I accelerated my pace in a panic and turned the next corner. What lay ahead? I knew only two or three schoolmates. Some of the tough boys of the neighborhood would be there. I was ready to run home when I found myself at the front gate of Marasleion. I went in – past the rose garden and the tall dark cypresses, past the Main Hall, climbed some steps, turned left and crossed the yard where boys and girls waited to enter the classrooms. Mr. Lulos, our teacher, assigned the seating. I noticed that Manolis, my nemesis, was in the class. This did not augur well.

The bell announced recess. Mr. Lulos opened the door, and we poured out into the yard. The girls drifted toward the shade of the fig tree chattering away. The boys gathered in the center not quite sure what to do until a stocky, tough looking Manolis stepped forward and took charge. "I'm Manolis," he said. "We're going to play Trojans and Greeks. I'm going to pick my team of Greeks. The rest of you will be Trojans." I didn't know it then but this was the beginning of a daily ritual with Manolis the de facto organizer and self-appointed leader of the event. No one ever dared challenge his status. He picked his small team of "Greeks", who were assumed to be the elite and invariably ended as the victors over the many but hapless Trojans. Miltiadhis and Tilemachos, twin brothers recently returned to Greece from America, were always on Manolis' exclusive list of privileged Greeks. I, who time and again ended up on the wrong list, was resentful but too intimidated to demand admission to the Club. I envied the two Amerikanakia, one of whom had long girlish curls and wore stylish sunglasses brought back from Chicago; his brother sported a dignified, serious demeanor under closely cropped hair. Their parents, I thought, must want maximum contrast in order to tell them apart. Manolis was clearly impressed by them. One by one he pulled his team from the crowd and shouted, *"Namaste i Ellines!"* (Here we are the Greeks!) - despicable. What followed, if not exactly battle scenes from the Iliad, at least a wild melee of chasing, shoving, tackling and screaming — the usual - with Manolis, as the bell rang, declaring unchallenged victory for the Greeks.

Many hours were spent in the Village Square listening to the magical sounds that came out of the new radio in a wood box with a curving top and an ornate façade which my father had likened to the Santa Maria Dei Miracoli in Venice, a small charming church he had discovered during a foray to the canals. "Shall we listen to Santa Maria?" he frequently asked after coming home in the evening. He would pull up a chair and put his hand on the dial, his head inches away from three lit green bands inscribed with tiny numbers, corresponding to mysterious "waves". As he fiddled with the dial, a rush of squeaky noises came out of the box interrupted from time to time by a variety of human or musical sounds. I found this very exciting. I tried to imagine where these languages came from. China? Africa? Russia? America? My father was not very helpful. He had strong opinions, said he hated or he ridiculed most of the languages. When he finally settled on a station, we were all happy to recognize a familiar language.

Santa Maria became increasingly the center of attention as world events accelerated toward what seemed the inevitable. News fluctuated from the comical to the tragic. For me much of it had a fairy tale, theatrical air — the royal succession flap in England for example. We listened to the ceremonies of George V's funeral in Westminster Abbey. Months of negotiations passed until his successor Edward VIII abdicated the throne to marry Mrs. Simpson. "He wants to marry that ugly American woman, can you believe it?" asked my mother, titillated by the delicious scandal. The coronation of George VI brought another solemn performance in Westminster Abbey. By then it was too much for my father. He didn't like the British anyway. In his view they had repeatedly betrayed Greece, most recently during the 1922 debacle. And he disliked the language, made yeowly, meowing sounds in mock imitation of the Archbishop's high English during the ceremony. Still we sat clustered around the radio even though no one could speak the language.

Two years before, we heard the news of the venerable Field Marshall von Hindenburg's death, the reputed hero of Tannenberg in 1914 and the man who appointed Adolf Hitler to be Chancellor of Germany, bringing the world its biggest disaster. My sentimental mother had wept. To her, Hindenburg was a Wagnerian hero, straight out of her youth's imperial glory years. She lit a candle in front of his picture on a little table in the village square. Niko too wiped away a tear. The rest of us didn't care.

When I look back I realize that my father had become a full-fledged Hitler enthusiast. He applauded the return of the Saar to Germany and rejoiced in the news of Germany's rearmament in defiance of the Versailles treaty. His unquestioning support of radical extremism continued beyond Germany. He was sympathetic with Japan's ruthless expansion into Manchuria and China. He was not shocked when Franco's Fascists assassinated Garcia Lorca and dismissed Lorca's genius as Communist provocation. He tolerated Mussolini's ridiculous posturing for the same reason he was impressed by Hitler's screaming tirades.

"Where is Ethiopia?" I asked one day as we listened to the news of Italy's invasion, Emperor Haile Selassie's flight and Mussolini's declaration that little Re Umberto was taking his place as the new Emperor. "But he is not a real Emperor," said the seven-year-old me of Umberto. "He is not a *neghros* like the people we saw in the pictures. Like Rosa."

The mood of the times even infiltrated athletics. On the radio we heard the first of the two historic fights between Max Schmeling, the swarthy German boxer idolized by the Nazis as a symbol of Aryan manhood and Joe Louis, the younger black American. My parents of course were rooting for Schmeling and cheered when Louis was knocked out in the 12th round. "Poor boy," said Papous. "What do you mean?" snapped his son. "He's just an illiterate son of black slaves. Didn't you see their pictures in the paper? Schmeling looks stronger and, besides, he has brains. He's the new Germany." Two years later we were listening again. The match this time was staged in New York's Yankee Stadium before a crowd of 70,000 people. Millions more were listening to the radio world-wide. Louis knocked out Schmeling in the first round. There was delirium in New York and glum silence in the Village Square until Rosa, who had been looking at the papers and knew who was who, suddenly jumped up and did a little dance clapping her hands. Papous laughed and clapped too, joined by his grandson. "Those Americans," said my father, "I bet they cheated. Schmeling is clearly stronger than that *Schwarzer*." Had my dear father forgotten that two years earlier at the Berlin Olympics another American *Schwarzer* had won four gold medals, causing fury and indignation among the Aryans?

Books began to enter my life. Some were still read to me, others I struggled with alone in Greek or the irritating Gothic German typeface. One of my favorites was *"Der Struwwelpeter,"* a color picture book originally published in Germany more than a hundred years before containing short admonitory tales for children. See what happens to you, it wants to say, when you misbehave. The boy Struwwelpeter was shown on the cover wearing old-fashioned clothes, his hair and fingernails shockingly long. He refuses to have them cut. Everyone yells *phui* at him and calls him *garstig* – filthy, horrid, loathsome. Another boy, Kaspar, refuses to eat. *"Ich esse meine Suppe nicht,"* he tells his mother, *"nein, meine Suppe ess ich nicht."* I won't eat my soup. He is shown growing thinner every day. The last image is a cross, with Kaspar's name on it, next to a tureen of soup propped on top of a grave. I liked the story of the *schwarze Bube,* the black boy who is teased and ridiculed by three white boys. St. Nikolas comes along to reprimand the offenders. When they ignore him he gets angry, picks them up and dips them in a large black inkwell. At the end the *Bube* is shown at the head of a parade, his tormentors now blacker than he, laughing no more. Rosa smiled but was not very amused when I showed her the pictures.

The Grimm Brothers offered entertaining tales of frogs turning into princes, evil witches foiled by children, kings promising their beautiful daughters as a reward for impossible feats. But these time-worn *Maerchen* were also rife with deception, treachery, bloody violence – scary enough to keep me awake at night, seeing monsters in the dark, wanting to crawl into bed with my Mutti and Pappi.

And then there was Homer. In a Modern Greek illustrated children's version of the *Odhyssea,* I discovered the appeal of Adventure. Yes, there was Polyfimos who ate people and had to be blinded by wily Odhyssefs, and evil Kirki who turned his men into pigs and the dangers of eating certain fruits. Scary stuff. But there was also the romance of travel, discovery, loyalty and love, of boats and the sea, of Kalypso, Nafsika and Pinelopi, models of female beauty, intelligence and virtue.

Movies also came into my life at this time. There was a particularly ceremonial and festive experience here, and quite wondrous. The process of going to the movies was an Event. It required getting dressed, leaving the house, taking a bus or street car and arriving before a huge painting of Charles Boyer and Greta Garbo in full costume as Napoleon and Queen Christina of Sweden mounted outside a theater downtown that may have been named Attikon or Titania or Pallas. On one side, next to the entrance, a small crowd was usually perusing a display of photographs of scenes from the film. For some reason, my mother, my usual companion, chose to ignore the starting time, and we entered the auditorium in the dark, the movie already flickering on the large screen. Although confusing, this experience increased the excitement. To find our seats and sink into plush comfort, we had to be helped by an attendant with a flashlight and a stack of programs. In winter and before the dawn of air conditioning, films were shown downtown in enclosed theaters. From June until November, the situation changed radically. Indoor theaters closed and empty open air lots in neighborhoods all over Athens were filled with rows of uncomfortable chairs, little tables between them for the ice cream and drinks sold during intermission. Frequently, the movie lot was hemmed in by apartment houses, their windows crowded with gatecrashers who had no choice but to join the audience until the show ended in the early morning hours and they could finally go to sleep.

I soaked up Hollywood's offerings. Laurel and Hardy were known as *o Xhondhros kai o Lighnos*, the thin and the thick man; Charlie Chaplin by his French moniker *Charlo*. Fred and Ginger were enchanting. Cowboy movies were an inspiration for make-believe games staged with friends during dreary winter afternoons when chairs, tables, cushions and drapes became stage props and the actors dressed up with grownup duds to act out impromptu scenarios of bravery in the face of deadly conflict. And then one day Errol Flynn and Olivia de Havilland came into town in full color as Robin Hood and Lady Marian to take from the rich and give to the poor. Smitten, I thought Olivia was ravishing. Niko too was enchanted. Forgetting his prejudices, he thought that American women were the most beautiful in the world, and said so right in front of his wife, especially Joan Crawford with her big sensuous mouth and dreamy eyes.

Still, these were uneasy times, what with revolutions, assassinations, putsches, demonstrations, strikes and such. In the dark, before falling asleep, I listened to the grownups sitting in the Village Square talking about troubles in the world. I felt secure under my blanket, the voices in the other room soothing even as they scanned the globe for the latest disasters. Eventually the conversation would return to cozier topics. "They say he has a new girlfriend every month. Now that the Nazis are in, Goebbels controls UFA, (the German Movie Production Company,) for propaganda of course, and with it his pick of starlets," Pappi said with unconcealed admiration. "Not only starlets," interrupted Jackie Saltiel, visiting with his wife Dora. "They say that even Annie Ondra slept with the little clubfooted twerp, and she a star." He spoke with some fervor, probably because he too was short and wore a raised shoe to equalize the length of his legs. "What a body," added Lotte, *"Busen wie noch nie!"* By now I had learned about *Busen* but "bosoms like never before?" Actually I found breasts quite interesting. The soft bulge on Mutti's chest was rather appealing. Sometimes, when I lay in bed next to her, I tilted my head to touch the side of a breast or let my hand casually fall on it, always pushed away gently but firmly, suggesting forbidden territory and making breasts that much more desirable. Once, I saw her come out of the bathroom naked; surprised to see me there, she smiled at me as she reached for her bathrobe. She was frequently provocative, almost erotically so, in her maternal ardor. She told me how beautiful my eyes were, called me *Ninchen,* (her diminutive for Niko,) let me trace her lips with my finger and repeated the gesture on my lips. When I saw her embracing and kissing my father, I ran over. "Kiss me too," I urged. She picked me up and planted a quick smack on my mouth.

I remember lying in the dark alone trying to understand, to fend off the idea of death. In movies I saw cowboys falling off their horses shot by other cowboys or Indians.

Once in a newsreel I watched a man with slick black hair and a funny costume stick a long sword into the back of a black bull. I was intrigued by the moment. What happens after? Is there anything? Kids say that you go to heaven, get wings and fly up into the clouds, join the Virgin, Jesus and all the saints from the calendar. It sounded vague, boring. Will Mutti and Pappi be there? Papous? Rosa? *Thia Toula* and Bebe? What if there is nothing? I didn't want to think about death. But it kept coming back.

In spite of troubles in the world outside, my parents were having a good life. My father's work seemed to be going well, they were young and enjoyed the company of their friends. Several photos show them posing on the roof terrace with a cheerful, worldly crowd. The men wore suits, vests and neckties, the women high heels and short skirts, their hair fashionably bobbed. Lotte seemed to be the center of attention, looking up flirtatiously at some man. At about that time Niko surprised her with a hand-cranked '78 record player from which its acoustical horn rose like a primordial bloom. One night I got out of bed awakened by laughter and bouncy music. I opened the door and blinked into the light. There they were – my Mutti and my Pappi in tight embrace, twirling around in the Village Square, their heads intertwined, hers on his shoulder, his resting on her locks. They smiled, their eyes closed. On top of the gramophone the disc spun around with them.

On the roof of the Andreou house, 1934. I stand between Papous and Dora Saltiel. My parents are on the left.

With aunt Toula and cousin Bebe. Andreou house, 1935.

My fourth grade classroom is on the second floor corner. The building still stands 80 years later.

With Dora Saltiel on the balcony of the Andreou house. The old monastery is behind.

UNTER DEN LINDEN

MY FATHER CAME bounding up the stair, flushed and smiling, unusual for someone who avoided exertion at any cost. He had exciting news.

"Balos paid up his fee," he said. "We have enough money for the trip to Berlin."

"I can't believe it," cried Mutti, overcome. "After so many years.."

"And you'll be there in time for the Olympics."

"Oh Ninchen, it sounds like you're not coming with us again."

He couldn't, he said. There was work to do.

My mother and I had shared the same passport on our first trip in 1930, six years before, when I was two years old. "Look at you," she said, pointing at our photo. "You were so adorable, with those black eyes, dark skin, like a little Arab. And that white beret!"

This and other photographs best describe that first journey for me. One is my favorite. My mother, my Grandmother and I posed for a street photographer. The picture was framed within an oval, cameo style. On one side stood Mutti, looking chic in white gloves and pocket book, a loosely belted frock, white open-necked blouse showing at the top, a fetching beret, silk stockings and patent leather heels – a pretty young woman, smiling, contented. By contrast, her mother next to her, looked to be already in her sixties, although it may have been the tight grey hair and wrinkled stern face over a frail small body that made her look older. Surprisingly, she wore a flower-print dress and dangling earrings, but the stiff leather pocketbook hanging from her arm, the shapelessness of the dress and the sturdy, laced brogues gave her away as an old lady, nothing coquettish here. Little me, who barely reached their waist, stood nestled against the folds of their dresses, skinny legs set apart, staring straight at the camera under a helmet of black hair. I wore a horizontally striped, tasseled, one-piece outfit probably buttoned at the crotch for easy access to poopy diaper. Behind us an older boy had stopped to gawk beside a park bench. Chestnut trees cast deep shadows on the cobblestones. Somber buildings beyond remind us that this is a city. Summer in Northern Europe.

On our second trip and after six years in Greece, my mother must have been thrilled to be back in her hometown with her mother and sister, in a still familiar environment, free for a while from that impossible language, able to understand and be understood effortlessly in her own. It was not the upscale Charlottenburg of her childhood, now a distant, idealized memory, but the humbler Gesundbrunnen district of five-story attached walk-ups near a freight train station. Families of tradesmen, small business men, clerks and minor government functionaries lived here, the wives cleaning house, shopping in the neighborhood, looking after the children who turned the sidewalks into playgrounds in the afternoon.

Still, it was Berlin. All through her life my mother would identify herself as *eine Berlinerin*, boast of her ability to *berlinern*, to speak in the tough street language of truck drivers and manual laborers, turning Gs into Js, and remember rowdy songs like *"Immer an der Wand lang."* ("Always along the wall," the drunk's need to hold onto a wall as he lumbers home). And occasionally she grew sentimental with *"Berlin bleibt doch Berlin"* (Berlin still remains Berlin) – even years later, after the second Great War had turned it into rubble.

Toward the end of her life in the *Altersheim* under the German church in Athens, she would still exchange stories with the ladies about life in Berlin as if she had always lived there. In fact, after that first trip, for the remaining sixty years of her life, she was to return only three more times for short stays.

That visit to Berlin passed in a blur of a few cameo images. I remember being taken to the laundry up in the attic by my grandmother. Large washtubs sat on a squeaky floor under dark roof rafters, their aging wood smell sharp but pleasant. Fresh wash was hanging to dry under a skylight. And I have a vague memory of glass spheres lighting a station platform on the train journey home – Munich? Belgrade? One story my mother told me a few years later stands out. She and I are in the toy department of Wertheim, the largest department store in Berlin. An employee puts me in the driver's seat of a shiny miniature Mercedes convertible, its top down. He strikes a conversation with the pretty young mother while I swing the steering wheel to the sounds of "toot, toot." Soon they are distracted by a pungent odor. They look down and find that the cute little boy's kaka has oozed out of his diaper onto the white leather upholstery – an embarrassment that Mutti soon turned into an anecdote to amuse her friends in front of mortified me.

And then there was the frightening incident my mother told me about some years later. "We were sitting in your grandmother's living room," she said, "when unusual sounds made us rush to the window." A group of men in brown shirts and shielded caps were marching in the middle of the street, singing. Tante Grete said that it was the SA, the Nazi storm troopers. They were singing the Horst Wessel song written by a young Nazi whom the Communists had killed a few days before. Suddenly, a roar came from the other direction, and the SA came to a stop. A mob of men in motley clothes and workers' caps, their fists raised, carrying clubs and yelling obscenities came rushing toward the Nazis. *Kommunisten!* shouted my aunt. People gathered to watch the melee, others leaned out of windows, some women screamed, traffic came to a halt. Raging male voices mingled with the crackling of sticks and the crash of thrown bricks and stones as if enacting a Shakespearean sword drama. Hats flew off, shirts were torn and bloodied and bodies lay on the pavement. Soon police car alarms and whistles joined the cacophony and dozens of *Schupos* (Berlin's black helmeted cops) entered the fray wielding their own clubs. My mother turned into the room and saw me cowering in a corner, whimpering. She picked me up and held me tight. She too was trembling.

"This happens every day now," Grete said, exasperated. "When will it end? All we do is hold elections. Ridiculous!"

Mutti remembered the troubles they had "with that little Jew, Karl something."

"Liebknecht," said Grete.

My mother was just twenty a decade earlier when Karl Liebknecht's Spartakists were battling the Reichswehr in bloody street fighting during an abortive Communist uprising shortly after the German surrender. Things were different now. The '29 crash and the great depression had swept away the few years of German prosperity my parents had enjoyed and had brought massive unemployment and political turmoil causing tent camps to spring up again. A great opportunity for extremists, mostly Hitler's Nazis, who had risen from obscurity to gain over six million votes in the recent elections and become the second-largest party in Germany, well ahead of the Communists. Unlike other parties they employed their own uniformed army, the Sturmabteilung, the Storm Troopers, or the SA - trained thugs eventually to number more than 300,000. Their job was to terrorize and harass the opposition, mostly Communists, to persecute Jews and generally promote a state of chaos. My aunt found them attractive — masculine, assertive, not pussyfooting around like the Social Democrats in that ineffective government.

At the train station in Athens, my father and grandfather were waiting. Niko eagerly took me in his arms and covered me with smoochy kisses. I had not seen him for two months. Who is this stranger with the prickly hair over his mouth? And the other one with no hair at all over his head? I turned to my mother and stretched my arms toward her.

"Ich will meine Mutti haben" (I want my mommy), I whimpered.

"Das ist doch dein Pappi" (but it's your daddy), cried my mother. Pappi was hurt.

"The child has forgotten his language!" wailed my grandfather. The worry proved to be unnecessary. I would soon be bilingual – German with my mother, Greek with my father, grandfather and playmates, and German when both my parents were with me.

In antiquity, *ta makra teixhi,* the two long parallel walls flanking the road that connected Athens (*Athinai*) with Piraeus (*Peiraias, Peiraiefs*) extended the fortifications of the city-state to its main harbor. From here, the mighty Athenian fleet sailed into the Aegean (*Aighaion*) to colonize the shores of the Mediterranean, spread their culture and language, and battle the occasional barbarian, but mostly other Greeks.

In 1936, along this road, now flanked by dismal industrial landmarks, the walls long gone, my parents and I rode in a taxi to board the ship that would take me and my mother to Venice, the first leg of our three-day journey to Berlin. Although the harbor was less than ten miles away, it was my first visit to Piraeus and my excitement was unbearable.

A boy, skinny legs poking out of a pair of shorts, was holding onto the railing of a ship next to a tallish woman in a white, mid-calf, mid-nineteen-thirties Ginger Rogers skirt and white blouse, her hair done up in a new *mise en pli*. My father was probably standing on the quay below looking up at us, having just asked an itinerant photographer to take the picture. The ship's name was *Grimani*, the twin of *Foscari*, both plying the Adriatic and named after famous Venetian doges. Soon the deafening baritone whistle blew and giant ropes were released from their moorings. As if in a Hollywood movie, my mother and I waved at my father who waved back, shouting *"Gute Reise"*. I felt the thrill of the big ship's slow movement away from the dock and saw my father's figure become smaller and smaller, soon to fuse with the crowd and finally disappear. Mutti wiped away a tear. Soon we were gliding past other ships, their destinations hinted at by names painted on their bows – Kerkira, Kriti, Istanbul, Alexandhria. As we came out of the harbor and entered the Saronic Gulf, the perspective behind us gradually changed. Above the blur of masts, smokestacks, cranes and warehouses rose the wide panorama of Athens and the mountains beyond.

"Mutti, look, the Acropolis!"

"Yes," she replied, "and over there…Lykavittos, just above our house."

"And Parnis…and Ymittos…and, way back, the top of Pendeli."

How could I have known on that sunny, happy day, that only eleven years later, on a cold February morning, I would again sail away from this harbor, for a much longer, fateful voyage, leaving behind parents, relatives, friends and the turbulent first nineteen years of my life?

Past Salamis and into the deep, narrow canyon of the Corinth canal we sailed, the boat seemingly motionless as the canal walls glided past us like giant geologic murals, under a ribbon of blue sky high above. We stood on deck, holding onto the railing, entranced. The sun reached the horizon ahead, the water gradually turning from red to purple to black, until sea and sky merged, and we traveled, suspended, inside a magic sphere speckled by stars and the blinking lights of the distant shores.

Next morning, a bright, sobering sky greeted our entry into the Adriatic. Past the dirty docks of Brindisi, we sailed north aware that something special lay ahead. That night we were warned to be on deck at sunrise, before breakfast. Lined up along the railing we felt the moist, cool air on our faces. The *Grimani* quietly slid forward as a miracle was unveiled before us, materializing gradually out of the morning's rosy ether. One after another the jewels of Venice gained clarity, arranged themselves, fell into place - domes, arches, spires, columns, cornices, walls — their distorted reflection rippling in the pink lagoon.

At first the passengers dwelled on the sight in silence, like worshipers in a cathedral. They pointed, looked at each other, smiled. Soon there were voices, exclamations. "…Over there on the right… Palazzo Ducale…lions on top…horses from… Saint Mark's… Byzantine…pink stone… the diagonal pattern…look, gondolas!"

"It's Turner," said somebody, "amazing."

"This is the real thing my dear. And better."

I turned to my mother. "Pappi says that this is one reason he became an architect."

"Yes," she said. "Yes … I understand."

Later, a small fleet of gondolas came to the side and we disembarked. Mutti screwed up her face.

"This water stinks, what's that stuff floating in it?"

"We better not find out."

A mid-day stop in Munich to change trains. I was exhausted and miserable. After two nights in a nice cabin with comfy double-decker beds, trying to sleep sitting up in a crowded second class compartment was torture. To make things worse, I suffered the agony and embarrassment that would plague me into my twelfth year - I wet my pants, condemned to sit in my own cold, smelly *pipi* as we crossed the Brenner Pass. Tormented, I looked out the window as the unfamiliar, majestic Alpine landscape rolled by. Normally I would be spellbound by the gushing streams, the steeply rising gorges, the quaint villages perched up high, the blue lakes and cow-studded meadows - all so unfamiliar for a boy raised under the parched slopes of Ymittos. But I was distracted by the two pigtailedgirls in the opposite seat. They seemed to be staring at me. Were they giggling? Have they sniffed out my secret? How awful.

"Mutti, I need to change," I whispered into her ear.

"All your clothes are in that suitcase up there," Mutti hissed back at me. "We'll just have to wait until we get to Munich. Try to sleep!"

Hours later, the train rolled into Berlin's Anhalter Bahnhof, a vast, cavernous space, ten times the size of Larissa Station in Athens, spanned by gigantic steel arches. We walked out lugging our suitcases through rushing crowds. I had never seen so many people moving around so quickly. And that strange new smell!

"It's the cigars," she explained. "People like to smoke cigars here, even some women do. Now let's find Tante Grete. She said she would wait under the big clock."

Tante Grete was a tall, thin, rather forbidding figure dressed in a straight, shapeless sheath, a little hat like an inverted soup dish, heavy black shoes, a large pocketbook slung over one arm. Her face was pockmarked. There were hugs and kisses, cries of joy, tears. "*Klein* Titzel," she said over and over, messing my hair. "Poor Enie," my mother had said. "A childless woman, longing for a family life she'll never have. Always wanted what I have."

A taxi took us along tree-lined avenues, past large colonnaded buildings, illuminated signs – *Konditorei, Buchhandlung, Kino, Warenhaus.* A large vertical one blinked PERSIL.

"What's *Persil,* Tante Grete?"

"It's a soap powder, *fuer die Waesche.*"

Soap powder? Laundry back home was scrubbed with big, thick bars of soap made from olive oil. This was another world. The streets were teeming with bright headlights, red taillights, throngs of people – the air charged with festive excitement. We passed more signs, some with "*Olympiade* 1936," others with the five intertwined Olympic circles. And now I began to notice the flags everywhere – tall vertical banners mounted on poles. Hundreds of them lined the avenues, red with a white circle in the middle. A crooked black cross filled the circle. My father had already told me about it. The new flag of Germany. The *Swastica, das Hackenkreuz.*

Away from the glitter of the *Mitte*, the taxi entered quieter streets, tree lined, cobble-stoned, with continuous walls of tall somber houses on both sides. Through a gateway guarded by two massive open wooden doors next to a tall courtyard, we reached a winding, creaky wooden stair.

"Do you remember?" asked Tante Grete. "You loved going up and down these stairs."

Outside a door on the third floor stood a small, frail woman, her arms stretched out. From pictures, I recognized the furrowed brow under wisps of grey hair, the timid smile betrayed by worried, watery brown eyes, the sharp nose. My *Grossmutti.* Old, like Papous, I thought. Except for the dress and the hair, she was not so different. I knew I was going to like her.

"Meine liebe huebsche Lotte," (my dear pretty Lotte) she cried throwing her arms around her daughter. "So many years."

"Yes, yes," said Lotte holding her mother's head against her own tear stained cheek. "But now we are together again."

"Ach, und da ist klein Titzel, schon so gewachsen!" He has grown so much, she says, bending down to press my head to her chest. Her only grandchild.

Through the hall we came into the parlor - a small, dim room, crowded with furniture. Two windows faced the street. Fruit, cake and sweets were laid out on a table in the middle. I smelled coffee

"Now let me show you to your room," said Tante Grete.

As the warm summer days went by I got to know my new environment. The apartment was small, quite a bit smaller than our house in Athens. Mutti and I shared a bedroom. Grandma Emma slept in another room. Tante Grete stretched out on a sofa, in the parlor. All these rooms opened into the entrance hall as did the kitchen, large enough for a small dining table. I still remember some oddities: two floors seemed to share a toilet located on the stair landing between them. That meant that some people walked up, and others down, when the need came, only to discover that someone was in there already. This was not so bad. I found that a chamber pot was tucked under each bed for around-the-clock use. And there were water pitchers and bowls on nightstands for washing. But I didn't remember seeing a bathtub or shower, just a portable metal washbasin brought down from the attic for the occasion. So much for Mutti's denigration of her adopted country as a primitive backwater. With the exception of Maroussi, our dwellings all had piped indoor plumbing.

I found other oddities.

"Why are there two sets of windows, one inside and one outside?" I asked one day.

"It's very cold here in winter," explained my aunt. "Double panes keep us warm. You don't need them in Athens." Little did she know.

I admired the massive floor-to-ceiling corner stoves. The semicircular front was surfaced with glazed tiles decorated with Alpine flowers.

"They keep us nice and warm in the winter," said Grete. "We put the coals in that iron door down there. On the shelf up here we keep food and our coffee pot. Every house has one."

Meals offered other novelties. At lunch and dinner Grossmutti put a bowl of boiled potatoes on the table, a staple, like bread, frequently accompanied by gravy, but most often salt would have to do. For breakfast, Tante Grete sent me down to the bakery next door, where the aroma of freshly baked goods wafted into the street. To the great amusement of the baker and his wife, the little *Grieche* stood on his toes and, in good German, timidly asked for *Schnecken* and *Krapfen* - sugar coated "snails" and round, plump jelly doughnuts. Another favorite was *Pflaumenkuchen*, the delicious flat plum tarts Mutti enjoyed with her afternoon coffee, frequently enhanced, without embarrassment, with the requisite *Schlagsahne*.

My big delight was berries, unknown down south, except for

strawberries and tree grown mulberries. I soon became quite a connoisseur, ignoring my mother's warnings about too much fruit. I learned names and flavors: *Himbeeren*, raspberries; *Johannisbeeren*, red currants; *Blaubeeren*, blueberries; *Brombeeren*, blackberries and my favorites, *Stachelbeeren*, the light green gooseberries. Berries had to be compared to my equivalent Greek favorites – grapes, *stafylia*, especially the seedless yellow and the small, tightly bunched black currants which I tore in big mouthfuls from the stem, too impatient to pick each grape one by one.

A rather shy boy, I would not venture outside without Mutti, Grete or Grossmutti.

We went shopping, sightseeing, visiting, usually by *U-Bahn*, the underground subway, but I preferred the more exciting surface train, the *Stadtbahn*, and even more, the elevated *Hochbahn* from which I could see the urban panorama, pretending that I was flying. (Years later, during my early days in New York I would experience the same thrill, a *déjà vu*, when riding the BMT or the IRT, and especially the third Avenue El.)

KDW (pronounced kah-deh-veh) and Wertheim, the two large department stores, became temples of lustful worship.

"We don't have the money to buy this *Mechano* set, Titzel. Put it down."

"Please, Mutti…"

"It's sixty Marks and very heavy. We're not schlepping this back to Greece."

"But Mutti…"

"Forget it. Just enjoy looking around."

"But what good is looking if I can't have things that I want?"

"Think of all the kids in your school who can't even imagine such toys. When you go back you can tell them about what you saw, they'll be very impressed."

But I convinced her to buy me little toy soldiers similar to the lead soldiers I had at home, except that these were bigger, made out of plastic, quite realistic, with movable limbs. They were German soldiers of course, some on horseback, others with drawn swords, helmeted and booted. I also found replicas of real people – Goering, Goebels, even Adolf Hitler. Their arms could be raised in the new Nazi salute. How exciting!

My shyness gradually abated and I ventured into the street alone. Some boys were playing on the sidewalk. At first I just stood around and watched. They ignored me. But soon I began to be noticed – who is this boy with hair the color of coal, shining black eyes, dark skin? He could be *ein kleiner Jude* (a little Jew) – new on the block, suspicious. Anyway, worth exploring. My heart jumped when one of them came up to me, not as tall as I but tough, with close cropped hair, a blond version of the despicable Manolis, the kid who tormented me in school.

"*Wie heisst du?*" (What's your name?)

"Titsian."

"*Was ist das fuer ein Name?*" (What kind of a name is that?)

"*Ein Griechischer Name. Ich bin aus Griechenland.*" (A Greek name. I didn't want to complicate things by saying Italian, I'm from Greece).

"*Wo ist denn das?*" (And where is that?)

"*Weit weg.*" (Far away).

"*Bist du ein Jude?*" (Are you a Jew?)

"*Nein.*"

"*Aber du siehst so aus.*" (You look like one).

By now a gang of little towheads in lederhosen surrounded me. I was asked to say something in Greek. They made faces, pointed fingers at me, laughed. "Du hast ein Vogel," (You have a bird in your head, you're crazy), said one. Another pushed forward and asked what the Greek word for bird was.

"*Pouli.*"

"*Poulee?* Ha, ha, ha…*Du hast ein poulee!*" shouted the wise guy. This is too much for the mob. "*Du hast ein poulee, du hast ein poulee,*" went the Teutonic chant pushing up against me. I slowly retreated toward the door and then bolted as the frenzy followed behind me.

But I came back the next day. After all I had experienced bullies in Athens and these were half as tough as the refugee gang. The *poulee* joke eventually wore out. They warmed up to me and included me in their play, running up and down the sidewalk, screaming and laughing. I almost felt I was back on Evzonon with my pals.

The radius of exploration around the neighborhood grew bigger and bigger. I ventured as far as the *Gesundbrunnen* train station to watch the freight train traffic led by smoky black steam engines. *"Komm mal her,"* said a fat lady one day, beckoning me over. Her husband was the stationmaster. They lived in a small house next to the tracks and inhaled the dirty, gritty air. *"Er ist so niedlich,"* He's so cute, she said. They thought that the scrawny, dark boy from the south was lovable and bribed me with sweets.

"Er spricht so gut Deutsch," He speaks such good German, they marveled.

I fancied myself an Olympic athlete and raced back home at full speed making people think that I really did have a *Vogel* in my head.

By streetcar or by train, but mostly on foot, we explored the city. Berlin was decked out to impress the visiting world with the glory of the Third Reich. Trains ran on time, streets and buildings were scrubbed, trees were blooming, fountains gurgled. A picture of wellbeing - prosperous, friendly, festive. You wouldn't know that three years ago the country was in dire straits. Adolf, Tante Grete said, took care of all that. Germany can be proud of itself once more. Thousands of foreign visitors here for the Olympics were impressed by what seemed to be a nation's peaceful rebirth. But then they saw the giant banners lining the avenues, the endless parades of goose-stepping, steel-helmeted soldiers, of boys in Hitler Youth uniforms all marching to the ominous beat of drums and glockenspiels. Not a peaceful sight, the visitors told themselves, but it quickened the pulse, made you feel good – after all, it was all part of a big celebration.

Unter den Linden was at the center of it all. Mutti and I walked down Berlin's Champs Elysees for nearly a mile from the *Brandenburger Thor* to the *Schlossbruecke*, the walk my father had taken as a young student.

"Ach, here is the *Zeughaus*, Titzel," said my mother. "We have to go in, you'll love it." The red uniform Frederic the Great wore in one of the battles of the Seven Year War was a prime display, along with swords, helmets, shields, spears, guns, machine guns, canon, artillery shells, armor, tanks, and hundreds of more objects glorifying war and conquest. I was enthralled and resumed pressuring my mother to buy me more of the plastic toy soldiers we saw in KDW the other day. As we left the museum, I pointed at the building next door. *"Wie die Akropolis,"* I noted. We were looking at a Doric colonnade. Two soldiers in knee-high boots, guns on their shoulders, steel helmets shadowing faces carved out of granite, were standing immobile guard in front.

"You're right Titzel!" Mutti was delighted. "It's the *Alte Wache*. They say the great Schinkel designed it as a guardhouse; he loved Greek architecture. Pappi will be very happy to hear that you saw it."

We crossed the bridge over the Spree.

"So many memories, Titzel," she said with a sigh. "I used to come here with my father. We sat in the Lustgarten, on one of the benches over there. It was always full of people, baby carriages, children… so peaceful…before the Great War."

She pointed out the Cathedral, *der Dom,* and the colonnade of the *Altes Museum.*

"And this big brown building?"

"Das Schloss, the Kaiser's palace!"

"He lives there?"

"No, no, Titzel. We have no Kaiser anymore. Herr Hitler is the leader now."

⌁

"Why can't I go to the Olympics, Mutti?" I was very upset.

"I could only get one ticket, *Suesschen*, besides you will find it boring, all these people running around, throwing things, a lot of shouting, that sort of thing." I suspected that she was not too keen on going.

"Look, Tante Grete will take you to the *Funkturm*, it's a very high tower for sending out radio waves. You'll go up in an elevator, you can see all of Berlin from there. Isn't that exciting?"

Going anywhere with Grete was a chore, she was always telling me what to do and what not to do. And by what right? She was not my mother. But we went anyway, and she even took me to lunch in the tower restaurant. The view was mostly sky, woods and tile roofs, Berlin just a blur in the distance.

"Look," she said pointing below. "There is Grunewald, our big forest, and right next to it the Wannsee, our big lake." Neither of us on that warm summer day could foresee the horror these names would conjure up in only a few years.

Mutti returned home that afternoon with a fresh tan, excited, though she pretended some ennui for my sake.

"It was all right, but tiring, and so hot," she recounted. "So many things going on at once. On one side there was jumping, you know the kind where you take more than one jump, several long leaps before you land in the sand. It went on and on." As she talked I remembered my father taking me to the old marble stadium in Athens built for the first modern Olympic Games in 1896.

"There was this amazing, skinny black man," she continued. "His shirt had the letters U-S-A on it, an American, they said. He had been winning all sorts of events. They say he got four gold medals. Some people were upset. Can you imagine, *ein Schwarzer!* "

"Did he look like Rosa?"

"Taller and thinner. Not bad looking."

"What was his name?"

"Something vowely your father would have made fun of – like Auen or Ouen, one of those English-sounding names."

"The *Ha Jot* was marching all through the night," Grossmutti told us one morning.

"What's the *Ha Jot?*" I asked.

"The initials for *Hitler Jugend*, Titzel, you know, the boys with the brown shirts and the short black velvet pants. You see them march by here sometimes."

"What are they marching for?"

"Oh, I don't know… to show their loyalty to the Fuehrer, that they love him. Besides, it's summertime - there is no school, they can stay up late and people like to see them march, like young soldiers, to hear the trumpets, the drums, the rhythm. It makes the blood run fast. It feels good after those miserable years."

"There is a big parade tomorrow in *Unter den Linden*, some big party anniversary I think." Grete announced. "Herr Knecht has invited us to see it from his office, on the second floor."

Next day we all took the *U-Bahn* to the Friedrichstrasse station and walked down Unter den Linden to an old building with large windows. Herr Knecht's secretary offered us coffee and *Schnecken*, and I was hoisted up on the high, wide windowsill. Huge throngs had already gathered below, people brandishing mirror periscopes to see over each other's shoulders, holding little Nazi flags. Rows of *Schupos*, city police in black helmets, lined the street keeping the crowds on the sidewalk. Huge banners hung from poles caressing the linden tree foliage. A steady buzz filled the air mixed with distant music. Loud commands resounded. Airplane formations cut through the sky. Our excitement rose along with the crowd's. Heads were turning to the left, something was approaching. The sound got louder as a big band came into view, dressed in full military regalia. A vanguard of glockenspiel players followed by piccolos, clarinets, trumpets, tubas and a herd of drummers and cymbalists kept up a steady, take-no-prisoners martial beat. Behind the band, impeccably precise rows of helmeted, goose-stepping soldiers marched in perfect company squares, each led by an officer holding an upright sword. I was ecstatic, clapping and cheering with everybody else. Suddenly the cheers rose into a huge roar. Something extraordinary must be coming, and all heads turned toward the commotion. Slowly, a cavalcade of limousines came into view, soldiers on motorcycles on either side, a long, black, open car in the middle. A lone man stood ramrod erect beside the driver, left hand on belt buckle, the other, held straight, was raised in salute. He too wore a uniform but was hatless, his hair combed straight, falling diagonally over his forehead. A little black patch rested under his nose. The face was forbidding, the eyes fierce. The very sight of him moved the masses to hysterical adulation, raised their '*heils*' to the heavens as for a pagan deity.

How can I ever forget this day when as an eight-year-old I joined my mother, grandmother, aunt and the thousands below to cheer the man who would soon cause more misery and destruction than any other in history.

A letter arrived.

Athens, 20 August 1936.

My dear Lotte.

It is three weeks since you left and I miss you both very much. I have received your two post cards, but they don't give me much information. How about a real letter, Lottchen? The weather here is unbearably hot, 40 degrees yesterday. I sweat a lot and worry about drafts. Gregoriadhis, you remember, the one with the English wife, came down with pneumonia, can you imagine, in the middle of the summer. But work goes well.

We had some big events here recently. You know that since the King was brought back last November, the politicians have been causing trouble, mostly the 15 Communists in Parliament and the labor unions. The King finally had enough. He declared a state of emergency and dissolved the Parliament. He got rid of those troublesome politicians and gave General Metaxas full powers - the way Hindenburg appointed Hitler Chancellor three years ago. Some say it's a dictatorship. Why not? Look how well things are going over there. Here, too, we need discipline, authority, order. So, I'm very pleased and feel optimistic about our future. I can't wait until you're both back, but write me a letter before that. I want all the details.

All my love.

Your Niko.

PS. Make sure the boy dresses warmly, especially in the evening. I remember the nights can be quite cool, even in summer. N.

I loved Berlin; everything about it excited me. I wanted to stay. "Why can't Pappi work here?" I asked my mother. She would love nothing better but knows it's impossible. So, we made the best of our stay. In Treptow we bathed in the *Badeanstalt*, a floating swimming pool set in the river Spree. We sat outdoors by the river for a *Kaffee mit Schlagsahne* and the inevitable pastry. Mutti bought a pack of cigarettes from a boy who walked around holding a tray strapped around his neck calling out his wares – *"Zigarren, Zigaretten!"* The ubiquitous aroma of cigar smoke filled the summer air.

On our last day in Berlin, a German shepherd bit my mother. She had wanted to buy some *Kuchen* for afternoon coffee but it was Sunday and the neighborhood bakery was closed. My indomitable mother went around to the back of the store where the owners lived. Their guardian dog met her at the door and dug his fangs into her calf.

I woke up on a cot. A man with glasses and a brown mustache looked down on me and smiled. "Aah, signora. *Sveglia.*" His voice was soothing. Another face appeared next to his.

"Mutti," I said, confused. "What's going on?"

"You had a little accident."

"Accident? Where are we?"

"You slipped and fell — the deck was wet."

"Who is this man?"

"Doctor Brusconi. He bandaged your head."

"I don't remember. Where are we?"

"We're on the ship, darling. The *Foscari*. On our way home. You hurt the back of your head. How do you feel?"

"Sleepy."

I remembered Tante Grete and Grossmutti waving good-bye at the station, the kisses, the tears. *"Kommt bald nach Griechenland,"* come soon to Greece, Mutti had shouted. We had leaned out the window as the two waving figures grew smaller and smaller under the giant arches. I seemed to have forgotten everything after that, even the return to Venice, until I saw doctor Brusconi's face looking down on me.

The ship entered the harbor of Peireas in the early evening. As we walked down the gangplank we saw my father rushing toward us. "What happened?" he shouted in panic. His wife was leaning on a walking stick, a bandage on her leg; his son wore a bandage around his head - like veterans returning from the front.

As the years passed and war approached, Berlin slowly faded away. Grete came to visit once at the Vassilisis Sofias apartment, but I never saw Grossmutti again. During the war we received a postcard from the Sudetenland. Mother and daughter had been sent there to escape the bombing, Grete working in a munitions factory. The card ended on an upbeat: *"Unser Adolf wird es noch schaffen!"* (Our Adolf will still get it done!)

I visited Berlin twice more. In 1963 I flew over from Colorado to explore the far out possibility of moving my practice there. My mother joined me from Athens and we had a few nostalgic days together. Berlin of course was not what it had been in its glory years three decades ago. Half the city, including Unter den Linden, lay now behind the Wall, a cruel monument to the Cold War. Kennedy had recently given his *"Ich bin ein Berliner"* speech there. One night while driving to a restaurant we came up to it, a menacing dark mass blocking our way. *"Ach, die Mauer, das ist die Mauer!"* screamed my mother, *"wir muessen umkehren!"* But we didn't turn around. The wall slowly approached us, an ugly pile of hurriedly thrown together stones, cement blocks, debris, mortar oozing out of joints, a mess of coiled barbed wire on top - symbol of new crimes added to those committed only a few years back. Right then I knew I had to go in and see for myself.

Next morning, having left my mother with an excuse, I parked near Checkpoint Charlie and walked toward Friedrichstrasse and the barricade just beyond the opening in the wall. The helmeted soldier examined my passport in studied slow motion, looked at me, leafed through the pages and pointed finally to a low structure beyond. Inside the guardhouse I was interrogated and asked to leave my passport and be back in three hours. Outside, I paused to orient myself in a landscape of desolation. In contrast to the West, little effort had been made to rebuild, at least not in the *Mitte*, the old center I remembered so well. Ruins still stood, apparently untouched since the last bombers returned back to their bases in England, two decades ago. Streets had been cleared of rubble however, the stones neatly piled, pyramid-fashion, on what once were sidewalks. I walked north along Friedrichstrasse crossing what looked like Leipzigerstrasse, once the elegant shopping street. I looked a few blocks to the left toward what had been Leipziger Platz and the giant Wertheim department store, site of that splendid toy department where I had made a contribution as a two year old. On I walked. A few streets up, I thought I recognized something - the ruin of a church? Could it be? Frazoesische Kirche? On the Gendarmen Markt? I turned right on what must have been Jaegerstrasse. And there it was, an empty space surrounded by the usual wreckage – and all at once I recognized the three carcasses: Schinkel's Schauspielhaus flanked by the two once-domed churches standing on opposite sides of the square - the Franzoesische and the Neue Kirchen, the cold wind rushing through hollows where once windows and doors hung. Classical carvings on brown stone blocks lay scattered on the ground - romantic ruins, archeological remnants - the low December sun casting grotesque shadows on them.

Suddenly I became aware that I had company. Two soldiers were approaching - fur hats, high boots, automatics slung over the shoulders.

"*Documenti,*" ordered one. I spread my arms helplessly with a small laugh.

"*Documenti!*" Louder this time.

"Passport…" I blurted, pointing to where I had come from.

"*Documenti!!*"

I desperately reached for my wallet and pulled out my Colorado driver's license.

"*Automobilski documento…Photografia egho…Americanski.*" I said pointing at my chest, amused at my own Esperanto.

"Passport …Checkpoint Charlie," I repeated for good measure.

A brief conference followed between the two. They have nothing else to do, I thought, I'm the catch of the day.

Finally the tall one said, "oh – kay, cow–boy," and waved me on with a smirk.

"Hasta la vista," I waved back for lack of anything else, relieved.

Later, further up, when I reached the wide expanse, I was shocked. This must be the avenue, but no lindens, hardly any buildings. More like an immense, empty football field. I looked left and right trying to find the spot. I could almost hear the roar of the crowd again. "My God," I thought, "I really saw that man…

saw the crowds…right here! I cheered with them! If only I could rewind the tape…play history over again." In the distance, to the left, I saw the columns of the Alte Wache, the mini-Partenon I had recognized as an eight year old, still standing. Now, standing alone among the ruins, the Alte Wache resembled the temple on top of the Acropolis even more. But then I recalled the two steely soldiers standing guard, the big banners, the cymbals and drums, the horror of the German occupation. No. No longer a Parthenon.

—⁓—

September, almost forty years later. My wife and I flew to Berlin. She had never been there and I was eager to revisit my memories with her. The city by now had morphed into its third rendition in six decades. Gone was *die Mauer,* Berlin once again *die Hauptstadt,* the capital. A great effort was made to restore *die Mitte* to its historic splendor. A debate persisted among the planners: should they rebuild exact replicas or should concessions be made to the New Architecture? As usual there was compromise. "Significant" oldies were restored. I was delighted, for example, to see the Gendarmen Markt group returned to its old self – the three buildings fully restored, their decorations brought back to life, mature trees, new pavement and the essential beer and *Wuerstchen* stand. The Reichstag however, after the Christo apotheosis, was topped with an ultramodern glass dome. And over, where the Wall had been traversing the footprint of the old Wertheim emporium, the gigantic Potzdammer Platz complex had risen, all stainless steel, tinted glass and glitter – the Mall of America transplanted from Minnesota, stylishly put together by world class architects in jarring contrast to what had been. Still attached to my old memories, I felt some regret. What would my father, the TH student have thought?

Arm in arm we walked the streets, I exclaiming and explaining as we came up to yet another site and she patiently listening to yet another story. But I sensed that she might have been disappointed. Expecting another Paris or London, she missed the essence of my interest, the effect Berlin had on me as a child, its connection with my parents and the stories they had told me about their time here in the 1920's.

"It's not only what I remember, or what I learned about their lives here," I told her. "You must surely understand how enmeshed in history all this is."

"I do, I do," she answered. "For me though, your reference to history, free of nostalgia, has a different meaning. You know very well that one of its darkest chapters was written right here. I can't discard this fact and think of Berlin as yet another pleasant city with monuments, museums, theater and all the other tourist attractions. There is a big, ugly, uneradicable stain here."

Still, we visited museums, heard Mahler's Second at the old Schauspielhaus, saw "Norma" at the Staatsoper, dined at chic restaurants and generally acted like proper tourists. One rainy day we queued up to climb the spiral ramp up to the Reichstag dome, able, as we went, to look down, through the glass, on the proceedings of the new German parliament. What would Niko have thought of all this? Democracy, he might chuckle, it just doesn't work. Too much talk and little action. On the other hand, he might be impressed – a united Europe, a dismembered Soviet Union... What do you think, Niko?

Not so bad?

Later, we crossed the Pariser Platz, past the Brandeburg Gate, to visit Frank Gehry's new Deutsche Bank building. Inside, we were admiring the giant oyster shaped conference auditorium, when a man came up to us.

"Are you Americans?" he asked.

"Yes?"

"A horrible thing just happened in New York. A passenger jet apparently crashed into one of the towers of the World Trade Center. It was just shown on television."

Our euphoria was suddenly shattered. New clouds had darkened the sky.

Joint passport, first trip to Germany, 1930

With my grandmother Emma on my first trip to Berlin, 1930.

Joint passport, second trip to Germany, 1936. Notice that my vain mother used her photo from the first trip. She also reduced her birth date by two years.

Mutti and I, second and third from the right on SS Grimani to Italy, 1936.

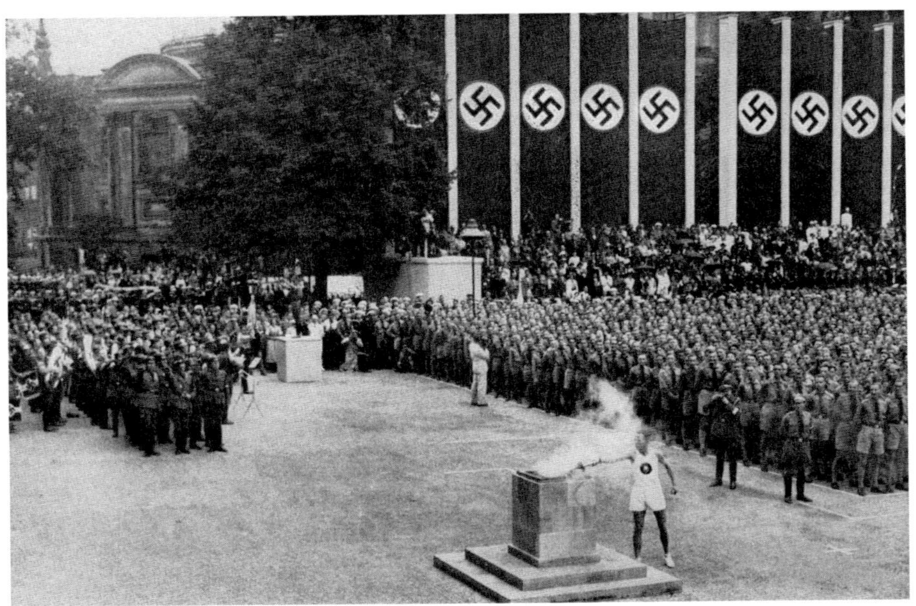

The Olympic flame is brought to Berlin, 1936. Notice Nazi flags and Hitler Youth.

Emma and Grete somewhere in Germany, ca. 1938.

HIPPOCRATES AND

HYPOCHONDRIASIS

THE DICTIONARY DEFINES hypochondriasis as a "morbid concern about one's health, esp. when accompanied by delusions of physical disease." Although there may be some exaggeration here, fear of illness and death was a persistent theme in my childhood years, principally conveyed by my father who was a keen product of that culture. His life-threatening injury in the military may have contributed to his disposition. An incident during his teens however, suggests more. While swimming in the sea one day – and he was apparently a good swimmer – he felt dizzy, panicked and called for help. He was dragged out and taken to a doctor who declared that young Niko had a weak heart and should stay out of the sea - forever. That's all my father had to hear. He rarely went to the shore after that. The few times I saw him at the beach he sat on a chair fully dressed surrounded by happy bathers, squinty eyed and grumpy. (Even on his honeymoon, you may remember, he wore his coat and tie on the beach.) His phobia, naturally, was transferred to me and I didn't learn to swim until I was thirteen.

Healing and preventing sickness was as much craft as science in those days. Faith-based intervention was on the top of the list - prayer, priestly blessings, kissing of crosses, crawling up hills on hands and knees – that sort of thing. Various curative and preventive potions, infusions and elixirs derived from grasses, flower buds and flowers like chamomile and *tilio*, had been popular folk medicines since antiquity. *Vendouzes*, like those administered to my grandfather lay somewhere in-between. Urban sophisticates, my father among them, preferred more scientific practices, i.e. medical doctors, although Greek physicians were looked upon with suspicion. It was generally agreed that German, Swiss, or French doctors were far superior to their Greek counterparts, and so, in the unfortunate case of severe illness, people had to embark on the long, costly and arduous journey by train to Zurich, Berlin or Paris. Otherwise, local doctors and lab tests, home remedies and preventive checkups would have to do. However, before anyone in our family saw a doctor or even considered pharmaceutical relief, he or she had already been subjected to my father's rigorous health test. Not surprisingly, I was the prime beneficiary (or victim) of his attention.

Every morning, while I was still in bed, my father would place his hand on my forehead for a preliminary assessment of body temperature. The slightest suspicion had him reach for the big thermometer, shake it vigorously to make sure the mercury had dipped to the bottom and shove it in my armpit. It was a familiar drill. After an interminable ten minutes, the thermometer would be removed. I could hear the big round alarm clock on the night table tick-tocking through the tense silence as Niko, holding the thermometer in both hands, close to his face, read the result and passed judgment. 36.6 Celcius was deemed normal, and I was free to go about. Between 37 and 37.8 lay the dreaded *dhekata*, the "decimals", considered a sign of impending trouble, although the patient might be feeling well. It was up to my father to evaluate the situation and pronounce the sentence, frequently "No school today." 38 and higher was *pyretos*, fever, deriving from *pyr*, the ancient word for fire. Even at the lower ranges, *pyretos* was a cause for alarm, requiring immediate bed rest, a possible aspirin and the summoning of a doctor. Beyond temperature, other symptoms demanded further action. Sniffles and coughs were treated with hot toddies, chamomile tea, lemon juice and honey, compresses, blue alcohol rubdowns, pills and syrups.

So far we speak only of wintertime, mostly respiratory ailments. Come summer however, attention shifted to the lower anatomy. Bellyaches, dizziness, diarrhea, constipation and vomiting were in. Occurring mostly in hot weather, these troubles were frequently the result of overindulgence in the season's cornucopia of figs, apricots, peaches and grapes - irresistible temptations. The public water supply may also have been responsible. The situation was not unlike that confronting tourists in Mexico, except that here the natives suffered along with the touristas. On average, at least one miserable week each season was dedicated to bed rest. In fact, this sort of malady was so common in Greece and so viscerally disliked, it was given a name of exaggerated meaning. *Amivadhes*, amoebas, conjured up the specter of microscopic creatures eating away at one's abdominal organs, causing, among other ills, the infamous amoebic dysentery, the summer's least welcome ailment and just around the corner from the deadly typhus. My father, like many of his contemporaries, saw the slightest indisposition as a potential crisis, and used the extreme word the way priests, shamans and medicine men try to ward off evil spirits. In my childhood, dangers like these lurked in the shadows and were known to strike unpredictably with disconcerting frequency, giving ample justification to widespread endemic hypochondria. During my childhood I overheard scary stories of wrenching diarrhea, of deaths and near deaths from typhoid, pneumonia, pleurisy, tuberculosis, etc. I still remember my mother's temporary paralysis, (or so she said,) during a bout of what was thought to be diphtheria.

For me, however, one word epitomized the miseries of summer: *lapas*. A slimy, mucoid, disgusting residue of boiled rice – unsalted, unflavored, of grayish tint, meant to coat the innards and soothe diseased intestines. "Have another spoonful, Titzel, it's good for you," my mother would say, making a face, barely able to stand the stuff herself.

In addition to the usual winter sniffles and summer diarrhea, I managed to contract measles, chickenpox, scarlet fever and a suspicion, never verified, of typhus and some of my mother's diphtheria. These ailments kept me out of school, sometimes for weeks, causing reentry anxiety – feelings of regret at having missed out on important events, having to treadmill ahead to catch up with what the class had already gone over and mastered.

I won my medical Oscar during a tragicomic episode, when I was seven years old.

One afternoon, as I stepped out of bed confined there by the usual winter sniffels, my left leg buckled and I almost fell down. My father, who was reading near by, snapped

"What happened? Why did you stumble?"

"I don't know."

"Does it hurt?"

"I don't think so."

"Let me see; walk around a bit."

I took a few hops forward. My leg was stiff.

"It feels a little numb."

"Numb?" My father leaned down and pressed my leg.

"Does it hurt here? Here?"

"No."

"How about here?"

"Nnn … o."

"Tell the truth!"

"A little."

He called my mother. "I'm going to get Verios." We had no phone in the house. "Something is wrong with the boy's leg."

Hours later came Dr. Verios, a pudgy, balding gentleman in his fifties, a carnation in his boutonniere.

"Had to leave my nephew's wedding," he mumbled as he felt my hamstring. "Very tight, hard to tell."

"You think it's serious, *Yatre*?"

"We'll have to X-ray. Bring him to my office on Monday."

On Monday, Verios let out a little whistle as he held the film against the light and pointed at a tiny whitish smudge.

"What is it *Yatre*?"

"I see a certain disintegration here."

My mother grabbed her husband's arm. "What mean this?"

"We had a case like this last year in Evanghelismos. A boy from Smyrna."

"Well?" My father's lower lip was trembling.

"Tuberculosis."

"Tuberculosis!?"

"Of the bone to be exact, a rare disease. Seems to have originated in Hong Kong."

My mother was helped to a chair and was given a glass of water.

"Not to get upset yet," says Verios soothingly. "I'll review this with Dr. Notaras. He's a professor at the University. I'll let you know in a few days."

"In a few days, *Yatre*? We must know immediately. Please!"

He ushered us out. "I'll do my best, he's a very busy man."

Some days later I lay between white sheets in fresh new pajamas, my bed once again in my parents' room. My left foot protruded from under the sheet, the big toe tied to a string leading to a pulley attached to the horizontal bar at the foot of the bed. A small bag filled with sand hung on the other end of the string was intended to pull the leg to a straight, presumably still position. The bag weighed about a kilo, not heavy enough to keep the patient from moving or bending his leg – something he did frequently. In fact, I was behaving like any normal seven-year-old, squirming and twisting, doing everything possible to defy the mechanism meant to keep me still. I actually seemed to be having fun, surrounded as I was by new lead soldiers, picture books and my favorite *fakos*, a flashlight I took with me under the covers to explore the mysteries of the deep. The sand bag was flying happily up and down, keeping pace with the leg it was assigned to control. "Stop moving so much, Tietzel," admonished my mother. "The doctor wants you to lie still and keep that leg straight." But it wasn't easy to obey when running out to play was what I really wanted. At night when the lights went out I was still awake. I could hear my parents in bed, whispering.

"Notaras says we should take him to a sanatorium, best hope for cure."

"Oh my God."

"Says Switzerland is the place to go."

"Niko, where can we find the money?"

"We have to sell everything. Move to Switzerland. I'll find some kind of a job."

"And I can go back to typing. Remember? I used to be good." She was crying.

I yanked at the pulley, turned away to my side and covered my head. I didn't want to go to Switzerland, I wanted to stay here in my nice house with Rosa and Papous, the canary and the new cat, my friends at school.

Another week passed. My parents decided to get a second opinion. The boy seemed to be healthy, bouncing around on the bed; the string had to be replaced twice, and the pulley oiled repeatedly to silence the squeaks. Two doctors appeared one day, looked at the X-rays, performed the usual palpations, took my pulse and asked me to stick my tongue out and say aah. They looked at each other and shook their heads. Mutti was holding my father's arm tightly. One doctor put his stethoscope away, took a deep breath and turned to them.

"Excuse me, but we can't find anything wrong. This is a perfectly healthy child."

"*Ach, mein lieber Gott!*" cried my mother falling on her husband.

"*Dhoxa to Theo*" (glory to God), whispered Niko, holding her tight.

They grabbed their befuddled son and smothered me with kisses. The two doctors backed off to escape similar treatment. But seconds later the real Niko reemerged, his face dark with new suspicion. Squinting at the two he asked,

"How can you be so sure? Professor Notaras has diagnosed tuberculosis, he is telling us to take the boy to Switzerland!"

Justifiable indignation followed.

"*Kyrie mou*, we too are professors! And this is our opinion. You may get a third opinion if you like, but we are certain that your son has been misdiagnosed. Get him out of bed and send him to school where he belongs."

And so, once again, after three weeks, I was back in school. My second-grade class had been quite busy during my absence. The teacher, Kyria Efstathiadhou, had the kids working on the production of an ambitious musical play, a kind of Greek version of *HMS Pinafore*. They had built the replica of a steamboat out of cardboard, complete with tall round chimney, bridge and gunwales, rounded in the stern, and ending in a sharp-edged prow. The officers and the crew were lined up inside that perimeter, too late for me to qualify for one of the leading roles. Miltiadhis, the short-haired twin from Chicago, was playing the captain, and thuggish little Makis, as chief petty officer, was able to boss the crew around – a role not unlike his schoolyard role. And what was left for me? Membership in the crew, along with the rest of the inept Trojans. Miltiadhis launched the show with a rousing aria – "*Vira tin anghira naftes stin plori,*" (Raise the anchor oh sailors at the bow). The crew promptly responded with, "*Laska, laska ta skinia sas…*" (Slacken, slacken your ropes…) and so forth. I put on a brave face and learned to sing along with the rest of the anonymous crew, crowded together in the aft deck. The audience, made up of first, third and fourth graders, clapped and whistled, showering kudos on the protagonists. I barely managed to hold back my tears cursing those damn doctors.

SUMMERS

FALL, WINTER AND spring were dominated by school, neighborhood playmates and family. Summer signified Unpredictable Change, since my restless parents, for reasons still unknown, chose a different venue each year, provoking the "where shall we go?" question come spring. So each summer was like opening a box of confections offering some previously unknown, exciting treat and I was curious for the surprises that lay ahead. After a year of regulated life, I was ready for the slow, indolent hours in the shade away from the dusty swelter of Athens, for days sweetened by the seasonal cornucopia of grapes, apricots, figs and peaches and the warm, pine-scented country air. I had no trouble adjusting to each summer house or hotel room having been exposed early on to house hopping and I found it easy to exchange new friends for ones I had left behind. As you will see, however, not every summer managed to fulfill spring's eager anticipation.

My father thought that in the summer, the cool, dry air in the hills and mountains was healthier than the sticky heat along the beautiful, endless Greek shoreline. His resolve never to swim again after his teenage seaside incident no doubt contributed to this preference. Only twice did my parents opt for the sea and both choices were less than felicitous. I would have preferred Berlin after that second trip in 1936, but it was not meant to be, and, with hindsight, I'm glad it wasn't.

My earliest summer memory goes back to when I was five or six. We had rented a rickety wooden cottage in the village of Pendeli nestled under the synonymous mountain, the white gashes from the ancient marble quarries still exposed. On the way to the public water fountain, the *vrissi*, in the village center, we would pass the stone perimeter wall of the monastery under overhanging branches crowded with walnuts, still green until their harvest in the fall.

The jerrybuilt cottage, set in a pinewood, must have reminded my mother of the rustic squalor of her days in Maroussi. But she took it well. "We live here like *prosfighes*, like refugees," she would say and laugh. Besides, it was summer and, despite the mosquitoes and flies, living mostly out of doors under the pines conferred a certain sense of novelty and adventure, at least for a while. The absence of indoor plumbing and running water was part of the fun. At least once a day, Rosa would take the clay *stamna*, the ewer-shaped, narrow-necked jug to the *vrissi*, noted for its frigid, fresh mountain water. Trailed by an entourage of local urchins, she would return barefoot, a towel wrapped around her head, carrying the *stamna* on her shoulder as if she had never left her Sub-Saharan village. Oil lamps illuminated the evening meal on the porch. "So *romantisch*," Mutti would say, trying to make the best of it.

Our white dog Putzi brought our mountain idyll to an abrupt end. His maleness had been a cause of concern. He disappeared regularly on amorous escapades for a day or two, only to return exhausted, hungry and happy. My mother let him go off like this although she knew that a rabies epidemic had been infecting cats and dogs that summer. One of the symptoms apparently was the urge to bite, causing animals not only to attack each other but human beings as well, resulting in several highly publicized deaths. There was panic in the air. Inevitably, the day arrived when Putzi began to exhibit strange behavior. A veterinarian came, diagnosed rabies and took the poor fellow away. Although Putzi had not bitten anyone, my father, predictably, insisted that I be immunized. We had to return to Athens where every day for two weeks doctor Stathopoulos would arrive with a cheerful "How are we today?" and pull a large, ugly syringe from his bag, load it with a clear liquid, ask me to pull my pants down and jab the long needle into my tender belly, evoking tears and cries of anguish. Naturally, having been told about the urge to bite, I kept a wary eye on the others.

A year or two later came our first attempt to summer by the sea in Loutraki, a resort on the Gulf of Corinth, known for its mineral waters, therapeutic mud baths and, more recently, for its bustling gambling casino. We had a room in an unbearably hot hotel my father had designed in the increasingly popular Bauhaus style. My mother and I knew nobody and waited in vain for my father to show up. Under a searing sun, she would drag me to the shore every morning to teach me the breaststroke, barely able to paddle around herself. Both of us hated the loud Athenian crowd, the sticky sand, the itchy salt water. We would soon give up and flee to the shelter of a beach bar to mope over tepid *gazozas*.

To break up the monotony one evening, we walked over to the casino restaurant and were shown to a table. Nearby, the sea was lapping the sand, still warm from the day's sun. Under a black sky, the lights of Corinth across the bay glistened, mirrored in the still waters. Mutti ordered her sweet Vermouth with a slice of lemon and an ice cube, and a lemon *gazoza* with a straw for me. Sitting primly next to her in my new one-piece sun suit, with its row of buttons down the front, my skinny legs and sandaled feet dangling off the chair, I surveyed the scene. A couple had just sat down at a nearby table, their two kids already chasing each other. The situation was irresistible, and before long I joined in the revelry leaving my mother sitting alone with her drink. She looked chic in her white blouse, the top three buttons carelessly left open, legs crossed to display a shapely calf, a wide brimmed black hat shading her melancholy eyes. Marlene Dietrich could do no better.

Some time later, I returned breathless to find a changed scene. A tall dark man was sitting next to my mother, leaning forward in intimate conversation. For a moment I thought I saw my father – the same white suit, made from light *koukoulariko* cotton, white shirt, white shoes. Only the straight necktie, instead of the bowtie gave him away. Mutti looked rather pleased, smiling guardedly, trying to suppress a giggle, playing with her locks.

"Titzel, darling," she said in her mannered Greek. "This is Mr. Kostas. He show us around the casino, help us with the games. Isn't that nice of him?"

Mr. Kostas was very polite, treated us to more drinks and guided us around the gambling tables, explaining everything. He bought my mother a few one-Drachma chips, and she squealed and leaned on him when the roulette ball landed on her color.

"Have you been to Monte Carlo?" he asked.

"Heavens no, just Athens and Berlin. Have you?"

"Oh yes," he said taking a deep drag on his cigarette, a man of the world.

"*That* is a real casino … glamorous people, heavy betting. A woman like you belongs there."

"Oh, Mr. Kostas!"

I tugged at her skirt, sleepy and bored by then.

As we walked back to the hotel, he said,

"I've always wanted to go to Germany, I love German people. They so admire our ancient stones." He smiled. "And the women are so beautiful, so friendly."

"Oh Mr. Kostas, you are a flatterer!"

"But it's true. By comparison, Greek women are arrogant, a bit hard."

Something Niko had told her many times.

Outside the hotel they shook hands, and he patted my head.

"Can I see you tomorrow?" That smile again. She looked away, trying to hide her pleasure.

"Possibly."

The white, hazy sky the next day promised another *kafsonas*, a scorcher, and another trudge to the seashore under a merciless sun. But I was not feeling so well.

"Mutti, my belly hurts," I complained, as I paced the floor in my underpants.

"I told you not to eat all those figs yesterday!"

"Mutti, ich muss kaka machen!" I was shouting now.

"I'll take you down the hall to the bathroom, let's go!"

But it was already too late. A sharp stink hit her nostrils. My underpants were bulging.

"Oh, Titzel, you naughty, naughty boy! What a horrible mess!"

She lowered my pants, wiped my bottom with a towel, grabbed the latest copy of the *Illustrierte* and wrapped the smelly pile in it as I whimpered, mortified.

"Just like when you were a baby and I changed your diapers," she hissed. "Now I have to wash myself, and the floor, and get rid of this *Scheisse*."

Soon, the two of us descended gingerly down to the lobby - I, holding the guilty package; she, smiling her *Kalimera* at the concierge - both of us picking up the pace as we rounded the corner looking for a discreet dumping site. In the afternoon we boarded the bus back to Athens.

"A suitable ending to a miserable vacation," said my mother. "What a fiasco!"

"Poor Mr. Kostas," I added, happy. "He'll wonder what happened to us."

The year after our summer in Berlin the question came up again.

"There is a village up high in the mountains of Peloponnisos," said my father. "It's in a forest of spruces. You'd like it there Lotte, it's a bit like the mountains of Bavaria."

Mutti, who had never spent time in the mountains of Bavaria, nodded with hesitant approval, although she knew that this meant weeks away from her husband, who might visit for a few days and then rush back to Athens.

The hamlet of Trikala, was perched some thousand meters above the sea. Our hotel room offered a view of Alpine grandeur. The air was fresh, fragrant with a mélange of bracing country smells – cow manure, burning wood, flowers and evergreens. Chickens and roosters clucked below; a donkey hee-hawed, hawks circled the sky.

"I think we'll like it here, Titzel," declared my mother taking a deep breath. "It's so healthy, and look at the *Tannen* - so straight, so strong, so fragrant." I knew what came next. "They make me feel so homesick," she said, her gaze aimed at some distant vision.

The cool dry air and Bavarian landscape were not enough. The village was primitive. We took walks. Mutti spent hours in the shade of the thatched gazebo chatting with other guests in her inimitable Greek, two attractive young men among them. I was alternately bored and mildly entertained. Playmates were hard to come by until one day Thalia appeared in the gazebo with her mother. She was a year or two older, as tall as I, with dark page-boy hair, long eyelashes, and pouty lips. We struck a conversation.

"I was named after one of the nine muses," she started. "I should have been called Terpsichori since I like to dance and sing. But it's such an ugly name, don't you think? I like Thalia much better. Don't you?"

"Yes…I think so." She was rather intimidating, but I couldn't stop looking at her.

"Would you like to hear me sing?"

"Sure…"

"It's a song from a film my mother and I saw in Athens. It was wonderful, lots of bouncy music and dancing. It's in English." She stood up and sang, *"I'm in xheaven,* (the 'h' is hard, a la Grec,) *I'm in xheaven,"* continuing with *"ta, ta, tas,* and ending with *"tseek, to tseek."*

She then grabbed me, stretched one of my arms out, put my other arm around her back and her own around my waist, all the while continuing her song. We twirled around a bit, her cheek pressed against mine, her breath in my ear warm and a little ticklish. This was quite astonishing but strangely enjoyable. Her cheek felt so smooth next to my mouth that I felt a sudden urge to take a bite. Meantime, as our legs intertwined down below to the rhythm of her *ta tas,* I became aware of another more urgent tension. Relief and frustration came together with the sudden appearance of my mother.

"Time for a walk," she commanded. Fred and Ginger had to unclasp.

A picture dated July 1938 shows me with my parents outside a small hotel in a place called *Varibombi.* Lotte wears a flowery, belted, mid-calf length dress; Niko is in his customary *koukoulariko* white summer suit, bow tie and white shirt. I stand between them – a splendid ten-year old specimen: straight black hair combed with a part slightly to the left of center; dark, tanned skin; bright toothy smile; slim arms sticking out of a plaid shirt; belted, short white pants exposing well formed knees and calves; feet in a pair of white sandals.

Varibombi lay in a valley north of Athens between two mountains, its location distinguished by its proximity to Tatoi where the King had his summer palace. Royalty always impressed my mother, who was nostalgic for the days of the Kaiser and pored over picture magazines following the antics of European royals. My father seemed to share her interest. He owned an *Almanac de Gotha,* a small red volume that listed the lineage of monarchies and nobility going back to the Middle Ages. He had found that most European bluebloods were related to each other, a discreetly incestuous linkage that, he said, explained royal afflictions like hemophilia, idiocy, insanity and the like.

"It's not only royalty," he told her. "It happens among ordinary people too."

"No!" She was shocked. "You mean…?"

"Yes, yes, especially in remote, isolated communities they say, like farm settlements high in the Swiss Alps, where it was revealed that brothers and sisters sleep together and have babies."

"Niko!"

"It's true. Families grow and grow and nobody ever has to leave the farm. And they do it with animals too, sheep, goats, even cows."

"Stop it! The boy will hear you. What a disgusting thing to talk about!"

The boy, who had only a vague idea of what "it" is, did overhear.

"I wish I had a little sister," he thought. "And I wouldn't mind sleeping with her or even with a brother. No fun sleeping alone."

On woven wicker chairs, under the pines, the small community of guests at the hotel passed the time chatting, dozing, snacking on watermelon, sipping lemonade, until mealtime when they shuffled to the restaurant for more eating, drinking and conversing. I fought off boredom in a culinary rut gorging every day on baby lamb chops, fried potatoes and a syrupy Levantine custard and filo desert called *ghalaktoboureko*. In spite of this diet I remained as thin as a rail, causing my father to squeeze my scrawny biceps and shake his head. "You're too thin," he declared. "We've got to fatten you up."

It was the following summer when I first tasted freedom and female betrayal.

My father had decided that we should rent a house this time. "It's much better than staying in a hotel for a month, with bad food and all those dull people." Mutti kept quiet. The food last year was not bad, I couldn't have enough of it, she loved being waited on, and it was nice to have company during those long hot days. Renting a house would mean cleaning and cooking, squabbling with Rosa, dealing with slow-motion Papous, entertaining her son and being bored while her husband was living it up in Athens with his buddies and God knows who else.

"For two months?" she asked weakly. "Where?"

"Ekali, I thought. It's so cool up there, so green, great views of Mount Parnis. Also very expensive. Maybe Kifissia, what do you think?"

"I like Kifissia. The big sycamores, the gardens, the sound of the water running down the side channels of the streets." She was perking up thinking of her friend Elfriede's villa and its luxuriant garden.

Listening nearby, I let my imagination fly. Gardens! I had just read a novella about a hidden, overgrown garden within whose walls two young lovers were happily imprisoned, enfolded in its deep dark arbors. Or perhaps a garden like the *giardini* in Pappi's Italian garden book, even with their stiff geometry. Or like the dreamy, lush Persian *bagh* I saw on a post card. Or, even better, the beloved, familiar oasis of a Greek *perivoli*, the walled-in garden, crammed with orange, lemon and apricot trees, intoxicating jasmine, glowing pomegranates, climbable fig trees…

"It's like moving into a new house all over again," Mutti cried, exasperated, a few days later. "We have to schlep all our stuff up there, to an empty house. A house? A concrete box is more like it!"

Niko, the architect, the aesthete, had really goofed this time. Away from the green center of Kifissia, the house we had rented, recently built, sat in a desert of empty lots. Far from Elfriede's villa, the shady sycamores and cool rushing water came to a sudden halt fifty meters from the house, looking like a distant oasis to a parched survivor in the Sahara. A flimsy wire fence enclosed a plot of earth that someday might yield a garden. In the middle sat a flat-topped concrete box, with square holes for windows, one corner missing to make room for a roofed terrace. The whole thing was painted the color of pistachio ice cream. If not for that color, it could be a bunker at the Maginot line — very much in the news these days. By mid-afternoon, the temperature under the roof would reach stupefying levels and only by dawn, when the slab has finally cooled a bit, would the air inside equal the temperature of the air outside. Rosa was the only one who seemed happy - probably reminded of her ancestral village in Uganda. "On the other hand," I asked my grandfather, "isn't black supposed to absorb heat more readily than white? Shouldn't she be suffering more than us?" Papous opened one eye, grunted and returned to his coma.

We spent endless days in swelter and boredom. Pappi arrived Friday night or Saturday morning from the train station in an *amaxaki*, the elegant, black, open cabriolet with the big wheels drawn by one horse, still popular in Kifissia, looking dapper, as usual, in freshly pressed white *koukoulariko*, white shirt and bow tie, toothy smile, black hair brushed straight back. Mutti swallowed her resentments and threw her arms around him. So did I who had missed his opinionated paternal presence.

"You look thin to me," he invariably told his healthy, sun-tanned boy. "Are you eating well?"

"Oh Pappi, you know I eat everything now. I'm strong, see?" I displayed the biceps of a scrawny arm. "And I ride a bicycle every day," I blurted, immediately aware of my faux pas.

Like a menacing Zeus he turned to my mother and unleashed his fury.

"You let the boy ride a bicycle here in the street, among the cars?!"

But we were prepared for the assault. By now his legendary nerves, his Greek *nevra*, had become old hat. Still, we cowered to pacify the beast, and soon the subject was deftly changed, to be picked up again more calmly later, or just put aside. We knew by now that underneath the furor there was no real threat, although sometimes I saw my mother teary after one of my father's eruptions. Still, in all these years, he had never raised a hand to hit me or my mother – or anybody else, as far as I could tell. A noisy bark, but no bite.

I relished my new-won freedoms - as long as my father was absent and with my mother's benevolent consent. I walked into town alone, bought myself a *tyropita*, looked at shop windows, gawked at the steam engines in the train station. At Kakoyannis' bicycle shop I paid for an hour's rental and took off, coasting down the shady lanes to the house, where I circled around, practicing tight turns, no-hands riding and balancing at standstill. In the process I had a chance to show off to the local gang of refugee toughies, who would like nothing more than to see me hit the dirt, so that they could grab the bike. They baited me, tried to push me, gathered outside the fence and challenged me. "Come out, are you a coward?" I just stood there looking at them. Eventually I turned around and slowly went in pretending I was a matador turning his back on the fatally wounded bull to the *oles* of the crowd. I sat in my room as the baiting subsided. I didn't like to fight. Was I a coward? Was it bad to be a coward?

Melpomeni lived in a whitewashed village house down the road. She had been watching me as I was going through my bicycle routines. One morning she came to the gate.

"What you want?" shouted Rosa, for whom the world outside was the Enemy.

"I want to see the boy who lives here."

"Titsiaaan! Someone want see you."

She stood there as I came out, a scrawny creature in a colorless sheath, a mop of short straight hair, bare legs in sandals. She looked like any other girl – except for the magnetic, challenging green eyes, a sight so shocking, that I felt the blood rush to my cheeks.

"*Kalimera*, I saw you yesterday."

"I saw you too."

"You shouldn't pay attention to those *khaminia*. They're no good."

"It's not easy."

"Would you like to do something?"

"Do you play *tavli*?"

"A little."

I brought out my father's heavy backgammon set and we rolled the dice for a while. She didn't seem to be interested in the game.

"Do you want to walk around? A boy I know near here has a swimming pool. We could go see it. Nobody is there."

We walked over, opened the gate and strolled around a fancy new house to find a rectangle of dirty water with a dead mouse floating in it.

"Do they swim in this?" I asked.

"Vassos says they do. They're rich. Are you rich?"

"I don't know. Are you?"

"My babas says we're poor. He says you and Vassos are rich, capitalists."

"We don't have a pool or a house. So I don't think we're rich."

"But you're richer than we are."

We moved on.

"I think that girl likes you," said Mutti with an annoying smile. "She's here every day."

"So, what's wrong with that?"

I liked having her around, waited for her every morning. A welcome change from the crude neighborhood boys, and so good to look at. We were inseparable until one day she said "Vassos is back. He's asked me over for a swim."

"Can I come too?"

"He didn't ask you. I don't know."

Now that Vassos was back, Melpomeni didn't drop by much anymore. I often saw her sauntering over to his house.

"Why can't we have a house with a swimming pool?" I asked my mother.

"I won't even answer such a silly question."

One day I walked over to her house to find her playing checkers with Vassos under the big olive tree.

"Can I join you?" I asked.

"Sure," said Vassos, who was actually a nice kid, even if he was a rich capitalist. The three of us chased each other around for a while until Melpomeni came up with an idea.

"How about a wrestling match? We can pretend you two are warriors in the Trojan war. One of you is Hector and the other

Achileas. The winner gets to marry me. I'm Helen."

"But Helen belongs to Paris, who abducted her," I said pedantically.

"Whatever," growled Melpomeni, eager for the match, her green eyes glistening.

Vassos and I squared off, circled each other and suddenly embraced like long lost relatives, our legs spread apart, our arms entangled in a heavy-breathing dance. Melpomeni hopped around us like a boxing referee. Soon we lost our balance, I falling first, Vassos on top of me, I desperately trying to get out from under but held in place by Vassos' weight. As I was lying there, my head squeezed sideways against the floor tile, Melpomeni's face appeared, inches from mine, grinning gleefully. I could feel her breath.

"Vassos is the winner! I'm going to marry him!" she gloated.

We got up slowly, dusted ourselves off and Melpomeni bestowed a kiss on Vassos' cheek. Once again a defeated Trojan, I slowly returned to the bunker fighting back tears.

It was during the end of that summer in Kifissia that war was declared. It did not exactly come as a surprise. Ever since our trip to Berlin, more and more disquieting news came over the radio. Around the city's kiosks, newspapers hanging on clothespins repeated ominous messages with screaming headlines. JAPANESE ARMY TAKES NANKING, GERMAN TROOPS MARCH IN VIENNA, CHAMBERLAIN, DALADIER YIELD IN MUNICH, CZECHOSLOVAKIA DISMEMBERED.

Greeks, down at the tip of the Balkan Peninsula, felt that these far away events were someone else's problem. Their own *Fuehrer* Ioannis Metaxas seemed to handle things well enough. My father was pleased.

Other summers followed. But the innocent years were coming to an end. I was growing up and the clamor up north was getting louder and drawing closer.

With my mother in Loutraki, 1935.

With my father, Trikala, on one of his rare visits. 1937

The three of us, Varibombi, 1938

Mule excursion, Trikala mountains. Mutti and I are third and fourth on the left.

GOODBYE EVZONON

NINETEEN THIRTY EIGHT, and we had been living in the Village Square house for almost four years. My father and our landlord Andhreou were having disagreements. Among other problems, Andhreou wanted to raise the rent. They had frequent noisy, impolite fights, typical in those days, given the volatile Mediterranean temper. As the heat of the argument rose, insults flew back and forth, mostly in the form of attributions like *ghourouni* (swine), *katharma* (scum), ktenos (beast, brute), *keratas* (cuckold).

This is a good place to say a few words about Greek curses. During my childhood, people of our "social level" would confine their insults to relatively mild expletives like those mentioned above. More shocking language entered an argument when it was fuelled by fury. The operative root expression was *ghamos*, (accent on the first syllable,) marriage. From here the leap went to the verb *ghamo* (accent on the more emphatic last syllable,) to fuck, (raw and vulgar, not the milder "make love" or "sleep with" or "have intercourse".) When *ghamo* was combined with the articles *to* and *ti* and the possessive pronoun *sou*, your, it became the basic component in a large menu of malevolent invective that might include such words as *mana* (mother), *Panaghia* (Virgin Mary), or *Theos* (God). So the curse *ghamo ti mana sou* may get the upgraded retort *ghamo* to *Theo sou* and so on. Today, decades later, an interesting cultural shift has occurred: *ghamoto*, (alone, without attachments and the article fused with the verb,) has become an expression of mild frustration, no longer an insult directed at anyone, a part of everyday parlance, passing through almost everyone's lips - spanning all ages, social classes and frequently heard on radio and television and found in newspapers. It has become benign, an expletive no worse than "dammit!" No one is shocked anymore.

Much to everyone's regret except possibly my father's, we decided to move again. Not only did we leave a house in which we spent four happy years, a generous, commodious dwelling with wonderful views, but even worse, we abandoned the lovely Evzonon neighborhood. I felt the loss more than the others. No wonder – all of my early childhood was cradled in that little street, even as my parents restlessly moved from house to house.

Once more, like gypsies, we piled up furniture, kitchen-wares, birdcage, and books on two horse drawn carts, to move only four blocks away. Down Moni Petraki Street we went, past the military hospital next to the army barracks, to Vasilissis Sofias (Queen Sofia) Avenue, a wide thoroughfare starting at Syntaghma Square in the center of Athens and running into the country road to Maroussi and Kifissia. Queen Sofia, as we recall, was King Konstantine's wife and the German Kaiser's sister. I rode on one cart holding Mookie, the new griffon sheepdog and Rosa in the other with Moushie, the calico cat we got last year.

Although there were some similarities to the Andhreou place, much was different. Yes, there was an outside marble stair leading to the second floor vestibule followed by a wood stair to the third floor where we entered a central room, similar, but disappointingly smaller, than the village square, from which doors led to all other rooms. But the similarity pretty much ended here. The house was set back from the avenue, making room for a small front garden. It reminded me of the Papamandelou house a few years back. The apartment was smaller than Andhreou's with fewer amenities and less charm.

Why did we have to move? Why, after nearly a decade and four moves did we abandon wonderful Evzonon Street, that cozy nest of my childhood? I was sad, nostalgic. Gone was Lykavittos, the Petraki monastery, the church, the little park. Our new home on Vasilissis Sofias featured a noisy parade of belching buses, wheezing trucks, clunky donkey carts and the occasional black Packard. Across the avenue lay empty, barren real estate slashed by the once mighty Illyssos river, now a gully fed by the sluggish effluent from the tarpaper refugee shacks clinging to its sides, that turned into a foaming grey torrent during the occasional downpour. Beyond, though, rose the blue-purple slopes of Mount Ymittos, still uninhabited in those days, where the sun made its cheery appearance every morning.

The move heralded a new phase in my life. I had finished Marasleion and entered the German school - a much longer walk every day. I spent more time reading – more serious books like the thick one-volume illustrated history of France and England. Jules Verne took me away on exotic, worldwide adventures to join the shipwrecked crew in the *Mysterious Island,* and I tormented Rosa with tales of the slave trade in equatorial Africa in *The Fifteen–Year-Old Captain.* From Daniel Defoe I learned how to survive all alone on my own wit – a lesson I would never forget. And one day someone gave me a book by Karl May, a German writer of adventure stories. The hero of the book was Winetu, an Apache warrior befriended by a German scout. Winetu had superhuman skills and courage - the ideal noble savage. May was a popular, prolific writer, cranking out dozens of squat, fat, gilded volumes aimed at young people like me. May's oeuvre went beyond Comanches and Apaches. Hooked, I amassed a minor May collection, devouring stories of camel-driving nomads in the Iranian plateau, treasure islands in the Indian Ocean and Bedouins in the Sahara. One day I was astonished to learn that none of these authors had ever left home - Defoe stayed in England, Verne in Paris and May somewhere in Deutschland. What gall! How disappointing!

In spite of my father's aversion to it, I found the sea very attractive and it had a presence in much of my reading. In Verne's *Twenty Thousand Leagues Under The Sea*, I imagined myself walking with captain Nemo and his comrades on the ocean floor to visit the remnants of Atlantis. In *Treasure Island*, I sailed with John Silver and his pirates on their ship and heard the creak of the ropes pulled by the giant square rigs. I put myself in the battle of Salamis – the crafty Athenians pouncing on the inept Persians in the narrows between the island and Attica, their oars their only means of locomotion, their shields and spears at the ready, their war cry terrifying. And in Trafalgar – Nelson in his admiral's uniform with gold epaulettes, braided high collar and inverted-boat hat, shouting commands under billowing sails, cannons blasting away, the French as inept as the Persians.

Still a boy, I spent time fussing with my *bakaliko*, a miniature of the traditional Levantine grocery store I got for Christmas. Everything the corner store up the street had to offer was here, small enough to hold in my fingers. I could fondle the little sacks of dry beans and lentils; barrels of feta cheese and *bakaliaro*, the dry, salty cod; tiny tins of canned fish and vegetables; trays of *dolmadhes*, wrapped in make-believe grape leaves and containers of black, green and purple olives. All were displayed and stored on shelves, bins, cabinets and counter tops surrounded by three "walls." Only missing was the delicious, musty smell of the real thing.

Occasionally, a boy or two would come to play. We closed the doors and stage-set the "Nautilus" interior with the big underwater window. I acted as the *regisseur*, both director and set designer, and assigned myself the role of captain Nemo. "You are the crew," I commanded. "We're sailing under the North Pole. Watch for the giant squid under the ice." One day, little Popi came over, a rare event. She wore her dark blue school smock with the white collar and a yellow bow on top of her head. Her knees were bare. I tried to stage an adventure with her, but she didn't seem interested in being a member of Captain Nemo's crew. She liked to talk and ask questions. So we stepped out on the balcony. *"Poh, poh,"* she said. "You can see so much from up here!" I stared at her − so much better looking than the boys I knew with their short haircuts, so different. "Look, look," she continued. "Down there somewhere is my house." She pointed at the shacks in the Illyssos gulch. "My parents and sisters and I sleep in the same room. Our house is small. Come over some time, we can wade in the river." I liked having a girl around, but what could you do with her?

One day Zouzou came to visit with her mother Lilli. Her looks were shocking. I had to turn away from time to time to hide my blushing. Boys didn't do this to me. Girls were troubling enough, but Zouzou provoked unfamiliar disturbing feelings. I was at a loss.

"Would you like to see my *bakaliko*?" I asked hopelessly.

We got down on our knees. She leaned over to point at something, her hair touched my cheek.

"What is this?" she asks, knowing full well what it is. "And what is that?" More leaning.

I was miserable, wanted to grab her and bite her lip. Salvation came from the other room.

"Kinder!" My mother's voice. "Come have some cake."

In the living room we sat properly at the table. Lilli was a beautiful woman, a ripe, voluptuous version of her daughter. German of course - "I think she's Jewish," my mother told her husband − married to a Greek merchant. Mr. Moschos ran a small, elegant, exclusive boutique in the Voukourestiou street arcade, around the corner from the Grande Bretagne hotel. Lotte walked by frequently and looked covetously at the display of luxury imports: Moroccan leather gloves, silk stockings from Paris, scarves from Milan.

"That little store is a goldmine," she told my father. "The prices are unbelievable."

"Did you buy anything?"

"Don't be ridiculous."

Lotte envied the Moschos' wealth, their luxurious penthouse apartment on Righilis street where room after room was decorated with oriental rugs and plush furniture. A wide terrace ringed three sides decked with wicker chairs and potted camellias.

"You know, they bought three of Achileas' seascapes. They look fabulous there."

"Good for Achileas."

"But I haven't told you the best story yet."

"I'm waiting."

"You won't believe this. Walking through the apartment we met this gorgeous girl, Lilli introduced her as Colette, a nanny supposedly, but guess what?"

"She's not a nanny."

"Exactly. She's his mistress! And she lives under the same roof. And Lilli seems to accept it."

"Amazing," said my father with a tremor in his voice.

Mookie, the hairy sheepdog, and Moushi, the calico cat, were lovers, in a Platonic way of course. They slept together like an old married couple. During the day he would sometimes lie under the kitchen table, front paws stretched out forward, head resting on them in a semi-snooze. Moushi would soon saunter over and with delicate cat steps, climb on top and snuggle into his thick, white fur. Before long she started to purr, kneading his pelt with her claws, provoking ecstatic growls from below. Like Puzzi of Pendeli fame years ago, Mookie was a sexually active male, disappearing for days on erotic forays. He'd come back like a veteran returning from battle – his fur filthy brown, a bloody gash on a leg, a half-closed eye. He was immediately given a big bath and rejoined the fold all perfumed and happy. But sooner or later the inevitable happened. The family noticed that the two were behaving strangely. Mookie kept shifting his weight from right to left paw uttering little whimpers. Moushi padded around the house randomly meowing. The vet came, diagnosed rabies and took them away. While the family mourned the sudden loss of two beloved animals, my father, true to form, brought up the matter of inoculation. Again it was decided that they should all just hope for the best - except for me.

"But they didn't bite or scratch me," I protested.

"It doesn't matter," insisted my father. "A little saliva in a tiny scratch, that's all it takes."

"What about the rest of you?"

"We'll be all right."

"What if you all die and I become an orphan?"

"Don't be wise. I'm calling the doctor."

In need of consolation, I brought new pets into the house. Not one or two, but a whole community. In school we had learned about a miraculous creature with the ancient name of *metaxoskolix*, the amazing silk worm.

"Why not raise some here at home, make your own silk," suggested Pappi.

"Me?"

"Yes you. I'll help you."

"No way," shouted my mother. "Disgusting slimy worms crawling around the house. I don't want them."

"But they don't get rabies, Mutti."

A couple of dozen tiny dots arrived in a shoe-box one day crawling around a pile of green leaves.

"Only in the bathroom," warned Mutti. "If they make a mess I'll flush them down the toilet."

And that's where they lived under my care. For several weeks I had to jack myself up the trunks of mulberry trees in search of food for my brood. My nature study was to culminate in a school report.

"The cycle began with nearly microscopic eggs laid in summer at an ideal temperature of 22 degrees centigrade. The worms emerged from these. They grew to a length of six centimeters and acquired twelve tiny 'legs' plus head and tail. The head was wrinkled and sad, like a basset hound's. The front three 'legs' are actually three pairs of 'arms' used for holding leaves close to the mouth. Mulberry leaves are the only food this particular species will eat. After about forty days the worms stopped eating, became transparent and spent the next three days weaving a cocoon around themselves. I cut one of them open and found a white oval object inside, - the worm had turned into a larva. After about two weeks, the cocoons opened one by one and a lovely white butterfly came out. There were male and female butterflies but I couldn't tell the difference. They climbed on each other. I think they were mating. Soon the females laid their tiny eggs and died. A new cycle was beginning but my mother wouldn't let me keep the new eggs. I was left with two dozen cocoons from which to make silk, but I didn't know how."

"Toula is taking Bebe to Switzerland, they're seeing a specialist in Zurich," my father said one evening. "The doctors here are totally baffled."

"I still can't get over it," said Mutti. "Remember last year, her ballet recital, how darling she was dancing to that little Delibes ditty? All curls, red cheeks, chubby legs?"

My cousin Bebe had contracted a mysterious malady. Ugly sores suddenly appeared on her legs and around her neck. She lost weight, was listless and ran a fever. To show their expertise, doctors took diagnostic shots in the dark – it's a kind of infection, blood deficiency, lupus, sarcoma… Various remedies were prescribed, this treatment and that – but no cure. Bebe's parents Achileas and Miranda gave up their marital bickering and rallied to save their child. The professor in Zurich prescribed some medicines and fresh mountain air. "It need not be Davos," he counseled, "but take her somewhere out of the city. You have such lovely mountains in Greece, *ja?*"

Back in Athens, they saw little improvement from the medicines. The sores seemed to be healing a bit but left ugly scabs; other sores came up elsewhere. Bebe was entering puberty; she cared about her appearance, wrapped colorful scarves around her neck and hid her legs inside long skirts. Feeling emaciated and disfigured, she suffered as much from embarrassment as from the malaise brought by her illness. Her parents rented houses in newly developing suburbs on the edge of farmland and pinewoods, hoping, in vain, for clean, curative air, a do-it-yourself sanitarium. What they frequently found however, was the disorder of work in progress – half finished construction, steel rods sticking out of concrete, unpaved roads, mounds of excavated fill and piles of lumber and bricks forgotten among the weeds of still empty lots. Still, there were mountain views and the pleasant stink from some still-functioning farm near by.

One Easter Sunday, my parents and I took the bus to Zoghrafou, a new development where uncle Achileas had found a second floor apartment. Cousin Tsanos was there with his parents, Stella and Dino, along with many other aunts, uncles and cousins mostly from Achileas' side of the family. The crowd had gathered in the large studio furnished with sofa, chairs, piano and, on one side, the paraphernalia of Achileas' work: easel, large table littered with squeezed, half empty tubes of oil paint, a mess of dirty brushes stuck in jars of smelly turpentine and a variety of still life props waiting to be transferred to canvas. The air was replete with the aroma of linseed oil. Achileas worked here now, a lecher in temporary remission, away from the temptations of his Kalithea hideaway. He was standing in one corner talking to my mother, gorgeous in her new crepe de Chine frock, white, with patches of a black pattern, deep cut V-neck, wide red belt meant to feature broad hips and ample bosom. Her light brown, shoulder length hair was set in a fashionable *mis en plie*. Still less than forty, she embodied woman at the height of her seductive powers.

"You look terrific," murmured Achileas, an insinuating smile parting a pair of sensual lips. "I'd love to paint you."

"Sounds like something you tell a lot of women."

"No, seriously. I'd like to paint you just as you are now, same dress and all."

Lotte laughed, flattered.

On the other side of the room, my aunts Stella and Miranda put their heads together. "I wonder what he's saying to her," whispered

Stella, who had never liked her sister-in-law and was a purveyor of juicy gossip specializing in her brother-in-law's escapades.

For the next several weeks, Mutti would take the bus to Zoghrafou for periodic sittings under Miranda's watchful eye. A large, lovely painting was unveiled one day to the oohs and aahs of the family. In it Lotte sat in a bluish grey upholstered chair, her legs provocatively crossed, one arm resting on the chair, its long fingered-hand dangling off the edge. The other, bent, was holding onto the red belt. She looked straight at you, the eyes melancholy, flirtatious above an ironic Marlene Dietrich smile.

That painting now hangs prominently in the living room of our house in Hydhra, once the beloved island hideaway of Toula and Bebe who left it to me.

In my room I pored over the fat one-volume history of France and England. My father had been subscribing for some time to a monthly publication called the *History of Nations* of which this was a part. It was written in flowery *katharevousa*, the prescribed language of intellectuals, official documents and most newspapers - a language that had been artificially put together during the previous century to "return the nation to its proper ancient and Byzantine roots." *Dhemotiki* on the other hand, was the everyday spoken language – spoken by all, even by professors and government ministers, as long as they didn't stand on a podium to deliver a speech or write a formal document. Communists, to their credit, along with most poets and fiction writers, chose to stay close to the people and be understood. They wrote in the vernacular.

Even though the book was touted to be a "deluxe illustrated" publication, its paper had the thin, yellowish look of cheap newsprint and the illustrations resembled smudgy black and grey newspaper pictures. For me however, the volume which my father had had bound in brown leather with gold letters, brought history to life – from Neolithic huts to the Restoration, from the caves of the

Dordogne to the Versailles treaty. As bad as the illustrations were, it was through them and their captions that I began to construct for myself some kind of image of the past. Pell-mell pictures of kings, queens, statesmen, soldiers, generals, battles, sieges, palaces, executions and tortures were converted into stimulants for learning. Here, for example, was the picture of a vast crowd in exotic clothing gathered around a platform, on which a man held up a head detached from a body lying horizontally next to a vertical contraption. "Paris 1793," it said below, "Louis XVI." And here was another picture of what appeared, through the smudge, to be a young woman. "One of the king's six wives," the caption read. "The king had her head cut off with an axe." ("What is adultery?" I asked Papous, who answered with a convoluted story of a young queen who got into trouble because she liked the king's son more than the king.) Then there was the picture of a handsome man with long hair and a Ronald Coleman mustache. The caption was rather long. "Turenne. This memorable portrait by Filippe de Chambain represents the great soldier at age 37. The color of the face is dark, almost coppery, it is the color of the soldier who lived outdoors." (Remember, these are black and white pictures.) It continues. "Below the protruding eye brows, the blue eyes gaze attentively in the far distance. The features are full of energy, calm and decisive. The wrinkle in the forehead and next to one nostril, betrays the habit of thought and the steady attempt by a man to concentrate his thought." (This is a literal translation of the caption.)

Now and then I found full-page illustrations on better quality paper – an angel on the façade of Westminster Abbey, a portrait of King Charles the First, with a big hat and boots, (I learned that he too lost his head) painted by someone named Van Dyke, a group of naked young women called "The Toilette of Aphrodite," (one of my favorites) by a French painter, and others. These, mind you, didn't necessarily appear in historic sequence, and I worked to fit them into what appeared to be the right time slot. Take for example the picture of an impressive building that caught my eye one day.

Domed, decorated and arched, its façade was mirrored in a majestic, tranquil pool. I thought it beautiful and gazed at it for a while. The caption intrigued me: "The Taj Mahal in Agra. At a distance of 250 kilometers southeast of Delhi, Agra is one of the richest cities in India in terms of monuments. Among them, the Taj Mahal is particularly worthy of admiration: it is a monument to conjugal love, built to the memory of his wife by Shah Jehan in the 17th century. It is all white marble and its construction took 17 years and 20,000 workers. Under the dome, in the location of honor, rests the body of Ardjumaunt, [sic] the beloved wife, next to whom her husband was eventually laid."

I wanted to know more. On the preceding page I found a picture of Catherine the Great of Russia (1729-1776) and on the next page the portrait of a man with a wig. It said, "Montcalm (1712-1759)" and described him as "one of the most beautiful visages in French history." I leafed back a bit and found the chapter heading "Government and Society about 1789." I asked myself, what do Catherine the Great, the Taj Mahal and Montcalm have to do with each other and this chapter? Apparently not much. Eventually I discovered that the entire section was about "Conditions that led to the French Revolution." The picture showing the beheading of Louis XVI had appeared in a totally different section. Oh, well. Thinking back, it may not have been a bad way to encounter history. My historian wife argues persuasively against the dull chronological recitation of events. Young people are bored by it. They need challenge, she tells me, the thrill of discovery on their own. It may well be that history, tossed around like a salad and flavored with flowery language and lots of pictures, was just what I needed.

Now and then the words *Ethniki Etairia* (National Society) would pop up in conversation. It turned out that my father had recently become a member of a hush–hush political club bearing the same name. He had been flattered when he was invited to join this group of officers, industrialists and key politicians, founded after the Fascist takeover in 1936, to advise the "Leader" General Metaxas on matters of state. Inspired by German, Italian, Spanish and other "nationalist" Fascist models, Metaxas sought to establish a party and a system to perpetuate his rule and *Ethniki Etairia* was formed to help him reach this goal.

My mother thought that Niko's membership in that cabal would help him in his lagging career. But he had angrily rejected the notion. Higher ideals were involved here, he told her, nobly. They would only be debased by the pursuit of personal gain.

"But these, you tell me, are such powerful people," she said. "They could help."

"Lotte, please," he was annoyed. "This is a serious political committee. I'm honored to be part of it. It would be embarrassing for me to introduce personal matters."

"I didn't mean…"

"Lotte, you don't understand! This concerns the future of what Metaxas is trying to do, what I've always wanted to see done – a new social order, a new party, progress without Communism. We are his advisors, it's not the place to promote my practice."

My father, nevertheless, managed to reap professional benefit from his Monarchism and his support of fledgling Greek Fascism. He was appointed head of a special urban planning task force for the "Capital" (the larger regional area of Athens,) launched by Kostas Kontzias, the newly appointed "Minister Governor" of Athens, an imposing man, as tall as a professional basketball player, his head crowned by a huge mop of frizzy hair. Sure enough, there was my Pappi in a photograph with little roly-poly Metaxas seated in the front row of a marble-clad auditorium, Kontzias towering over him, Niko and other functionaries behind them looking serious and attentive. Other pictures show him informally posing with his staff in a high ceilinged, colonnaded hall in the building that was once a stately royal palace, later converted to house the

Parliament and, since Metaxas dissolved it two years ago, modified for the use of various government agencies. It was a jolly crowd of young, good looking men in shirtsleeves and pretty women in black lab-style smocks who seemed to be having fun at their work surrounded by drafting boards with large, messy rolls of drawings on them. My father, in his early forties, appeared to enjoy this youthful camaraderie. But there was a serious side to the fun.

One of Niko's professors in Berlin had been the noted city planner Dr. Hermann Jansen who had won an international competition to modernize Ankara as the new capital of Turkey under its President Kemal Ataturk, the same man who had routed King Konstantine and the Greek expeditionary force in the catastrophe of 1922. Supported by Kontzias, and Jansen's success in Ankara, and probably inspired by Baron Haussman's draconian overhaul of Paris eighty years before, my father's team embarked on a similar venture for Athens – planning its orderly expansion and carving out new avenues to relieve its clogged arteries.

Alas, not much was to come out of this ambitious project as events would soon show. Athens inevitably grew but its size and shape today would inflict despair in the hearts of the young crew that valiantly struggled to bring modernity and order to their ancient city.

As it turned out, Metaxas and his cohorts did not limit their operations to edifices and grand planning projects. True, their aim was to establish an efficient, tightly run state, the way the others up north were doing. To accomplish this, however, they had to quash parliamentary opposition, control the press, suppress the labor unions and, most important, exterminate the Communists. Such an elaborate operation fell in the hands of one Constantine Maniadhakis, euphemistically known as the Minister of Public Safety. Under him functioned two police organizations – *Gheniki Asfaleia* (General Security) and the quasi-secret *Idhiki Asfaleia* (Special Security). It was not clear which of the two was more ruthless in the pursuit of Law and Order – and the persecution of Communists. Suffice to say that they will both loom large in this story.

Sina Street rises in a steep incline from Panepistimiou Avenue next to the University, past the French Lycee, straight up toward the Lykavittos pine wood ending at the stark, white stucco bell tower of the German church. Once, maybe twice, my mother took me to the Christmas Eve service there before our own traditional tree-and-presents ritual at home. The church interior, like the exterior, had an airy, simple feel to it, modern, one would say. The nave was open, tall, uncluttered with neat rows of dark stained oak pews. A carpeted aisle led to the raised altar dominated by a huge stark wooden cross and an altar table draped with an embroidered cloth. Wooden chairs and a lectern stood on the sides. The pastor wore a plain gown with a white accordion collar, like those in the Frans Hals paintings I had seen in an art book. He read a few lines from the Bible in clear German. Then the congregation rose to sing, holding the hymnal books kept in the backs of the pews. Then we all sat down. Then the pastor read again, and so forth. Everything was straightforward, understandable and brief enough to avert boredom. No elaborate gold-embroidered costumes, no beards, no endless incomprehensible chanting, no crossing, no wandering around, no whispering in the corners, and everyone had a place to sit. If this meant being *Evangelisch*, I was for it. Who could argue with such orderly efficiency, such brevity and synchronized obedience? This however, turned out to be a short-lived attraction.

I thought back to this experience a decade later when I was required to attend the Anglican Sunday service in the glamorous Gothic chapel (more a cathedral, actually,) of my American college. I found the performance pompous and boring as did many of my schoolmates. Sitting there, half asleep, my mind wandered back to the little church on Evzonon when as a six-year-old I had ambled in with my pals during Easter week. I thought of the warm, smoky intimacy, the pervasive smell of incense, the glow of the thin yellow candles, placed one by one in the tall brass candelabras by worshipers as they entered, crossed themselves and planted a kiss on an icon. I could hear the sharp, melodious baritone of the Papas standing in his brilliant costume and gold crown under the *Pantokrator* fresco glowering from the dome above.

By the time I reached college, I had lost any attraction to religion I may have felt as a child. I was grateful that my parents did not press it on me – either her modern, scrubbed Protestantism or his musty, oriental, ancient Orthodoxy. It gradually occurred to me that they didn't care much about churches and religion. Although they observed certain rituals – Christmas, Easter, baptisms – they mostly stayed out of churches. The vision of my great grandfather had long since receded into distant irrelevance. It had become a curiosity.

Downhill, not too far from the German church, on Araxhovis Street, stood another building in the Bauhaus style – the three-story German school, known by the Greeks as *Ghermaniki Scholi* and *Deutsche Schule Athen*, by the Germans. In September 1938, age ten, I enrolled here as a fifth grader (although my grade was called *Sexta*, Latin for sixth, in an inverted system that named the last high school grade *Prima*, First, rather than Twelfth). I remained here for the next five years. Above the front door hung two flags – the Greek white and blue and the flag I had seen all over Berlin two years ago bearing the black swastika, the *Hackenkreuz*. Soon it would also be raised on the Acropolis, to be seen by all of Athens.

"The Sexta classroom is in the annex over there," said Fraeulein Lueber. "We'll go over and meet Frau Poumpoura, the Greek teacher, and maybe Herr Boehme who teaches the German subjects."

The classroom was on the ground floor. People peered in as they passed by. Three rows of desks were separated by two aisles. Two boys or two girls shared a hard wooden seat attached to the desk forming one piece of furniture. The inclined top lifted revealing a shelf for books, paper and half eaten candy. A groove kept pencils from rolling down.

The shock of my new environment was soon eased by the presence of two friends. Dennis and I had shared a desk at Marasleio and did so again here. Physically the opposite of Dennis, Vassilis was short and chubby and took the class by storm with his polemic, no-nonsense manner, challenging the teachers at every opportunity. And he seemed to be hormonally more advanced than the rest of us.

"I see you looking to the left a lot," he said to me one day.

"What do you mean?" I blushed, knowing what's coming.

"That little Aliki is very cute…or is it the other one?"

He was referring to the twin sisters who were not only endowed with matching good looks, hair and bodies, but also came to school wearing identical blue smocks with round white collars, confusing classmates and teachers. "Are you Aliki or Eleni?" they were frequently asked. But I, smitten, knew the difference. Aliki wore a graver, more melancholy countenance, and her lips were fuller – although Eleni was not so bad either…Anyway, I had decided to focus on Aliki who sat to my left, two desks ahead, studying her profile, until my eyes met Vassilis' devilish grin. What a rascal.

Kyria Poumboura, a short, plump woman with a frizzy permanent, was writing on the blackboard with what appeared to be gray chalk. We liked her. She was bright, friendly, informative and quite amusing. Patient with *orthographia*, the endemic Greek spelling problem, which most of the class had still not mastered, she skillfully guided us through its minefield. "Now remember," she cautioned. "There are five different ways to write the 'ee' sound: iota, eta, ypsilon, and two diphthongs, omicron-iota and epsilon-iota." We knew this already, but when to use which where? And why is all this necessary? Her explanation that sometime long, long ago each of these letters stood for a different sound didn't satisfy us. Why not one letter per sound? Oh no, she retorted, it's part of our tradition, our culture. I knew that this confusion didn't exist in German, but in a few years I would find it in English. By then I had concluded that spelling had to be learned by rote.

The class did not like Herr Boehme; the opposite of Kyria Poumboura, he was tall and thin. Her soft friendly features glowed, where his mean blue eyes exuded merciless threat. Her patience and care could not compare with his righteous fury. Herr Boehme's right hand, moreover, was deformed and he wrote with his left hand in a downward, diagonal, spasmodic stroke. Like many German teachers, he wore an NSDAP button on his lapel. It stood for *Nazional Sozialistische Deutsche Arbeiter Partei*, the Nazi party.

We read and wrote stories in German and did some arithmetic. A number of students struggled with the language. Herr Boehme liked discipline, Order. Humor was a foreign word; he detested chit-chat and giggling. He would hurl a piece of chalk at an offender with awesome ferocity, clear across the room. Later in life, I was not surprised to learn that left-handed pitchers were much in demand in baseball. I was once beaned on the forehead by a Boehme fastball, leaving me dazed and my face and clothes white with powdered limestone. When even such attacks failed and mayhem spread, Herr Boehme exploded, bellowing, *"Maul halten! Es ist wie eine Judenschule hier!"* Shut up! It's like a Jew school here!

Dressed for children's costume party. 1938.

My German School class, still wearing short pants, 1941. I'm in the back as usual.

Lotte and Grete with Evzone. Easter, 1938.

Left:
Niko at his drafting board.

Right:
Niko's name displayed before one of his constructions. 1938

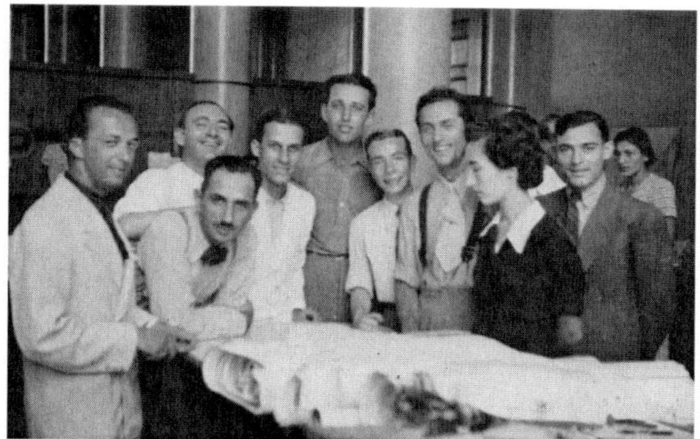

Niko, arms on table, with colleagues at work, 1939.

The "Leader", Ioannis Metaxas, sits in the center next to tall Kontzias, Governor of Greater Athens. On the right we see Niko with his team of planners.

KRISTALLNACHT

I HAD BEEN attending the German school for a few weeks, exposed to Herr Boehme's abuse and the new Nazi regimen, when this happened.

All through the night of November 9th, 1938, violence raged in Germany. Using the assassination of a minor German diplomat by a Jewish youth as an excuse, the Germans launched a well-orchestrated pogrom against Jewish - German citizens, among them decorated veterans of the Great War. The attackers damaged, torched or destroyed almost all Germany's synagogues and cemeteries. They vandalized some 7,000 Jewish shops and dozens of department stores. There were numerous killings, brutal beatings and endless humiliations. In a preamble to later events, more than 30,000 Jews were taken to concentration camps. Streets were littered with shards of broken glass from the many ravaged store fronts. The night of broken crystal - Kristallnacht.

I don't remember hearing about the events of that night on the radio or in discussions at our house - the way we had talked about the abdication of the King of England or the Schmeling-Lewis fights or the invasion of Ethiopia. But my father must have read about it – if not in the Greek papers certainly in the *Voelkischer Beobachter* (People's Observer). For some time, shortly after Hitler's ascent to power, he had been subscribing to what was the official daily newspaper of the Nazi party, printed in Berlin since the 1920's. He had several issues bound into heavy, folio-sized volumes in luxurious grey linen. They disappeared soon after Italy and Germany invaded Greece.

Curious, after all these years, to see what my father had been reading, I went to the New York Public Library. The November 10, 1938 edition of the *Voelkischer Beobachter* carried a short article on a back page. In reaction to the murder by a Jew of the Paris Embassy attaché von Rath, the article said, an outraged German population "let off steam against Jewish intrigue" and smashed display windows of Jewish owned shops. I found that nearly every other issue contained some attack against the "nefarious Jew" – his world conspiracy, his criminality, his dominance of capitalism in America and… his control of the Politbureau in the Kremlin! Most of these stories appeared on the front page, many under screaming banner headlines in block Gothic type. Read today, the outspoken vitriol coupled with the knowledge of what was soon to come strike like a blow to the head.

My father, who kept himself well informed, must have known all this. And so, if he had known, why didn't he discuss it, as he did other news – he, an astute, uninhibited commentator on world drama? And he was well aware that my mother and I, just two years before, had stood in front of Wertheim's department store admiring the displays in the same windows that now lay shattered on the sidewalk. But wait a minute. Had I not seen those headlines myself – a ten year old boy, quite literate in two languages, who lapped up news at his father's knee, aware that Jackie Saltiel, the Myllers, the Mordos, all close friends of my parents, were *Juden*? Wasn't it I who had cheered Hitler two years before?

But that's not all. The *Beobachter* from the mid thirties on, shows the unmistakable, deliberate drumbeat to war – the taking of the Saar, the invasion of Austria, the Munich surrender, the rape of Czechoslovakia and, on the eve of war, the astonishing non-aggression pact with the Soviets. Germany wants nothing but peace, the *Beobachter* declared. Churchill and Roosevelt are the real war criminals. *Der Fuehrer,* our revered Leader, has been generous, but they better not challenge his patience. Today, over seventy years later, it's easy to find this vicious drivel posing as journalism, almost comical in its absurdity. Not at all amusing, however, was my father's respect for that vulgar instrument of propaganda — enough to want it consecrated in a position of honor among the Platos, the Goethes and the Rousseaus he so proudly displayed on his shelves.

I remember more…Two or three books extolling the rise of Hitler, (they too disappeared at the appropriate time) with pictures of him as a soldier in World War One, looking gaunt, sporting an elongated mustache; standing outside the beer hall with Ludendorf and other codefendants from the Putsch; traveling through the German countryside before adoring, flag waving crowds, little girls in dirndls offering flowers; looking up at "Das Braune Haus" the Nazi headquarters in Munich; relaxing in lederhosen under the Bavarian sun. And of course pictures of him after he took power, by now wearing his booted, belted, tunic uniform, black hair falling diagonally over the brow, eyes fierce, the countenance that glared at me from the walls in the German School. *Der Fuehrer.* And although I don't remember seeing it, there must have been a copy of *Mein Kampf* tucked away on some shelf since my father referred to it now and then. I bought a copy recently, curious to find out what he had been exposing himself to. Need I say now what I think of it? It was all there. The world didn't seem to have read it, or just didn't listen, or pay attention, or care. But Niko had.

There is much that baffles me about my parents in their relation to Jews. Through the years I had heard them make disparaging remarks, mildly derogatory or mocking. There were several incidents.

Once, I must have been as young as four or five, I heard Niko repeat a refrain that originated during the 1931 pogrom in

Thessaloniki when Jewish Greek citizens were attacked by bands of Greek "nationalists" – beaten, their houses burned, their businesses ruined. Amazingly, I have retained its sound and words.

Klapsete Evraii Tromeri Ioudhaii To Meghalo Sas Kako…

Weep you Jews, terrible Hebrews, (for) your great evil…

Then there was the time I heard my mother make light of another event in Thessaloniki later, during the German occupation when thousands of Greek Jewish men were summoned to the central square, forced to stand hatless in the summer sun, kicked and humiliated and ordered to do calisthenics before a crowd of jeering Germans and gentile fellow-countrymen.

Another time, my mother and I went to see "Jud Suess" one evening in a summer movie theater. Suess was a Jew in eighteenth century Germany who, having gained the favor of a local potentate, became powerful, greedy and ruthless. He was a caricature Jew — dark complexioned, hooked nose, fat, lascivious lips, his accent heavy, eastern. In one scene, his eyes aglow with lust, he is chasing a blond Aryan beauty around a big bed. It all ends with the blackguard in a cage, his clothes in rags, his beard long and black, being wheeled to his execution, as crowds of upright German folk throw rocks and shout obscenities.

For me, such memories have come back, some quite recently, as virtually new discoveries, lying dormant in my subconscious all those years. I could say today that I was too young then to care, that I trusted my parents who could do no wrong. It was only later when my own thinking and my own emotions came into play that I understood…

In the light of such stories, and while anti-Semitic persecution was raging in Germany, it is interesting that my parents willingly befriended a number of Jews in Athens. Their attraction to people who spoke my mother's native tongue must have overcome their prejudices. It didn't seem to matter that a few Jews were among their German-speaking friends.

Take the Saltiels for example. A Sephardic Jew from Thessaloniki,

Jackie spoke excellent but accented German and Greek, (although a Greek national, he grew up with Ladino as his first language) and worked for Osram, a German manufacturer of light bulbs and electrical equipment. Short, clubfooted and not particularly good-looking, he was a charmer and a flirt with a rollicking sense of humor and an upbeat, happy personality. Women loved him, my mother among them. His wife Dora, a mousy German Gentile, was his opposite. When everyone laughed at one of Jackie's jokes, she remained deadpan. A permanent look of disapproval seemed to reside on her features. Children annoyed her, probably because she had none of her own. Dora didn't like Hitler and the Nazis, "they are so vulgar," and early on she would argue with Niko about the Third Reich. Dora had one big passion: she adored all things British, especially the Royal Family, whose genealogy she knew intimately, back to the Norman Conquest. She was outraged by Edward's insistence on marrying "that American floozie" and abandoning his throne. My father, who liked to ridicule British Royalty countered that those imperialist hypocrites had repeatedly double-crossed Greece and would do so again. Despite such anomalies, the Saltiels and my parents had been friends ever since I could remember.

The Myllers had fled Germany soon after the Nazis came to power. One day my mother took me to their suburban villa in Psychiko where I met their two sons Rolf and Ulrich. They spoke fluent Greek although they were blond and wore lederhosen. We cemented our friendship by wrestling on the grass, while their blue-eyed mother Liselotte chatted with my hazel-eyed mother Lotte sipping drinks under a sycamore.

Dr. Ernst Myller had been a promising young obstetrician in Nuremberg. He and his family lived happily in a lovely modern house. The Nazi takeover in 1933 came as a shock to them. Their families had lived in Germany for generations and thought of themselves as Germans. Ernst was a decorated World War I veteran. But the persecution was relentless. In a later memoir, Liselotte recounted how Jewish doctors, lawyers and businessmen were randomly rounded up by storm troopers and forced to perform menial, humiliating tasks like pulling up grass with their teeth from between cobble stones. Unlike others, the Myllers understood that they had to leave Germany. In an earlier trip they had made some friends in Athens and decided to settle there and become Greek citizens. Ernst got his medical license and set up his clinic in an elegant big house in Kolonaki. His reputation spread and patients flocked to him. His *kliniki* was the talk of Athens, clean and efficient, furnished with the latest equipment brought down from Germany – a far cry from the environment of Greek health care. Traditional xenophobia was put aside when it came to trusting the competence of professionals trained in "Europe," doctors in particular, and in Dr. Myller's case, one who was not only "European," but also German, a highly prized pedigree ...

Dr. Myller's reputation was seriously challenged however when my father came down with appendicitis and was rushed to Dr. Myller's clinic. After the operation, Niko was transferred to a room where a nurse put a hot water bottle under his feet. He came out of his sedation the next morning in great pain. The water had been boiling hot and during the night his feet had slowly roasted to a crisp. Dr. Myller was devastated. After his patient was brought home by ambulance, the penitent doctor came to visit every day to comfort him and peel layers of black skin off the bottom of his feet. He refused to accept the sizable fee for the operation. But my father, in a familiar display of noblesse oblige, insisted.

"You must be out of your mind," Mutti shouted afterwards. "For three weeks you've been away from the office, your clients wonder if you'll ever come back. Why do you always behave like a prince, when we are paupers? Don't you see how the Myllers live? Villa in Psychiko, car, fancy vacations, servants. They don't need our miserable money!"

But German and Germany kept Liselotte and Lotte together. They saw each other frequently.

"I'd never have guessed that they were *Juden*," she told Niko.

"They don't look at all Jewish, so fair, so... German."

"He has a bit of a hooked nose."

"You have a rather big one yourself, my dear."

"Touché."

The Myllers introduced my parents to the Mordos, recent escapees from Prague, where Renato had been director of the Opera. The Minister of Cultural Affairs had invited him to Greece to revive the Athens Lyric Stage. Soon he was staging a production of *Die Fledermaus*. Lotte and Niko were invited to the gala opening night. Papous, Rosa and I stood in the foyer to admire them as they were leaving. Mutti looked terrific in a long red gown and a black velvet cape. Her neck and earlobes were adorned with faux gold jewelry and her hair had been set that afternoon in a new bouffant. Pappi seemed ill at ease in a borrowed smoking, a black overcoat and homburg. Rosa and I giggled.

"The King was there," said Mutti on their return, flushed with excitement, brandishing a gigantic program with gold letters and red ribbons. "And Crown Prince Paul with his new bride Frederica. She's the Kaiser's granddaughter, you know, the niece of Queen Sofia, the Kaiser's sister."

"Ah, the Kaiser," said my father with some irony. " Anyway, the music was wonderful. Mordo did a great job, such beautiful sets."

In spite of threatening rumblings up north, life in Athens was good for me and my parents, for the Myllers, the Mordos, for Jackie and Dora Saltiel and for most other people. Somehow, my father and mother managed to reconcile these friendships with their admiration for Hitler and the virulent hatred emanating from Germany. The Myllers and the Mordos thought they were secure here. They could not possibly be reached in this ancient, welcoming land, under the warm Mediterranean sun. No Kristallnacht here.

KODRINGTONOS

END OF AUGUST 1939. Dora and Jackie Saltiel came for a visit. As usual, their opposite personalities were a welcome source of entertainment. But today the news was shocking. The Germans had just signed a non-aggression pact with the Russians.

"How could they make a deal like this with the Communists?" said my father, beside himself.

"You're a purist, an idealist as usual, my boy," replied Jackie, who knew his Realpolitik. "It's very simple. Hitler wants to cover his derriere before attacking Poland. Instead of fighting him, Stalin will help him gobble it up. And not only Poland, my friend. The same fate awaits those little countries on the Baltic. Mark my words."

"Ridiculous!"

"Not at all. Piece by piece, the two dictators will carve up Europe. Half of it will fly the *Hackenkreuz*, the other half the hammer and sickle."

"They may take Poland, that's all," said Niko, but then, thinking back, he added, "of course, if the French attack… they will be forced to open a western front…"

"Aha. You see how sweet this non-aggression deal is for Hitler? Not only is he safe in Poland, but once he's finished there he can take his revenge and attack France without a threat at his back."

"We shall see," answered Niko, excited by the prospect. "Meantime, it looks like war is inevitable... but it will never reach us down here in Athens."

"Hmm... I'm not so sure, Niko..."

> *On September 1, 1939, a few days after Hitler and Stalin signed the non-aggression pact, the Luftwaffe started bombing Poland. The Second World War was launched on September 3, when France and England declared war on Germany. It would not end until six years later - the deadliest conflict the world had ever seen.*

My father was whistling *"Die Deutschen in Polen,"* the current campaign song played every day on the radio, as the Germans raced toward the Vistula, sowing death and destruction. He openly voiced his pleasure and support of this new aggression. The injustice and humiliation of Versailles would be corrected - finally. A new order would sweep over Europe. Communism would be held back, defeated even. The infamous treaty with Stalin was just a ruse.

Somehow, though, Jackie's uncertainty lingered in my father's mind. What if the war did come down this way? After all, the Balkans had been a notorious tinderbox in the past. What then? Would the city be bombed? What would be the prime targets? Military installations of course. Wasn't there a major military compound behind the high wall right next to our house on Vasilissis Sofias?

"We've got to move," he announced to my mother.

"What? Why? We moved here only last year. It seems like yesterday."

"Athens may get bombed. There's a whole army garrisoned next door to us. You know that."

"You're out of your mind. You yourself said that the war would never reach here."

"I changed my mind. We've got to get as far as possible away from the center."

"I can't believe it!"

On Mutti's insistence they looked for a house to rent in Psychiko.

A desirable address, it was the closest suburb to Athens, barely a half-hour from Syntaghma Square by bus. Rich people lived there; some of them even owned cars. Mutti dreamt of a small house with a garden. We would squeeze in somehow. But the rent was prohibitive and there was a long walk to the bus to get into town. So, instead of Mutti's dream house in a lovely suburb, we moved to an apartment at the other end of town, near the parade ground of the old Military Academy where Niko had marched as a cadet, now converted into a park.

Again on the third, top floor, our new apartment stood at the corner of Kodringtonos Street (after Sir Edward Codrington, a British admiral who helped bring about Greek independence,) and Tritis Septemvriou (Third of September Avenue, a date of uncertain significance). Far removed from the upscale Kolonaki district, the location had few positive qualities. The new park on the Evelpidhon parade ground, the Archeological Museum with its own small park and music pavilion and the neo-classical Polytechnic on Patission Avenue were redeeming features, though some distance away. But I couldn't get the old neighborhood out of my mind. I missed them all: the dirty old monks of Moni Petraki, the little Byzantine church, the pines of Lykavittos, Marasleion, Kolonaki Square and the *kafeneion* where Papous had coffee with his cronies, and even the menacing bulk of the Evanghelismos hospital. But most of all I missed Evzonon, the street of my happy childhood, a haven compared with this neighborhood of screeching trolley cars, belching buses, dour facades and joyless humanity. Of the seven dwellings I had shared with my parents before leaving the fold, I would live here the longest — all of seven years, a period almost equal to our entire time on Evzonon. The contrast between those two segments of my life could not have been more poignant. The first — composed of sweet, hastily receding memories - was to be followed in this graceless neighborhood by exciting, tumultuous times. It was here that I discovered budding manhood. It was here that I began to learn and to dream. And it was here that we three encountered life threatening danger and the terror that came with it.

Evzonon was the beginning. Kodringtonos defined the future.

There was nothing particularly novel about the floor plan. An indoor stair came up from the street to our front door and a small entrance hall. There were two bedrooms, one for my parents and one for Papous. Two rooms at the end of the hall, a dining room and a sitting room, were separated by glass doors. The maid's cubbyhole was perched over a tiny kitchen and a storage loft above the lone bathroom. The predictable spiral stair led up to the roof terrace. A small balcony protruded over each one of the streets. All in all, a far cry from the Village Square!

My father designed the new dining room furniture in a bulky, curvilinear, stripped down Louis Quinze style painted a garish blue, the chairs upholstered in bright red velour. A matching *vitrina* with glass doors and shelves displayed Mutti's colorful *Roemer* stemware, Bavarian porcelain, and Chinese tea set. Under the table lay a large Persian carpet. Next door, the sitting room featured our new folk collection of hand- carved, dark stained walnut in the style originated on the island of Skyros. I slept here on a small day bed next to Santa Maria, the wooden radio with the curved top that had played such an important role in the Village Square and would continue to do so as future events would tell.

Our new decor signaled a substantial shift of sensibility for my father. One would think that his 'twenties Berlin modernist training, up to now evident in the exterior of his buildings, would also be applied indoors, with light Bauhaus tubular steel, bentwood furniture, that sort of thing. But Pappi now spoke with some admiration of Albert Speer, Hitler's favorite architect, the designer of the new Berlin Chancellery and the mammoth Party Congress complex in Nurnberg. "Isn't it amazing?" he told me as we looked at pictures of the huge model of Speer's megalomaniacal expansion of Berlin. He pointed at a building at the end of a long, wide, avenue. "This is going to be the biggest dome in the world, 250 meters in diameter, sixteen times bigger than the dome over St. Peter's Basilica in Rome!"

My father was not the only one attracted by Speer's blocky, ponderous version of classical architecture. Its mass and size brought forth, in the most direct way, the power and authority of the State, *das Reich*. Although intimidating and pompous, it soothingly conveyed a sense of security, erased all doubt, eliminated the need for alternatives, for choice. The Nazis had declared Bauhaus Modernism a subversive, "Jewish" invention although some of its greatest proponents, Mies Van der Rohe and Walter Gropius among them, were not Jews and had to flee Germany to practice in America. My father may not have been aware that the vile Joseph Stalin had abandoned the Soviet Constructivist pioneers in favor of a bloated, colonnaded, "socialist" neo-classicism. He didn't see the commonality of it all, the imposed linkage between style and dictatorial authority.

There was little about 30 Kodringtonos Street that warmed my heart.

Across the way, from a half basement, came the sounds of hammering and sawing, a carpentry shop, I thought – how nice. Then one day I saw a man hoisting his recently completed work out of the depths: three or four pine boxes, each large enough to contain an adult human body. He propped them up against each other on the sidewalk, whistling and humming, cracking jokes with passers-by, happy, unaware of the bonanza that lay ahead. Next door, a seedy corner store sold *psilika* – cigarettes, thread, pencils, cheap knickknacks and, from a rusty Socony Vacuum pump outside, petrol to the occasional motorcyclist and the taxi men who lined up at their stand further up the street. Their long-snouted, lovingly polished 'twenties Buicks and Packards glistened, their trunks decorated with white-walled spare tires, chrome headlights and radiator grilles flanked by stylishly curved fenders. In winter, an old man sat on a stool at the corner under the corrugated iron awning, selling roasted chestnuts from a black brazier. He warmed his hands over the charcoals fondling his merchandise, croaking from time to time, *"kastana, zesta kastana!"*

Above the stores lived a young couple with a baby and what I thought was the younger sister of the wife. Through the open windows I could see them walking around in their underwear. They ignored me as they leaned out to air their bed sheets in the morning, and I stood there staring at them. I was also intrigued by the mysterious little house next door to them on the right, a remnant of old Athens. An iron gate opened into a long narrow passage, a dark jungle of giant philodendrons. Unlike the apartment next door, the shutters were always closed. Rumor had it that a once-famous opera singer of legendary beauty and talent lived here in seclusion and modest poverty, wishing not to be seen any more. Curious, I kept a keener eye on the closed shutters and the dark foliage after I glimpsed a small white figure scurrying out of a side door.

The view from the other side of our corner apartment was less interesting mostly taken up with a large three-story house of Palladian pretensions, similar to our own, appointed with black iron-railed balconies and heavy projecting roof cornices where swallows built their nests each spring. A stonewall enclosed a yard next door. Corrugated iron sheets stretched along two sides sheltering stacks of firewood, charcoal for cooking on braziers and anthracite for heating stoves. Wine was stored in two huge wooden barrels that lay horizontally on racks under the shed. Twice a week, Papous sent me down to the *mandhra* with an empty bottle. With his sooty hands the coal merchant stuck a newspaper cone into the bottle and held it under one of the massive wood spigots as the foamy, yellow retsina gushed out. The combined smells of coal, wood and wine were such a perfect blend, so intoxicating that I took a swig now and then as I walked home.

This, in sum, was the stage set at the corner of Tritis Septemvriou and Kodringtonos, where dramatic events would soon act themselves out. Two other sights are worth noting. I soon learned that a grey building further back to the side was the headquarters of *Eidhiki Asfaleia*, the ominous "Special Security police". And straight out to the south, viewed from two windows and one balcony, seemingly detached from the roof tops, levitating like a biblical miracle, floated the Parthenon and its stony satellites – I *Akropolis ton Athinon*. It shimmered in the morning sun, turned to gold at sunset, paled to snow white against the black clouds of a thunderstorm – but most of the time, it was graced by a blue sky, little puffs of vapor fluttering about it like *putti* in a Tiepolo heaven.

The bell rang. I opened the front door. Next to the potted ficus at the top landing stood a teenage girl.

"I came for the job. My name is Kaiti" – a smile on a pretty oval face.

In those days I blushed frequently, especially when confronted by girls, and this one was particularly challenging in her clinging frock and bare legs.

"Ena lepto," one moment, I mumbled, leaving her standing to go find my mother.

"The new maid is here," I whispered. Kaiti stepped in to meet Mutti's keen, searching eyes.

"I come from Meghalopolis in Peloponnisos, high in the mountains."

Mutti lit up. "Oh, I know place. I visit friends in Vitina. They have beautiful, how you say, *Tannenbaum* there, like Germany. You know Vitina?" Kaiti didn't know Vitina.

"My parents have eight children, too many. So they sent me to the city."

"Have you done this work?"

"At home, since I can remember. But I still finished High School."

She was a proud girl, bright. I kept looking at her. She threw me a smile. More blushing.

"All right," said Mutti, thinking of Niko. The girl was so attractive. "Bring your things. You staying up there, over kitchen."

I was happy – she was so much better looking than Rosa. The same oval face as the slave girls in the Ingres paintings…and so cheerful. My father came home, looked at Kaiti with approval. Mutti would be on her guard.

But what of Rosa? By the time we moved to Kodringtonos, she had been with us for ten years. I had known her as long as my parents, saw her and Papous as members of my family. But Mutti had grown tired of her and increasingly found fault with her. And Rosa too had had enough. All these years she had been confined to one house, serving us, tied to our moods and wishes, deprived of friends, society, entertainment. Someone told her of a job in a hospital where she would be working with other people, men and women. She would have her own place, probably make more money. She would make friends, go to the movies, eat out sometimes. Lately there had been some shouting and yelling in the house – more than usual. And then one day she was gone. No tears, no good byes. I felt singularly unmoved. What did this small, illiterate woman mean to me, I would ask myself in later years. There must have been a kind of love when I was small and she held me in her arms, fed me, wiped my bottom. She was not good to look at, like Mutti, but she cared for me. She did all the dirty chores and more, giving my mother the freedom to go out, to read her German magazines or sometimes a book, or to write letters to her mother and sister. To her credit, Mutti did not act like a *grande dame,* like the other Athenian ladies who had servants to clean their houses and care for their children, giving them time to shop for elegant clothes, have their nails and permanents done, meet their friends or lovers, or go to the movies in the afternoon. Mutti did care about her house, and spent time with Rosa planning meals, composing shopping lists, supervising cleaning chores. And since

Rosa's skills may have been limited, Mutti frequently performed these tasks herself. She was an excellent cook in both German and Greek cuisine. She worshipped her husband. She was passionate about me. When I was not in school she would frequently take me along on her expeditions – shopping, walking in the park, sitting in a café, visiting a friend, seeing a movie. But her affection for Rosa was limited. There was little communication between them beyond daily domestic matters. Most of the time, Rosa lingered in the background, a silent observer, not a participant. Come to think of it, Papous frequently suffered similar exclusion. The trinity of father, mother and son was the critical center of the household. The others, often unnoticed, simply occupied space.

—

"Kindhinis has a little dog," Pappi announced one day, "a little wirehaired terrier. They want to give it away."

"Do we want a dog again?" said Mutti, looking at potential trouble. "Is it a male?"

"I think so. If you…"

"Niko, you know what's going to happen. Remember Mookie and that mutt up in Pendeli?"

But I, who had heard, interrupted. "Yes, yes. Please, Mutti."

"Who's going to watch it? We can't let him go off by himself like the others. Will you walk him? Do you want more of those injections?"

"I will, I will."

Next day Pappi and I went to pick him up.

"We call him Rudi," says Mrs. Kindhini. Rudi came to greet us waving his stubby tail. His short, rough fur was mostly white, with black and rust smudges here and there, floppy ears, longish snout and a glistening black button of a nose. I picked him up to get a slobbery kiss - love at first sight. The dog quickly fit into the household, although not quite the way Mutti had foreseen. I soon reneged on my promised duty. Rudi never got to walk in the street, the leash languished in a corner. Instead, he was allowed to climb the black spiral stair one flight up to the roof terrace, a wide expanse, paved with soft stone tiles, where he could run, jump, pee and poop to his heart's content. The space was enclosed by a high parapet, and poor Rudi could only see the sky, occasionally to bark at some passing pigeon. But soon he discovered his favorite perch on one of the two balconies, sticking his head through the iron railing to scan up and down the street and bark with relentless enthusiasm at whatever moved – cats, birds, people and donkeys, even cars and motorcycles. Naturally he reserved most of his energy for members of his own species, some of whom might look up and bark back, starting a prolonged duel of canine insults. In winter he spent hours looking at the world below from behind glass, sitting primly on a little pillow on the desk next to the window, whimpering from time to time, aware that barking was futile. He fooled around with me, racing me on the roof terrace, retrieving, rolling, pulling at a rag, growling. He was a happy, lively fellow. The mood changed, however, when I sadistically inflicted my own form of psychological torture on him. I lifted him up on top of the bookcase and made horrible, threatening noises, grimacing and waving my arms and soon Rudi, in terror, began to whimper and tremble.

"I wish he'd take a bite out of you," noted Kaiti one day as she passed by.

On a sunny May morning in the Deutsche Schule, Herr Schwebes gathered his gym class for an important announcement. He beamed from ear to ear. "At dawn today, German Panzer divisions rolled into France, Belgium and Holland. They are advancing rapidly toward Paris." He raised his arm and shouted "Heil Hitler!" I was among some of the twelve-year-olds who cheered.

We had been waiting for this day, led by my father's keen partisan interest - no doubt stimulated by his readings in the raging *Voelkischer Beobachter*, the newspaper of the Nazi party. He had mourned Germany's ignominious defeat in the First War. We read the papers, listened to the radio and tried to follow the battle on the map. News poured in quickly and before we could put it all together the British had slipped out of Dunkirk and the French surrendered in the same railroad dining car in which they had humiliated the Germans twenty-two years before.

End of June, 1940. Deutsche Schule Athen closed its doors for the season, its Nazi faculty satisfied with the Wehrmacht's conquests and probably looking ahead for more. Pretending that all was normal, we searched again for summer escape. Still smarting from last year's fiasco in Kifissia, Pappi found a charming stone villa in Aghia Paraskevi, a village not too far from the city, on the cool slopes between Ymittos and Pendeli. Aunt Toula and Bebe had rented a house uphill and I was looking forward to a summer near them. The villa was spacious with high ceilings, large green shutters and a stone terrace overlooking a pine wood and I soon found local playmates – Kostakis and his sister Voula. There were bicycles to rent, and an outdoor movie theater in the village that showed last year's Hollywood productions dubbed in French with Greek subtitles.

Warm, lazy days went by. Pappi returned every night from the city in his bow tie and white cotton suit. Papous dozed in the shade. Mutti and Kaiti bustled around the house, came back from the market laden with summer plenty – tomatoes for stuffing or salads scented with oregano; *melintzanes* and *kolokithia* (egg plants and courgettes) for making *imam baildi*; green and yellow peppers, cucumbers and a bounty of fresh herbs. The annual parade of fruit started in June - strawberries and *mousmoula*, the yellow eastern plums, had already made their appearance in May - with white and orange apricots and red and yellow cherries. *Visina*, the sour, black cherries that made *ghlyka tou koutaliou*, thick, sugary preserves eaten with a spoon off a little silver dish, and *visinadha*, the delicious summer drink, would come later. July greeted the large, red peaches and who could resist the arrival of *karpouzi* and *peponi* melons, competing with the onslaught of endless varieties of grapes, each with their own name, color, size and shape. August brought the huge, honeyed purple figs, the royal figs, sweetest of all. The parade continued well after summer when school began, until every last tree and vine had been plucked bare, and the season of winter fruit was upon us.

One day, Kostakis and I rented bicycles and circled the house of Sofoula, a saucy preteen charmer near by. We waved at her and smiled. She waved back.

"Let's stop and talk to her," suggested Kostakis.

"No, no," said I, "let's go back."

"Coward."

Later Lotte asked, "Where were you?"

"Riding with Kostakis."

"Where?"

"Down the street."

"And what was there?" Silence.

"Come on Titsian, out with it. Something was going on."

"There was a girl Kostakis knows," I blurted, aware from past interrogations that there was something to feel guilty about. I was not quite sure what. Lotte was relentless.

"You are too young for this sort of thing."

"What sort of thing?"

"Don't talk back to me. You know what."

Visions of Thalia, Melpomeni, Zouzou, Aliki, Frosso, (my God, had I known that many girls?) passed through my mind. What was the problem? I tried to imagine. There must be something there, I thought, something forbidden. My mind wondered to the paintings of naked women in my father's art books, to the bulging sweaters of some of the girls in school. Mutti would not explain and, as usual, I didn't dare ask further.

And then there was Kostakis' sister Voula. We had been chasing each other breathlessly among the pines. She picked up a stone and threw it at me. I threw one back at her. In school I fooled around with boys, wrestling, chasing, kicking a ball around, that sort of thing. But this was a different kind of fun. We hid behind tree trunks, ducked out to throw a rock and jumped back behind the tree. Suddenly I saw blood running down Voula's face. My stone must have found its target. "Mamaa!" she was screaming, running to her house. "He's trying to kill me!" It was time to flee, I decided, before Mama came out. There was a lot of shouting that night as my father tried to settle the matter with Voula's Mama who ended up calling him *skatokokaliari* (shitty pile of bones), a description rather close to the mark given Niko's skinny frame. For a day or two, I was confined to the premises. No more play with the neighbors.

"And stay away from those girls," shouted my mother. "That woman nearly killed your father."

But Kaiti was there. All three male generations in the house enjoyed her presence. When at work, she pulled her hair up and back in a bun, exposing the lines of a fragile neck and soft round cheeks in the manner of the young women in the ancient relief sculptures of Kerameikos, whose thin robes barely hid their pubescent breasts. Kaiti was industrious, well tempered, and when not bustling around the house, sat under a tree, her face in a book, legs primly kept together.

Mid afternoon, siesta time. The big midday meal was over, the grownups asleep. The lazy rhythm of the cicada chorus barely cut into the stillness of the air.

"What are you reading?" She looked up, surprised.

"How come you're not sleeping?"

"I told you, I can't sleep in the afternoon. I only pretend because they want me to. Sleep is such a waste, even at night. There is so much to do and so little time. So, what are you reading?"

She lifted her book.

"A brief history of Socialism. This chapter is about Mateotti, assassinated by Mussolini's thugs years ago. Sad, but I'm also amused by his name."

"Because it means 'in vain' in Greek?"

She laughed. "It also means vanity, conceit."

"Don't let my father catch you reading this. He hates the Left."

"And loves the Right."

"He fears Communism. I think he has a social conscience but he's also very much a patriot, a nationalist."

"Therefore National Socialism, or Fascism. Is that the answer?"

"I don't know, Kaiti. I admire my father. I want to think that he's right." I was looking at her. "You're so smart, Kaiti. You should be in school, the University."

"Some day," she sighed. "Some day when I have some money, or when I marry somebody rich. Then I can learn, travel, see the world. Meantime I have to do this, be a *dhouliko*, work for my keep, maybe save a little. It's not so bad. I'm still young and I like it here. A nice family, a comfortable house."

I was sitting on the ground next to her, hugging my knees, her own legs close by, a breath of air fluttering her skirt. We grew silent. Ahead, under a searing white sky, pines cast their dappled shadows on parched soil.

Summer rolled languidly along. July came and went followed now by the dog days of August when all was ripe, full and sensuous. Pappi fled his office and the inferno of the capital to stay for some days with the family. I found new friends, spent afternoons with Kaiti under the trees, visited Toula and Bebe who was feeling a little better, although far from recovered. They had rented the top floor of a house set in a grove of apricot trees uphill from the village. A large terrace overlooked the houses below. Just above loomed the foothills of Ymittos. After sunset when the air was cool and fragrant with the aroma of freshly irrigated soil, mother and daughter reclined on canvas deck chairs among potted geraniums chatting, enjoying the view. I joined them with news of the day and a recap of disquieting world events. What will the Germans do now that they have swallowed up France and isolated the Brits on their island? This was the question everybody was asking.

"I heard on the radio," said Bebe, "that Churchill is now Prime Minister, rallying his people to fight to the end."

"Your *ghermanofilos* father will be very happy if England falls," Aunt Toula told me. "But I'm worried."

She was a tough woman, fiercely protective of her ailing daughter. When her landlord made some crack about Bebe the other day, Toula tore into him with shocking street language.

"I'm worried about Mussolini," she continued. "He's trying to imitate Hitler's predatory ways. Last year he took Albania. Are we next? Will Metaxas resist or are we going to buckle like the Albanians? I bet that's what your fascist father would like."

I remained silent - the loyal son. I petted Taitu, Bebe's black Scottie who growled at me. Bebe had named her after Haile Selassie's wife, the Empress of Ethiopia. Both were in exile now after the Italians took their country and Mussolini made little Re Umberto the new Emperor.

The night darkened. Above us, the black sky was speckled with a myriad jewels — a giant dome, a whole universe, yet warm, protective, almost intimate, safe. The real world seemed far away. Here, all was well.

—

August 15, *tis Panaghias*, the All Holy Virgin's day, the day of Her ascension to heaven, the day She joins Her Son and His Father up there, the second most important holiday of Orthodox Christianity after Easter. Church bells had been ringing all day. In late afternoon, breathless heat was finally giving in to dusk. Papous sat on the shady side of the terrace fresh from his nap, a straw hat covering his baldness, whistling, as usual, Siebel's refrain from Gounod's Faust. Mutti and Kaiti, perched on the parapet nearby, were reviewing the evening's menu, a light one after the midday feast. On the steps below, I was tickling Rudi's belly provoking ecstatic growls. My father suddenly entered the peaceful domestic scene with incredible news.

"The navy destroyer 'Elli' was torpedoed a few hours ago in the harbor of Tinos, in broad daylight. Thousands were there for the festival… sank in flames right before their eyes … went down with most of the crew and all its holiday flags and decorations."

We were stunned.

"They say that the torpedo came from an Italian submarine." His voice was hesitant like an afterthought.

"I knew it, I knew it!" cried Papous. "Something was going to happen after Mussolini invaded Albania. That was only the first step in the plan."

"What do you mean, plan?"

"I bet Hitler and that ridiculous Mussolini cooked this up. They want all of Europe, including us."

"Nonsense, you don't know what you're talking about, Baba." Niko snapped back. "The Germans have nothing to do with this. That clown Mussolini is just exploiting their victories to make his own empire."

"Don't fool yourself, Niko, Hitler is in on this."

"Baba, the Germans like Greece and Metaxas. They won't let the Italians harass us."

Kaiti could no longer contain herself.

"Forgive me, but let's not forget that Hitler and Mussolini are allies, collaborators."

Kaiti's eyes shined, she was surprisingly eloquent. The Germans, she said, have been encouraging Italian conquests to suit their own ends. They stood by with the rest of the world while the Duce swallowed up Ethiopia. They approved when Mussolini called the Mediterranean 'Mare Nostrum', Our Sea.

"You sound pretty sure of yourself, my dear," said my father, dismissively.

"The girl is right," said Papous from under his straw hat. "We are the next to be swallowed up."

Later, as we sat around the dinner table, our small talk was hushed. In the darkness outside, crickets had joined the cicadas in a serenade. Moths flew in through the open glass doors to buzz the lone bulb hanging from the ceiling. The summer idyll was coming to an end.

Late September. People wished each other a premature *kalo xhimona*, have a good winter, although they still wore summer clothes and went to the seashore. In the markets one still found a plethora of summer fruit and vegetables – with grapes predominant – pink, red, yellow, green, purple, black; with and without seeds, large and small, oval and round; names like *rhodhites* and *soultanes*. With warm, clear, sunny days and the weight of deep summer lifted, there was a sense of optimism in the air. The fear of immediate threat brought on by the sinking of 'Elli' was waning - but not for long.

Distracted by the excitement of the new year at the Deutsche Schule, I looked ahead eagerly. I was entering Quarta, seventh grade. Classes were held in a bright room lit by large windows in the main building, a great improvement over last year. I admired my new notebooks, their pages lined, a place on the cover to write my name; I fondled my pencils and little pencil sharpener and lovingly sniffed the fresh-print smell as I flipped through my new text books. There were courses in both ancient and modern Greek; German; Greek and German history; chemistry and physics. Arithmetic was now called mathematics. Serious stuff. The class was divided into two sections – one for Germans and Greeks who spoke German well, like me, and one for all the others. Greek students came together for subjects taught in their native tongue. It was not clear what the Germans did during that time, since we took all their subjects with them. Instruction in National Socialist dogma? The origins of Aryan culture?

Turnen, physical education sessions, were held in the school yard or, when it rained, in the *Turnhalle*, the multipurpose room used also for assemblies, music, school plays and Christmas celebrations. We began by running around in a wide circle, Herr Schwebes standing in the middle, a whistle in his mouth like a circus ringmaster. Swedish exercises followed with much hopping up and down, arm waving, bending this way and that. The class concluded with a combative game: a heavy ball hurled back and forth between two teams was to knock out opposing players until one side lost its last player.

This was clearly a male contest, performed with such ferocity that it looked like training in a military barracks — befitting the rising mood of the times. Superstars and weaklings quickly came to stand out at each end of a bell curve. I was happy to hide in the anonymous mediocre center. One superstar towered above all others: Hans Juergen, known as Ha-Jue, German as you might have guessed, was tall, muscular, blond, blue eyed and very good looking — a perfect Aryan specimen. His throw in the knocking-out ball game was devastating. He could run and jump like a demon. Girls withered before him. Boys, especially the dark, athletically deficient Greeks, or half-Greeks, tried to rein in their desire to see him dead.

Most of the German teachers were men, their hair cut very short with a little tuft on top. Herr Meine taught German literature with frequent references to the poetry of Schiller and Goethe, Fontane and Lenau. But he ignored Heinrich Heine, who wrote the classic *Lorelei*, the poem about the deadly seductress of the Rhein, which every German child knew by heart. I learned why one day, when I read that Heine was a Jew. Herr Boring, in charge of science, lit Bunsen burners under glass bottles creating puffs of acrid smoke. In German medieval history, Herr Fleischer told us about the precursors of the Third Reich, emperors of the Holy Roman Empire, the various Ottos, Heinrichs and the brazen Kaiser Friedrich Barbarossa. The venomous Herr Boehme, our first teacher, was not to be seen — to no one's regret.

More than the faculty, the administration represented the Third Reich. Dr. Romain, the principal, was known as *der Herr Direktor*. Ramrod-erect, steely-eyed and scowly, hair cropped a la Himmler, he took evident pride in the facial scars he garnered as a student duelist in Heidelberg, the requisite mark of manliness in pre-1914 Germany and once again de rigueur. He wore the NSDAP Nazi button on his lapel as did most of the German teachers. Herr Kaspar, the associate director, a bantam-sized martinet, walked the halls looking for reasons to shout, reprimand and punish. I got a taste of his wrath when he saw me fooling around as the class was being marched up the stairs. *"Her kommen!"* (come here!) he barked, pointing at me. A searing sting crossed my entire left cheek as my head was swung violently to the right. *"Maul halten!"* (Mouth shut!) boomed Kaspar and I staggered on.

Romain showed his own mettle one day when the door to my classroom was suddenly swung open and Romain marched in followed by his retinue.

"Who is Thanassiadhis?" It sounded like a command. A small arm rose in the back.

"Come here!"

Thanassiadhis slowly moved forward and standing before the director, looked up at him.

"I have been informed that yesterday you called Karl Stoll *'ein Deutsches Schwein'*, a German swine. Take your things and get out immediately! You are expelled from this school." And he followed up with a crackling slap across the boy's face.

"Raus!" Out!

At the start of a school assembly, with the entire faculty and all the students sitting in neat rows in the gymnasium, the *Turnhalle*, Kaspar would stand up on the podium and announce, like a medieval herald: *"Ich melde den Herrn Direktor!"* (I announce the Herr Director!) A few well-calculated seconds later, Romain would stride in, raise his arm and boom *"Heil Hitler!"* in almost perfect imitation of the Fuehrer's body language.

Students made up several categories. The Greeks, as noted, fell into two groups: the purebreds and the half-breeds like me. In spite of my command of the language and familiarity with their country, I had no friends among the Germans, who felt superior and culturally detached. The German girls were pretty but haughty. Prominent among the boys was one Hans Wrede, a little Nazi who strutted around in his Hitler Youth uniform, a born heel clicker. His father, an archeologist, had written a book on ruins in the Attic peninsula. He also happened to be the head of the Nazi Party organization in Athens. By contrast, Horst and Klaus, sweet, gentle boys, occasionally exchanged words with the natives and often abstained from uniformed drills, to the contempt of their Nazi compatriots. Youths from other countries made up a third group. Their parents may have been diplomats, expatriate businessmen, artists, writers, archeologists, all more or less in love with the blue skies, the wine-dark seas, the romance of ancient ruins. Some were refugees, like Diran, an early friend, whose Armenian parents long ago fled some Anatolian massacre. He spoke faultless German, accented Greek, and his handwriting was the envy of the class.

I knew less about the girls. They were still a sub-category, but not for long. Argyro, a full Greek, and voluminous, was gregarious and fun loving – an early promoter of fraternization between the sexes, a precocious matchmaker. Her close friend Hannelore, one of the half-breeds, sported blond *Zoepfchen*, braids, curled around her ears, telegrapher fashion. Among the Germans, Waldtraut and Irmgart, one blonde, one brunette, smiled and laughed a lot but kept a guarded distance from the Mediterranean crowd. Denise, a saucy, dark-haired girl, said that her family came from Rumania, but "we are *Volksdeutsche*," a Nazi term used to identify German speakers in countries about to be devoured. Many of the boys and girls came to school from elegant apartments in Kolonaki or houses in Psychiko, some arriving in cars driven by chauffeurs or by taxi. Among them was Kostas, a jovially dim fellow, scion of a ship-owning clan based in London and Geneva. He often spoke of uncle Aristotle who owned a fleet of freighters.

The Acropolis as I saw it from my Kodringtonos Street window.

I stand in the center between my parents.
Papous is on the right and our new maid on the left.
Ag. Paraskevi, summer, 1940.

Mutti and Rudi on the balcony, ca. 1942

On the roof of the Kodringtonos
house, 1942.

Rudi resting on the balcony,
Kodringtonos house.

WAR

OXHI!

AT DAWN I heard the sirens wailing. Still groggy, I staggered to my parents' bedroom to find my father standing before the open window looking at the grey sky.

The streets below were deserted.

"This doesn't sound like a drill," he muttered. "Too early, no warning."

"Could it be real? Should we be doing something?"

"I don't know. Let's turn on the radio."

Kaiti was already down from her loft as we crossed the hall on the way to the living room.

"What's going on?" said Papous coming out of his room, adjusting his beret.

Sitting on the edge of my bed next to the radio, I fiddled with the dial. Five heads leaned forward to hear a voice – the tail end of an announcement: "… general mobilization. Meantime our courageous soldiers are holding their positions along the border and have already inflicted heavy casualties on the enemy…Fighting is intense…This message will be repeated with appropriate updates as further news is received. *Zito I Ellas!* Long live Greece!"

As if on command, we all stood up to the sound of the national anthem.

"Damn!" My father's voice came as a shock.

"I saw it coming," said my grandfather. "You wouldn't believe it Niko, but it was all there. The invasion of Albania, the sinking of *Elli*, the harassment."

"It's easy to say now."

"It should have been obvious to all of us. Mussolini saw Hitler gobbling up country after country and wanted in on the action. After Ethiopia and Albania, we're the next easy target."

"Right," chimed in Kaiti. "After Austria and all those others, it's our turn. They will devour all of Europe and more, just as Napoleon did."

"I bet Hitler doesn't approve of the attack," said Niko, quieter now. "Greece is of no interest to him. And don't forget – Germans respect Greece, its history, its culture. They would never attack us."

The previous evening – October 27, 1940 – Prime Minister Metaxas attended a reception at the Italian legation. There were toasts, smiles and handshakes amid the tinkle of champagne glasses. It was still dark in the early hours of October 28 when the Italian ambassador came to the Prime Minister's residence and presented him with the ultimatum: Let our troops enter Greece, or we'll come in by force. Like Leonidhas at Thermopilai, Metaxas gained admission to the Greek Pantheon by uttering just one word: Oxhi, No. That small word would be repeated every year on Oxhi Day, a national holiday to commemorate the defiant act of the little dictator who introduced Fascism to his country, was known as a friend of Germany and had opposed entering World War I as an ally of France and England. Now, when so many other countries had succumbed to Hitler's juggernaut and Britain stood alone to oppose him, Greece became, voluntarily, her only fighting ally.

I cheered when I heard that schools were to be closed indefinitely, eager to enjoy late mornings in bed and long afternoons in the company of Dumas' Musketeers.

"If you think you're going to lie around all day like a lazy *tembelis*, forget it," warned my father. "You will continue your lessons as if you were in school. Mutti and I will be your teachers."

Daily sessions were organized. Lotte was my morning teacher, with German subjects. In the afternoon, my unemployed father tutored me in Greek and math. He was a good teacher having distinguished himself in both the Military Academy and the Technische Hochschule and a stickler in the daunting intricacies of Greek spelling and grammar.

But he was not just about syntax and numbers. As never before, those sessions revealed a man of scattered interests – from calculus to Goethe, from Mantegna to Cavaradossi, from galaxies to Pascal. Although his knowledge did not run deep, his mind was alive and cast a wide net. He was a hungry accumulator of facts that he frequently converted to ideas, some useful, some profound and some unfortunately misguided, as I eventually concluded. For my purposes though he was an ideal teacher - a stimulator of curiosity, an opener of doors. Fear and anxiety may have been raging in the world outside, but there we were during those chilly winter afternoons, sitting next to each other, talking - secure in our intellectual cocoon.

The winter was particularly harsh on the battlefront up north. To everyone's amazement the small Greek army had pushed the Italians back into Albania. One after another the cities fell – Koritsa, Arghyrokastro, Aghii Saranta, names one had not heard before. "Soon we'll take Tirana, the capital," the saying went. "And then we'll push the *makaronadhes*, the spaghetti eaters, into the Adriatic." But winter and rough mountain terrain frustrated the dream and slow, numbing attrition took over. The army was not equipped for snow and ice; frostbites and exposure became the real enemy. The country back home rallied to help. Socks, mittens, scarves and sweaters were knitted by the thousand, and Lotte carried her needles and ball of wool around the house, even in bed and into the bathroom. The famous *chanteuse* Sofia Vembo, known for her muscular voice, cascading locks and hefty chest, had abandoned her signature ballads of love's pain for rousing songs of victory and ridicule of Benito Mussilini. We all felt good about ourselves. For a while at least, our own little dictator was a hero and the country was united.

In the cold dark night the sirens whined again. We jumped out of bed, put on our overcoats, grabbed some blankets and a flashlight and found our way to the front door.

We were not allowed to turn on lights during an alarm – windows had been shrouded and the glass panes x-taped for protection. Down the stair we stumbled, holding onto each other. Fear had shaken off our sleep. In the basement we huddled, shivering, together with the people from the other two floors. Halting, nervous conversation, some feeble jokes, floated in the dark.

"We should bring a deck of cards and play bridge down here," suggested the elderly Mrs. Vafiadhis.

"And some backgammon sets. It looks like this is going to happen a lot."

"Maybe we should just sleep down here. Bring some mattresses down. A little *kamineto* to make coffee."

"I prefer cognac. Heats the blood. Calms your nerves."

Outside the bang-bang of antiaircraft fire sounded oddly reassuring, like summer fireworks. Suddenly an explosion shook the floor of what seemed to be next door, and all breathing stopped.

"Panaghia mou!" a voice came out of a corner. A woman crossed herself. My mother grabbed me and pressed me to her chest.

"It's far away," said my father, who years ago had been trained to gauge the proximity of artillery fire. A few more distant explosions were heard, the rat-tat-tat stopped and the soothing monotone of the all-clear finally brought the neighbors to their feet and up the stair to their beds.

Even though it was hard to muster enthusiasm for Christmas, my mother remained undeterred. For her, it was still the most important event of the year. Having been weaned on its glittery magic, I naturally was a willing accomplice.

"Where on earth are you going to find a tree?" her husband asked. "There is a war on."

"Don't worry about it *Schatz*. We have our ways."

Trees were not yet a customary part of Christmas celebration in Greece. Furthermore, spruces, the appropriate trees, known as *Tannen* in Deutschland, could only be found on mountains above a certain elevation. The nearest was Mount Parnis, but its summit where spruces grew, was covered by snow. A man had to travel up there by truck or donkey cart to bring a tree down. There may even have been a law prohibiting the cutting of such trees since forest fires and drought had turned spruces into an endangered species. Such problems did not restrain Lotte. Every year since she had come to Greece, she managed to cajole somebody to bring her a spruce. The more readily available pine simply would not do.

"The needles are too long, the branches irregular and the trunks are crooked. Besides, Greek pines lack that nice *Schwarzwald* smell."

So, one evening, as if carrying contraband, a man came up the stair, dropped a small tree at our threshold, took his money and fled. It was indeed a spruce — not the size of past years, but still a spruce — its sylvan aroma soon to penetrate every corner of the house.

Happy and full of energy, my mother, with Kaiti's help, went to work. They managed to find ingredients to make *Pfeffernuesse*, the delicious, jaw breaking, spicy biscuits and the yellow pound cake, her favorite *Kuchen* that goes so well with afternoon coffee. (Where did she find the eggs?) And in honor of Greek custom they also baked *kourabiedhes*, the nut-filled cookies rolled in powdered white sugar, ideally suited for showering neckties, bosoms and carpets. When the big night finally came and Papous, Kaiti and I were invited to enter the living room, all seemed as it always had been. Candles had been lit, the old music box from Berlin played *Heilige Nacht* and kisses were exchanged. The little tree had been elevated on a table and under it lay one or two presents for everyone. Lotte had done it again. For a few moments it seemed as if nothing had changed, that love and peace still reigned, that all was well in the world.

One day in February, as I was walking down Patission Street near our house, I saw a strange crowd milling around the square outside the Archeological Museum. They didn't look like the tourists who would have been seen there in past years, nor like demonstrators assembled to stage some protest. They were dressed in military uniforms but their varied headgear and features were not Greek. Some wore turbans and black beards, their demeanor a bit wild and menacing. Others had slanting Mogul eyelids and small, lithe bodies. Still others, more European, sported a kind of cowboy hat, one side of the wide rim turned up white hunter style. As I came near I heard what seemed to be several different languages, none sounding particularly familiar although I had been pleased with my ability to identify languages on the radio.

"Who are they?" I asked a man who acted like a tour guide.

"With the British army. They just arrived two days ago."

"They don't look British."

"They're not. Colonials. Those with the turbans are Sikhs, from India. The others are called Gurkas, also from there somewhere."

"The others over there, they don't seem to be Indians."

"Australians – those with the cowboy hats. The ones next to them with the peaked hats I think are from New Zealand. Nice people. Our allies."

But some Athenians were suspicious.

"They found the head of a girl in Khalandhri. Still looking for the body," the green grocer told Kaiti one day. "It's got to be those Indians, those with the beards and the towels wrapped around their heads. They look like killers, carry big knives. Watch out *koritsi mou*, don't get mixed up with those people."

"I haven't seen any knives," I told her.

"They're rather good looking, so big," said Kaiti. "But how do you speak to them?"

"Better not."

> *Ioannis Metaxas died in January 1941 after a brief illness. The King appointed Alexander Korizis to succeed him. Korizis invited a British expeditionary force to join the Greek army against an expected invasion by the Germans, something Metaxas had been hesitant to do either for fear of provoking them or thinking of them as friends, as he did during the first World War. Hitler was getting fed up with the inept Italians. He rolled unopposed through Rumania and Bulgaria and on April 5th 1941, Panzer divisions attacked Greece and Yugoslavia. Greek and British generals failed to coordinate a line of defense, and soon the Wehrmacht was charging toward Athens, while the Commonwealth troops, after a half-hearted effort, abandoned the Greeks to their fate. Koryzis committed suicide. The King fled to Crete, where the British staged a brief defense until German paratroopers took the island, chasing the King and his ministers to Egypt.*

April 27, 1941, was a lovely spring morning after a day of eerie silence. I stepped out on the balcony and took a deep breath. Rudi next to me had stuck his head through the railing looking right and left for something to bark at. To the south, the marble of the Acropolis was catching the early sun in a rosy haze. Across the way, swallows, fresh from Africa, crisscrossed the air shrieking, looking for material to build their nests under the heavy roof cornices. The man at the corner store below was raising the roll-up shutters. Most other windows were still closed, the streets empty. I heard sounds up the road to my left and turned toward the intersection of Kodringtonos and Patission. There was traffic there, quite a bit of traffic I now noticed: a continuous stream of trucks, cars, motorcycles and what looked like big guns all painted a drab military gray and moving toward the Center, toward Omonia Square, in an endless silent procession. I turned and ran into the house.

"Everybody," I shouted, "come to the balcony, quick!" Kaiti was out first.

"My God," she whispered, her voice deep. "They're here…the Germans…the enemy."

"Amazing," said my father. "They got here in twenty days. Blitzkrieg. We didn't stand a chance, even with the Brits helping. If you can call that help."

I saw my mother shiver.

Looking at his son, Papous had the final word. "I told you so."

The German occupation began that day. Four years of misery lay ahead – for us, for Greece, for the world.

Along with the Germans came the Italians, who at first assumed the larger burden of the occupation, since the Germans had bigger fish to fry up north. This was too much for the Greeks.

"Can you believe it," said my grandfather. "We beat the hell out of them in Albania and now they're strutting around like roosters. Look at them, with those ridiculous feathers on their helmets." He was talking about the elite Versailleri platoons that at times jogged through the streets holding their rifles diagonally across their chests. Athenians pointed at them, laughed and yelled obscenities. After all, they said, the Italians may be ridiculous, but they're rather harmless.

"I saw some of them carrying a gun on one shoulder and a guitar on the other," I told Papous.

"There you are," he laughed. "These people are lovers, not soldiers. I rather admire that. I've always liked the opera better than war. Your father seems to like both."

The Germans were less visible at first. On rare occasions, a small formation would march by in black-booted rhythm, singing of *Heimat*, the fatherland, or of comrades fallen in the battle of Sedan – in 1870? 1916? 1940? It didn't really matter as long as the relatively tame, sentimental songs kept the pace. The take-no-prisoners Prussian grandeur of the Wehrmacht was revealed in full force during a parade I witnessed one day – a *déjà vu* of what I had seen in Berlin just five years before. Freshly shined boots hit the pavement with machine precision to the relentless beat of drums and the steady crash of cymbals accompanied by trumpets, piccolos and glockenspiels. The Germans knew and used the power of the military band well. Not only did it provide the necessary stimulus for marching, it also served as a rousing propaganda tool for the general population. The emotional and kinetic power of music can entice people to dance. But martial music, especially old Prussian marches like "Frederikus Rex," has a way of arousing different feelings – of aggression, patriotism, masculine prowess. It makes young men want to go to war, to kill. Is this what I found so exciting in Berlin in 1936?

"Will I be going back to the Deutsche Schule?" I asked my father.

"I'm afraid there is no choice at this time. We might be in trouble if you were to pull out now."

"Would they arrest you?"

"I don't think so. I'm not sure what could happen. Better to be cautious now. We'll see what we can do later. Do you mind?"

"I don't if you don't. But they are the enemy now. Right?"

"Yes…of course."

In mid May we gathered in the schoolyard to resume classes for a few more weeks. The Greeks spoke in hushed voices. Were we embarrassed? I was surprised but also relieved to see that everybody had come back. Their parents must have felt the same way my father did. The Germans of course were gloating, especially that little Nazi Wrede prancing around in his Hitler Youth uniform, his blond hair shorn down leaving a little tuft on top a la Himmler. How long was this going to last? The Germans now occupied most of Europe – from the Arctic Circle to Crete, from the Atlantic to the Russian border. England stood alone. After relentless bombing by Goering's Luftwaffe, there was talk of its invasion by the powerful Wehrmacht. But before the short school year ended the news was quite different. Instead of England, Germany had invaded the Soviet Union, the country with which it had signed a non-aggression treaty less than two years ago.

Having recently brought under his power half of Poland, Rumania, Bulgaria, Yugoslavia and Greece, Hitler had ordered troop concentrations along the Soviet border. Suddenly, on June 22, 1941, without any negotiation, warning or ultimatum, German armies moved into Russia in a war the world had never seen before. Millions of soldiers and thousands of tanks and aircraft would face each other from the Arctic Ocean to the Black Sea, along a battle line one thousand eight hundred miles long.

Ludicrously, in the midst of such cataclysmic events, my parents looked again for summer refuge as if all was normal. Nikos Kyriakos, an old army buddy of my father's, offered to share his house right by the sea opposite the island of Salamis not too far from Athens. (Kyriakos was dear to my father for having been jailed in an attempt to assassinate Venizelos in Paris.) Mutti was apprehensive.

"You mean the five of us are to live with the five of them? It must be a large house."

"Not exactly. But we have little choice these days, darling. We can squeeze in, they're nice people. The boy and you can have a dip every day, right in front of the house. I think I might even do some fishing. I was good at it as a kid."

It worked out better than Mutti thought. Beds and cots filled the house and we shared the one bathroom and the cooking and shopping chores. Children read, swam and played, men talked politics and world events and did little else. For me, living in an extended family, in a camping-out mode, was the essence of fun. And I loved the sea.

Anastasia and Katia, the daughters, were spirited girls, a year or two older than I. The three of us spent hours frolicking in the tame sea and the sandy beach in front of the house. To my embarrassment, I couldn't swim, although I was thirteen years old and to avoid further taunting I allowed Katia to become my teacher. The lessons involved inevitable body contact which added to the thrill of learning for both teacher and pupil. "You don't have to grab me every time you think that you are sinking," Katia would admonish and giggle. Soon though, I was able to paddle along, still careful to keep my nose out of water.

De facto segregation between boys and girls was still the rule in school. This summer though, the daily proximity of Katia and Anastasia began to alter the situation for me.

I enjoyed their company as I did Melpomeni's two summers ago in Kifissia. But a disturbing change had crept in. I had grown up with the natural awareness that boys were not the same as girls, that my mother was a woman and my father a man, that there were two kinds of animals – male and female - and that, somehow, out of this two-someness small creatures emerged that grew up to be as big as I and then continued to grow and be as big as my mother and father and later become old and look like Papous.

Years before, when I exposed myself dancing with the two little girls in the Papamandelou kitchen, I learned that I had something between my legs that they didn't have but the revelation didn't leave a big impression. Still, I found girls interesting – their clothing, their longer hair sometimes decorated with a bow, like little Aliki's in fifth grade, their oddly different behavior. I liked them although, like other boys, I wouldn't spend time with them – until Melpomeni, who rather aggressively had sought my company. But it was still all rather innocent, virginal, undeveloped.

In later years, the memory of a certain incident came back to me that, along with some others, played a lasting role in my behavior toward girls – and eventually toward women. I am five or six sitting next to my mother in a dark movie theater. On the screen I see a group of men and women in a room, talking, drinking, smoking. At one moment the camera turns toward one of the women reclining on a couch. She is laughing, holding a glass in one hand, a cigarette in the other, her lips and eyes dark with makeup, her long hair resting on a cushion. She is totally naked. Almost immediately I feel a hand over my eyes and hear my mother's voice hiss "don't look." Until that moment, partially or even totally naked men or women had been abstractions since I had never seen one in the flesh, so to speak, except for that very brief glimpse of my mother when I was even younger. In my father's art books, or in the Archeological Museum, I had perused with some curiosity but no shock, a maiden's bare breast peaking out of her robe or a naked youth's genitalia displayed as naturally as his fingers and toes. White marble or bronze or paper somehow put a distance between me and flesh-and-blood reality. However, once my beloved Mutti uttered the words *"Guck nicht,"* nudity, especially female nudity – and by extension sex – became forbidden territory. On that day my mother established, and thereafter kept trying to enforce, her own Hollywood decency code.

I enjoyed cavorting with Katia and Anastasia – in the water, on the beach in front of the house and indoors. One incident stands out. The three of us were lying on the big bed in their parents' bedroom wrestling and tickling each other amid giggles and little shrieks. It was here that I became acquainted with the tactile pleasures available in the female body – the fleeting touch of a pubescent breast lurking under a thin summer blouse, the accidental caress of a thigh as a skirt lifted. At which time one or the other asked, breathless, "what is that hard thing under your pants?"

"Yes," said the other, her hand firmly clasping my *putsos.* "Tell us what it is."

"It's …nothing…nothing," I blurted.

"Oh, yes," growled the first, tugging at my shorts. "Let's pull his pants down and see."

"No, no," I shouted, panic rising, suddenly thinking of my mother. I quickly untangled myself and staggered out of the room followed by shrieks of laughter.

~

With the war and the occupation, my father had to depend on his pension as his only income. He had a lot of free time and thought he could indulge himself a little. Neither a swimmer nor a beach idler, he decided to take up fishing.

"You want to go to Athenas Street with me?" he asked me one day. "I'm buying fishing gear. To fish in Aghii Theodhori."

"To fish? I've never seen you fish."

"I've told you. I used to fish in Anavysos as a boy. Was quite good at it."

"Why go to that market? Just meat and vegetables there."

"You can find anything on that street. Wait and see."

My mother had dragged me through Athenas Street a number of times when I was small. I remembered it as a hot, smelly, dirty, noisy place, the nearest thing to a Middle East souk, the central market of the city, a relic from the years when Turks ruled the country over a hundred years ago. It had grown over the years, a model of rudimentary commercial energy. Athenas (named after Athena - accent on the last syllable - daughter of Zeus and goddess of wisdom after whom my native city Athena was named – here the accent falls on the second syllable) starts on Omonia Square in the center of the city and runs through some of the oldest neighborhoods to end in Monastiraki Square at the foot of the Acropolis not too far from the remnants of the small Roman Forum. Action thrived on both sides of the street, much of it outdoors, possible in this benign climate with its grudging rainfall. Vehicle traffic was minimal, mostly hand or donkey driven carts, occasional streetcars. Automobiles were rare – rumor had it that once one ventured in, it might never be seen again. Pedestrians were the undisputed masters. The last time I had walked through there, just before the war began, Athenas was still bustling. Near Omonia, tables were set up selling cheap hardware, knick-knacks, clothing – the kind of merchandise one would find in a flea market. Further down came the victuals - fruits and vegetables piled up on outdoor stands, heaped high in bright, shiny pyramids and rows, their colors, shapes and sizes responding to each season's cornucopia. Cheeses came in chunks, wheels or floating in barrels of brine. Open tin cans contained the great varieties of Greek olives –maroon, green or black, shriveled or smooth, large and small. Triangles of sticky, sweet *khalva* were displayed next to stacks of little white sugar-powdered cubes of *loukoumia*, Turkish words, among the many left behind, mostly food related.

A strong smell signaled the approach of the fish market housed in a high, arched hall. Mongers in clogs, handlebar mustaches and floor to shoulder aprons stood tall on wooden platforms above pools of brown water shooing flies away with horsetails, loudly hawking their wares. Fish lay in rows on tilted racks next to shrimp, octopus, squid and sea urchins. The din of shouts reverberated off the skylights above, mingling with the stench. You had to love fish as much as my father and I did to stand this scene. But it was tame by comparison to the meat market next door where bloody carcasses hung on iron hooks, illuminated, even on the brightest summer day, by flocks of bare bulbs on limp wires. Swarms of flies and wasps brazenly attacked the meat unfazed by the swatting horse tails.

"You can tell a war is on," said my father as we walked down a much quieter Athenas Street. "It's going to be a rough winter. Look, there're hardly any vegetables, very few grapes, and it's mid summer. Remember last year? We had everything. Who could have thought this would happen?"

Past the meat market he hesitated, took a few more steps, looked around.

"Here it is." He stood in front of a tiny stall at the corner. A man was hidden behind piles of fishnets, spools, racks of hooks and lures. He wore a seaman's navy blue cap. His sumptuous gray mustache grew over a landscape of dark leathery skin.

"It's ready, I've got it right here," he said pulling out a flat basket, its rim lined with cork holding dozens of little steel hooks, each carefully tied to a separate thin line, all the lines laid down on the center of the basket in a neat spiral.

"Beautiful," said my father.

"Be careful to release the hooks one by one, in sequence," said the old man. "Let the lines unwind and fall in the water gently as you move the boat. Don't hurry, otherwise you'll get in a tangle."

"Yes, yes, I know," said Niko a little impatient. "I have experience in this, don't worry."

I was very impressed.

A few days later, I heard my father get up at dawn. Holding the fishing basket he walked toward a rowboat pulled up on the sand next to the still, gray sea. Across the way, over the low hills of Salamis, the rosy pinks, yellows and oranges heralded the sun. Barely awake I had staggered behind him.

"Why can't I go with you Pappi? I won't be in the way, I can help."

"Let me try this by myself first," he said. "Next time we'll go together. I promise."

I helped him push the boat, watched him climb in, put the oars in the oar-locks and slowly row away into the morning mist. I stood looking for a while, the sea lapping gently at my bare feet. Niko was wearing a wide rimmed straw hat he had just bought for this occasion. He looked ridiculous.

"Pretending to be an old salt," I thought grumpily as I turned to go back to bed.

The sun was already hot by mid morning. I was playing backgammon with one of the girls. Between rolls of the dice, I dipped my hand into the bowl next to me to pop another grape into my mouth.

"Here comes your father," announced Anastasia as Niko approached, oars lifted, letting the boat slide into the sand. Up the stone steps he came, his face already broadcasting failure.

"So?"

"Amazing, not a single bite."

"You had about fifty hooks on that line," said Papous from his favorite corner. "Did you put any bait on them?"

His son glared at him. "Of course I did."

"Maybe you were rowing too fast. Remember back in Anavysos, how I taught you to be patient?"

This was too much for Niko. He turned and entered the house. A door slammed.

"You were a bit too harsh with him, Papou," said Lotte.

Upset by my father's embarrassment, I asked Anastasia to join me for a ride. In the boat we found the basket buried under a tangle of twisted lines and unbridled fishhooks, some bait still attached here and there.

Later that afternoon we gathered on the terrace with the Kyriakos family to watch the sun set over the Korinthian mountains and enjoy homemade *vissinadha*, made from sour cherry syrup. Soon the conversation shifted to the inevitable.

"I hear they're approaching Leningrad," said Kyriakos. "They've already taken Minsk and it's only August."

"We forget the huge distances there," said Niko. "It's not the way it was in France last year."

"Not only distance, everything is in a totally different scale. Look at the size of the armies on both sides, millions, all spread out – and the equipment, the weapons, the huge supply lines."

"That explains the slower pace. They have to wait until their supplies catch up with them. Otherwise they'd be in Siberia by now."

"Probably so," Kyriakos laughed. "One thing puzzles me though," he continued, turning serious. "We thought that the Russians would have collapsed by now, the way the French and the English did. After all, they're oppressed people. You'd think they would have opened their arms to the Germans, greeted them as liberators."

"You old soldiers seem all excited by this war," interrupted Kyriakos' wife Xhariklia. "This is not a Hollywood movie, you know. By the time this is over, thousands of young men will be killed, even millions, not to speak of the poor civilians – women, children and old people who will suffer from hunger and cold, lose their homes, die. Look at what happened during the Albanian war."

Kyriakos glared at his wife. "Serves those Bolsheviks right," he shouted. "They asked for it."

"Shame on you!" she yelled back. "We're talking about human beings here, not political ideologies."

"You know why the Russian armies have not collapsed?" Kaiti broke in, unable to contain herself. "They're fighting for their country, that's why. The way our boys fought last winter. Even though they hate the dictatorship they live under."

"Bravo Kaiti," said Papous quietly.

"How about some dinner," ordered Kyriakos, looking at his wife.

One of my many drawings of Papous. Winter, 1940.

My mother as I saw her, ca. 1942

THE WINTER OF '41

SEPTEMBER 1941. I entered *Terzia*, eighth grade in the German school. I was thirteen years old, and, like my silkworms, exhibiting signs of metamorphosis. My nose was growing to a disquieting prominence. My voice suddenly sounded screechy, and little pimply spots were erupting on my face. I spent considerable time looking at myself in the mirror of my mother's makeup cabinet, where she sat every night in her silk robe to apply copious amounts of cold cream on her face in the manner of a circus clown. I didn't know why she did this, since her skin was soft and smooth, and I loved to stroke it and bestow kisses on it. It was I that should be using the cream, I thought. But when I tried to put it on one day, it was a disaster. The stuff felt greasy and hard to control. It penetrated my nostrils, stung my eyes and got on my hair and shirt. Its taste on my lips and the heavy perfume of its scent felt suddenly repulsive, and I ran to the bathroom to wash it off and wipe myself vigorously with a towel.

I was troubled. What happened to the pretty, dark-eyed boy the girls used to tease? The long lashes were still there, so was the delicate mouth, the straight black hair dashingly parted to one side. But now the nose dominated all, a nose that came dangerously close to looking like my father's. I didn't think my Pappi was particularly good looking, even if Mutti seemed to think so, certainly not when compared to the actors I had seen in American movies, like Clark Gable and Ronald Coleman.

And now a new outrage was added to destroy further my boyish features: a pair of eyeglasses. I was walking with my father along Green Park on Mavromataion Street, when he pointed at a street sign and said, "let's turn over there, at Derigny."

"How can you read that far?" I asked.

"You mean you can't?"

"Of course not."

My father, not one to let such an opportunity go unchecked, proceeded to give me an amateur eye examination. He pointed at store signs, house numbers, newspaper headlines posted outside kiosks, each time asking me to recite.

Next day I found myself looking at eye charts in Doctor Xhalkidhis' office.

"Simple myopia," he said, "but quite severe. How did you manage all this time?"

"Will I wear these for the rest of my life?" I asked my father who didn't wear glasses.

"You'll get used to them," he said, sounding pleased with himself.

The next day in school I noticed that the writing on the blackboard had turned white — a definite improvement. But I was bothered when the girls looked at me and snickered.

In October the Germans at school were still strutting around. Their armies were knocking at the gates of Moscow and Leningrad and Rommel was rolling toward Cairo.

It will soon all be over, they said. The Greeks were glum. Not only was the news depressing, but here we were, attending a school run by the Enemy, pretending that all was normal. Mavridhis couldn't stand it.

"I hear that a resistance movement is starting," he whispered during recess. "We have to join. My brother is thinking of going."

"Going?"

"To the mountains, what else?"

"But your brother is older. Aren't we too young for that?"

"Nonsense. In Russia, children younger than we are have been throwing Molotov cocktails at German tanks."

"Molotov what?"

"You're hopeless," hissed Mavridhis, disgusted.

But things got even worse. What seemed to have been a skimpy supply of food during the summer, was turning into a major crisis. Athenians soon learned that the occupying armies – the Italians, the Bulgarians, but mostly the Germans, were plundering the country, living off the land like locusts. Food supplies and crops were confiscated; private and state property was looted; huge taxes, called "occupational costs", were levied. The *Katoxhi*, the *Besatzung*, the Occupation - four years of famine, inflation, fear, misery and death – had begun in earnest coinciding with one of the coldest winters in anyone's memory.

After school one November afternoon I went shopping with Kaiti.

"Get whatever you can," said my mother. "We can't be choosers anymore. All I found this morning were some dry beans. See if those people are out on Patission. They come there when it's dark."

We bundled up and stepped out in the dusk. The baker was closed, his shelves empty for days. On the avenue, at the bottom of Alexandhras, some dozen men and women were lined up against the iron railing of the Italian Institute, where the flag of the defeated army hung once more. Crates were stacked in front of the peddlers and each makeshift counter carried minimal merchandise: a few potatoes in a pile, a sack of lentils, bunches of beets, some walnuts, some chestnuts.

"How much the *patates*?" Kaiti asked the shadowy figure behind the crate. His answer was barely audible.

"This is robbery," she said, shocked. "Shame on you! I'm going to tell the police!"

"You do that, *aghapi mou*" (my love). The man's loud guffaw was echoed by the rest of the lineup. "By the time they get here, we'll all be gone and you'll get nothing, sweetie. And your mistress will be very angry when you come back empty-handed. Ha, ha, ha!"

So we bought a few potatoes and some beets and started back. It was quite dark by now. Streetcars rattled by, their lights on, the long rods on top squealing against the network of overhead electric wires. People inside were packed together, the overflow hanging perilously outside the open doors. Undeterred by their hardships, they had gone to work the same way this morning and every day since it all began. Other people rushed by on the sidewalk, their collars turned up, exhaling puffs of condensed air. Kaiti took my arm and drew me close. I could feel her breath as we walked, the softness under her thin coat.

—

Papous was not well. His mild, doe eyes were red, a bead of mucus hung at the end of his nose, he coughed. After school, I would find him lying on his bed bundled in his black winter coat, *kaskol* around the neck, beret perched forward, looking straight ahead. How many times had I sat next to this gentle old man, heard his stories, sketched that gnarled profile? I took his hand.

"Your hand is cold, Papou."

"*Tha pethano, paidhi mou.* I'm going to die, my boy." The voice was raspy.

"Nonsense, Papou. You've been saying this for years. Just a little cold, everybody has it, it's very cold outside. Here, I'll put a blanket over you."

"We have no heat."

The apartment's "central heating" no longer worked. The stove in the entrance hall had been the only source of heat. It had to be stoked by anthracite from a large bucket next to it. Coal dust had to be swept off the floor periodically, some of it inhaled. But coal was not available this winter. On occasion, Papous had alarmed the family by filling a soup dish with rubbing alcohol and lighting it.

We caught him now and then rubbing his hands over the flame.

Later in the evening we set up a table in his room, and helped him up. A charcoal brazier in the corner was meant to stem the frigid air leaking in through the window. We all wore overcoats and hats, even gloves. But noses and ears went unprotected and gloves had to be removed to guide food from plate to mouth. How did Scott and Amundsen do it in the South Pole?

"I have no appetite," said Papous. "I'll just sit here and watch you eat."

"Come now, Baba," urged Niko. "You need to eat something. Good for your cold."

"I'm not hungry."

"How about some of these *ghaelettes*?"

Niko was referring to the dry, round biscuits, 5" in diameter, made of white flour and very hard, that had mysteriously appeared during the occupation. Because of their preservative qualities, they had substituted for bread during long sea voyages in the old days.

"Too hard for my dentures."

"But they get soft when they are soaked in water, Baba, you know that."

"No thanks." Papous wrinkled his nose.

"You're right, Papou," I laughed. "It's awful stuff. Tastes like wet cardboard."

"But you'll have some of these nice boiled potatoes," said Niko glowering at me.

"Look, Lotte put some vinegar on them, and some oregano, they're delicious."

"No *ladhi*?"

"We had our last olive oil for lunch, Baba, remember? Titsian and Kaiti couldn't find any."

"I'll drink a little water."

"Or maybe a nice cup of chamomile?" asked my mother with an endearing smile.

"Yes, that would be fine."

On December 6, Saint Nicholas Day, the first in the string of year-end holidays ending with Epiphany on January 6, men and boys named Nikolaos celebrated their Day. As it was probably the most common male name in Greece, *Tou Aghiou Nikolaou* was one of the most important holidays, or so it seemed to me who had been the key secondary beneficiary of the attention traditionally showered on my father. This year, although the need for diversion was, if anything, stronger, the means for celebration was seriously lacking. Still, visitors were trickling in bearing some ersatz concoction or some "fresh mountain greens" or some schnapps left from last year. After all it was the intent that mattered, and the opportunity to gain strength from common fellowship, from shared misfortune. And conversation had shifted away from the usual gossip of births, marriages, divorces, love affairs, in-laws, houses, maids. The talk now was of shortage, inflation, danger, unemployment, combat, fear.

"They're having trouble over there. Stuck outside Moscow."

"Toula, there is a city near Moscow named after you. Huge battles there."

"You think it's cold here. They say the oil is freezing in their engines."

"We should be getting credit for delaying them. They had to postpone Russia to come here and rescue Mussolini."

"You can't get anything outside the black market anymore."

"Did you know what I paid for half an *oka* of rice the other day?"

"What's going to happen to us?"

"When will this end?"

Two days later, my father came home with news from another part of the world.

"Amazing," he said. "The Japanese sank almost the entire American fleet in the Pacific Ocean. A surprise attack."

"Aren't the Americans friends with the British, and the Japanese with the Germans?"

"Quite so. And you know what? Hitler and Mussolini have declared war on the United States."

"Wonderful! That means…"

"Exactly, my boy. Although they're far away and have their hands full with the Japs. Still…"

"Don't forget Pappi, they helped win the last war. It's a big powerful country."

"It's not the same situation. Hitler now controls all of Europe."

I looked at my father. "But it's the first ray of hope. And the Russians are holding on."

"I guess so…"

Sometime before Christmas, when all was bleak, my mother produced a Santa Claus. Wolfgang, a thirty-something schoolteacher in civilian life, was serving as a lowly private in the Wehrmacht. He was tall, with dark hair and fleshy, gentle features. There seemed to be a wife and children back in Hanover and no apparent Nazi affiliation. No one knew where and how Lotte found him. He came up the stair carrying a small suitcase, took off his coat and put down his load in the middle of the living room floor. My mother, Kaiti and I watched as Wolfgang unclasped the locks and slowly lifted the top. Breathing turned into a slow whistle and we sank down on our knees, like worshippers. Had the suitcase been filled with diamonds, pearls and rubies we would not be more dazzled. With thumb and forefinger, like a jeweler, piece by piece, he brought out his treasure – bars of dark chocolate, jars of blueberry and raspberry jam, canned *leberwurst*, a tin of biscuits, packages of pumpernickel, canned sardines, shrimps and duck confit, flour, sugar, tea, coffee, cocoa, and – holy of holies – two loaves of dark sourdough rye bread - ordinary German army issue highly prized in the local black market. Overwhelmed, the two women threw their arms around Wolfgang who explained that he was happy to bring so much pleasure to a nice family. I wondered how he had managed to gather such a cornucopia in the middle of the war. This could not have been a part of his normal diet, even for a member of a victorious army. Such loot would have been luxury under normal conditions before the war. I felt a brief pang of guilt. This was the Enemy after all – not a bullying loudmouth Nazi type, like some of my teachers at school – but still the Enemy.

And how did my mother find him? Had she met other soldiers? Where? Like worms, such thoughts began to slither into my head. But not for long. As I smeared a heavy slab of *leberwurst* on a thick slice of that army bread, all symptoms of remorse vanished along with those sneaking suspicions.

Outside, though, raged a deadly famine. Looking out the window one day, I saw a small crowd at the corner of Septemvriou Street. Curious, I ran down, crossed the street and pushed my way in. A man lay on the sidewalk, prone.

"Is he dead?" a woman whispered.

"Dead as can be," answered a man and gave the corpse a little kick. "They're dropping all over the city – out in the country too."

"Those pigs are stealing all our food," said another voice, louder.

"Whatever is left goes to the black marketers. We have to take things in our own hands."

Another day, after school, as I was walking down Massalias Street behind the University, a truck passed me and came to a stop ahead. On it seemed to be a pile of clothing. Two men jumped out of the cab and opened the tailgate. I stopped with a gasp as I suddenly understood what I was seeing – a pair of legs, a head or two, some arms sticking out of the tangle – a truckload of corpses! One by one the two men picked up the bodies like so many sacks – limbs, heads hanging, swinging, unrestrained in a grotesque ballet. I was looking at death, shocked to see how different it was from life, expecting to see some gesture, some familiar movement, to hear voices. These people, fully dressed, could have been on their way to work or out to dinner together. I realized that I was standing in front of a city morgue.

The wooden radio with the arched top, the old Santa Maria dei Miracoli, still with us, sat on the little side table in one corner of the living room between the daybed, (my bed) and the sofa from Skyros with the carved dark oak back that matched the ornate bookcase and the two arm-chairs. The radio had recently acquired the status of a shrine. Like worshipers, we all gathered around it every evening for the 8 o'clock Greek-language broadcast from London. The local station offered slanted news and Nazi propaganda. The BBC broadcast began with the sound of a Roumeli shepherd's flute playing a simple, plaintive melody that lasted a few seconds but had assumed, in the darkness of this miserable winter, the power of a paean, a Beethovenian ode to defiance and hope. This brief overture was followed by *"Edho Londhino,"* here is London, delivered by a mellifluous masculine voice. This evening we were told of the Wehrmacht's retreat from the gates of Moscow and Hitler's firing of Feldmarschal von Brauchitsch to assume personal command of all armed forces. The Fuehrer simply would not accept retreat.

"Isn't Brauchitsch the one who came to Athens last spring?" asked Kaiti.

"The very same," said my father. "Walter Wrede, the archeologist, gave him a tour of the Acropolis."

"How the great fall," I said. "How satisfying."

"It's their first defeat." This, from Niko who, some months before, had been cheering them on.

The other news was less bracing. In the back-and-forth North African front, Rommel once again was advancing, threatening to reach Alexandria.

December 1941. Ludicrously, Christmas was here again. Wolfgang's goodies had already been consumed but my mother remained undaunted. She made ersatz *Pfeffernuesse*, a meager little tree was found, candles were lit, some presents were given and *heilige Nacht, froeliche Nacht* was played on the old music box from Berlin. But it was hard to ignore the world outside – the raging famine and bitter cold, the dying, the brutal occupation, the despair brought by a dark future. And, most important, Papous' health was rapidly declining. Sitting by his bedside, rubbing his hands and feet, I tried to cheer him up.

"Remember when I would sit here," I told him, "and you'd tell me stories of Kyparissia when you were a child? Of my great grandfather, the priest? How he would beat you with his belt? You'd call him 'the devil' behind his back."

For a brief moment, Papous' lips would part a bit in a faint smile. Then, serious again, he coughed.

"Tha pethano agori mou," he whispered.

"You keep saying that, Papou. You're not dying. It's a bad winter and you're a little weak."

"Tha pethano."

"You should be eating your broth. Come spring you'll be *mia xhara*, just fine."

"Tha pethano," like someone facing the gallows.

Kaiti and my mother fussed around him, adjusted his bedding, gave him alcohol rubs, coaxed food into his mouth. My father took his temperature, consulted with the doctor who came every day and shook his head.

On a Sunday afternoon in January, I was sitting by his bedside while my parents were napping and Kaiti was in her room reading. Papous seemed to be sleeping, his breathing heavy, out of rhythm. I couldn't keep my eyes off him. After another long pause I leaned over to listen for breath. Suddenly, his mouth dropped open and I heard a gurgle.

Now there was total silence. I slowly moved my finger to touch his temple. His head slowly flopped over to the side and his beret fell off. Papous lay there as I had always known him – bushy gray eyebrows, furrowed cheeks, brown liver spots, virile mustache, prominent, aristocratic nose. The eyelids were closed. He could still be sleeping. I got up and rushed next door to wake up my parents.

"I think Papous has died," I whispered.

It was the first and last time that I witnessed the ending of a human life.

The next day, three men in dark suits brought up a simple pine box that looked much like the ones made by the casket maker across the street. They dressed Papous in his best suit, including vest, white shirt and necktie, socks and street shoes. My mother stayed in her room but Kaiti and I joined my father to look on.

"It's like the El Greco," I whispered. "Jesus brought down from the cross."

"And many other paintings," added my father. "A timeless picture of sorrow."

As the men lifted the body and my grandfather's head and limbs flopped around like so many sticks, lifeless as a marionette, I was reminded of the cadavers I had seen in front of the morgue. The shock now was greater. The dreadful desperation of this winter, the tragic sweep of this entire year, had struck home. This was no stranger down on the sidewalk. Placed for eternity in the box before us, was my beloved Papous, my childhood companion, the wise, gentle anchor of our family.

I wished I could cry, but no tears came. As the men took him away, I realized how much a part of my life he had been and yet, in all those years I had taken him for granted. My close interaction with my parents had made his presence less conspicuous, less important. Like other older people, he existed on the margin of our lives although he hung around the house most of the time. In his mild, halting way, he tried to join the company of my parents, their friends and relatives, especially when his daughters came to visit. His presence frequently annoyed my mother and sometimes my father – they saw him, I think now, as a man from another era, slow-moving, with fixed, quirky habits, peripheral to the ideas and customs of their own time, willing to ignore his innate wisdom, the perspective of a long life. As for me, I knew that I would miss my afternoons and evenings with him – his stories, the tunes he whistled to himself, his affection.

But I wasted no time to take possession of his room. I was a teenager and felt that it was time to inhabit my own space although Papous' spirit held sway over every corner. I inherited his bed, left in its position along the outside wall, close to the window with the Acropolis view. The square table in the center of the room was removed together with the nightstand, the washing bowl and pitcher, the chamber pot and the icon of the Virgin and Child. (The icon still sits on a shelf in our house in Massachusetts). Soon, a large desk with drawers and a tall, wide modern cabinet meant to store books and dishes were brought in. A year or two later, when our first telephone and a new typewriter took their place on the desk, I found that my parents had gradually expropriated "my" room as their office to write letters and speak on the phone about some new business they had embarked on… But I still slept on my grandfather's bed and managed to do my homework there.

The famine and bitter cold of that horrible first winter of the occupation continued. As in a silent movie, people walked the streets in fast staccato movements, black and gray shapes wrapped in dark cloth, mouths shielded from the wind, hats pulled down to the eye-brows, bent over in wordless despair. What occupied their time? Were they civil servants in the impotent government, merchants with nothing to sell, veterans of a defeated army? Here and there you saw a child, skinny bare legs purple from cold, arm extended, begging for food. *"Peinao, peinao,"* I'm hungry, came the plea. Was there a mother somewhere? Misery was worst in the refugee settlements where the wind whistled through the cracks in the wooden *paranghes*, the jerry-built shacks I knew existed up the hill somewhere and around the city's perimeter. I saw some of the kids from there wandering around Syntaghma and Kolonaki, their rags, bare feet and shaved heads challenging the conscience of upright citizens who shooed them off or looked away. Some boys who could afford the equipment, practiced the time-honored occupation of boot-black. A small rectangular box contained the tools and materials for their work: bottles of brown, black and neutral coloring liquid, wax polish, brushes corresponding to the stain colors, a long cloth for final polishing and square pieces of cardboard torn from used cigarette packs inserted on either side of the shoe to keep the customers' sox from getting stained. A brass foot stand was attached to the center of the box. Boys, and some men, in a row along strategic sidewalks or squares, sat on low stools behind their work stations calling out or hitting their box with a brush to attract business. German soldiers with their high jack boots were lucrative targets. The boys had quickly learned the magic call. *"Extra prima Stuka Putz,"* they shouted, evoking the power of the deadly dive bombers of the Luftwaffe to extol the quality of their *Putz*, their polishing.

***

The trek to school from Kodringtonos was particularly trying that winter. I still wore the short pants and low socks of pre-adolescent boys even though my shorts were already bulging with the equipment of manhood that strained to be released from captivity whenever I found myself squeezed against a girl in a crowded street car. But today all was calm down there as I crossed the *Pedheion tou Areos*, the vast new park that was once my father's parade ground when it was part of the *Evelpidhon*, the Military Academy, and I could only feel the cold on my legs and think of the long boring slog ahead. After the park, my daily route took me down the spiritless streets behind the Archeological Museum and the Polytechnic, through the Exarchia neighborhood to the steep ascent up Araxhovis street and the gates of the Deutsche Schule, just below the German Church. Entering the school was like entering another world - one of order, warmth and reason – or so it seemed. For a few hours, I left behind the purgatory of suffering and despair I had encountered on my way there. Never mind the Heil-Hitlers, ignore the clipped, snapping commands, tolerate the haughty demeanor and self satisfied smirks, suppress your guilt. Concentrate on Learning, on Art, Literature, History; focus on Xenophon's *Anavasis* and the intrepid "Ten Thousand", the Greek mercenaries who shouted *"Thalatta, Thalatta!,"* the Sea, the Sea, as they approached the shores of the Black Sea after years of warring in the Asian plains, eager to get back to their Greek homeland. Think of the heroes of the 1821 War of Independence, the freedom fighters whose lifeless marble statues in the park I passed every morning on my way here.

I sketched myself and my new glasses, aged 13.

Bodies delivered to the Athens mortuary, winter 1941.

INGRES

AND THE WATER NYMPH

I WAS SITTING in my new room after lunch. Kaiti and my parents were resting. I enjoyed those few hours of privacy in my grandfather's room, a room that now was more or less my own. Today I was leafing through one of my favorite art books. I had lately been admiring the Ingres women − not so much the formal portraits of bourgeois ladies in low-cut satin gowns, as the voluptuous, fleshy odalisques lolling about stark naked in Anatolian harems, or equally naked nymphs from revived classical antiquity. One in particular had been attracting my attention: a young girl with lovely breasts, wholesome thighs and blank face holding with one frail arm an overflowing ewer over one shoulder, the water caressing her contours on its way down. For some days now, this image had been provoking strange stirrings in my pants accompanied by a shortness of breath. The experience was clearly not new, what with last summer's peccadilloes and other minor transgressions. Lately, at school, the boys and I have been titillating each other with risqué stories, jokes about the female anatomy, that sort of thing. The other day, Franz, the Swiss boy who consorted with the Greeks, told us about his encounter with Amalia during recess in the schoolyard. "She was leaning against the big pine tree," he said in a confidential tone as all heads leaned forward, "one leg bent up propped against the trunk, her skirt poised above the knee, eyes closed, smiling." He walked over to her and whispered in her ear, as if offering a bon-bon, *"willst Du ficken?"* Would you like to fuck? Without opening her eyes, still smiling, she answered dreamily, "ja, *und Du?"* yes, and you? This was too much for us. Some snickered, others laughed too loudly, one turned around and walked away.

"Well, did you?" I asked.

"Nothing happened. Besides," he added confidentially. "I don't think she understood, her German is a bit shaky." More guffaws.

I stared at the Ingres girl again today. Her face was oval, a bit like Kaiti's, with a lifeless Mona Lisa smile, abstract. But her body came to life as my eyes focused to take in this mysterious, unfamiliar vision and my own body responded once again, tensing. The bulge in my pants was becoming unbearable. The room around me had disappeared and all I could hear was my own racing heartbeat. "I'm going crazy," I murmured as my hand went down to discover the tormenting thrill of my own flesh, the heat and urgency of this magical instrument that seemed to have a power all its own. I had to suppress my scream as the explosion came, a release of indescribable beauty, a pleasure so sharp it could have been pain, exquisite pain. "My God", I whispered still panting. "Did I do this?" As my breath began to slow down and I was once again aware of the room, another image appeared before me – my mother's censorious face. Terrified, I jumped up, grabbed a newspaper from the desk and wiped the sticky white mucous off the floor. In my panic, I still noticed the interesting pungent odor that I had smelled before in my pajamas. I quickly changed my underpants. Where to put all this evidence? She was sure to find it. For now, let's just hide it behind the bed. But why did I feel so guilty? It was nature after all – those thousands of little spermatozoa racing to pounce on a bevy of defenseless ova. I returned to sit at the desk and stared ahead, smiling. "I'm a man now," I thought. "I can procreate."

As I revisited my nymph day after day during those spring afternoons, a new awareness began to dawn. The girl's oval face seemed more and more familiar. I recognized the full lips, the hair demurely pulled back, the dark provoking eyes. Her languid arms were there too, her slim ankles, shapely calves, her knees …"My God," I whispered, "it's she, right here in my house. I see her every day, we joke together … and she sleeps above the kitchen … every night, only a few meters away from me!" I knew now why the recognition had not come sooner. "It's the two *Majas*. I see them every day, both the *vestida* and the *desnuda*. I just didn't put them together – until now. How wonderful!"

The bell rang. I rushed to the door, always eager for a new visitor. A voice boomed from below.

"Ya sou, Titsian. Irtha me to podhilato." (Hi, Titsian, I came with the bicycle).

"Bring it up," I shouted, happy to hear the voice of my favorite uncle. Achileas was so much fun, even though other members of the family thought of him as a black sheep. He had solved the wartime transport problem by riding around Athens on a rickety old bicycle, the back always loaded with something or other – groceries, a rolled up painting, a chair. I remembered the day I rode on the back together with some bags as Achileas huffed and puffed along Kifissias Avenue on the way to visit my aunt Toula and my cousin Bebe in the suburb of Ekali. Trucks and buses were speeding by spewing pollution as the bicycle weaved this way and that. If that were not enough, Achileas, an incorrigible girl watcher, would raise the level of danger by turning his head to follow the swing of some woman's skirt as she trudged along the highway. "Watch out!" I would scream as we swerved into the traffic.

Today Achileas wheeled his bicycle up two flights to reach the landing and the front door. His broad chest was heaving for breath but there was a triumphant grin on his handsome face. He carried the rakish insouciance of a Clark Gable. The necktie hung loosely around his open collar, the proper business suit was rumpled and needed dry cleaning. Toula, no longer in love, referred to him by his surname – o Varvaressos - in addition to other less flattering names. "What a bum," she would say, and her brother agreed. Family and friends were scandalized. A *ghynekas* they called him, a womanizer, he's never held a steady job.

"You know what he's doing now?" said a cousin the other day. "Drawing mockups for new inflated Drachma bills the government issues every other month. Can you believe it? And only because of connections with the Central Bank, through his brother. I bet it won't last."

"He's always fussing around that land in Kalithea, pretending to be a farmer," said another.

"Did you know that he's declared himself a Communist?" fumed my indignant father. "What does he know about the proletariat, that good for nothing voluptuary? He should stay home and take care of his family, his sick daughter, the poor thing."

But I liked him. Achileas was an Artist, a Free Spirit, a Mario Cavaradossi. So what if women loved him. People were just jealous, I thought, stuck as they were with their boring lives, their fat spouses and whiny children. But then, I didn't think of my parents that way. Mutti certainly was not fat, not like some of her German friends, like Elfriede or Frau Wark. And Pappi after all is an architect, a kind of artist, although not really a free spirit. To be fair, both my parents admired Achileas as an artist, if grudgingly. His large portrait of my mother, set in an ornate gilded frame, hung prominently in our living room together with a foamy seascape and a picture of a shoreline featuring a lonely tormented pine. "Not exactly a Courbet," said Niko, "but better than most of the pretentious junk you see around."

Achileas leaned his bicycle against the wooden coat rack in the front hall, took off his jacket, rolled up his sleeves and wiped the sweat off his forehead with his arm. "Brought you some green olives from Kalithea," he said offering a cone of greasy rolled- up newspaper. Kaiti came out of the kitchen and took the precious package with a smile. *"Sas efcharistoume para poli,"* she thanked him profusely, using the polite form. *"Dhistichos dhen echoume kafe, ena neraki?"* (Sorry we don't have coffee, some water?) We sat down in my room. Kaiti came in with some water and sat down with us. I could tell that she was enchanted with him, and soon Achileas gave her all his attention.

"What is a lovely girl like you doing here?" he purred and she blushed. "You could be a model."

"Oh, *Kyrie* Achilea, you are a flatterer."

"No, no. I know these are difficult times, but still there is room for someone like you in a couturier's salon or an artist's studio …"

I knew where this was leading. Surprised by my sudden pang of annoyance I asked "How is the family up in Ekali?"

Achileas looked at me askance, the tete-a-tete was over.

"I'm going there today, haven't seen them for a week. I've been busy with a new commission."

"And what are you painting *Kyrie* Achilea?" she asked still captivated. I stared at her – why did this bother me so much?

"Come up to Ekali," my uncle told me as he finally took his leave. "Bebe is asking about you. We can ride up on the bicycle together."

"Thanks, I'll take the bus."

A few nights later I was in the bathroom. Its window looked out on the spiral steel stair that led up to the roof terrace. Up behind the stair I could see Kaiti standing by the window of her room. She was in her underwear, elbows raised, combing her hair. I pulled back – had she seen me? I stepped forward again; I couldn't keep my eyes off her, the black tuft under her arm, her soft profile. Suddenly she turned toward the open window. "Do you like what you see?" Her throaty voice coming across the winding steps startled me. It was not her usual matter-of- fact tone. I fled - mortified, confused. The incident passed without comment, except – was that a little ironic smile I saw the next morning? There was a change though, certainly in my manner, but also in hers. The easy big sister-little brother affections — a kiss on the cheek, the passing muss of hair — seemed to have stopped. Irony and innuendo became more common, plus bumps and brushings dismissed as accidental with a polite but smirky *"sighnomi,"* excuse me. Until one day, when we were alone in the apartment, an accidental bump was followed by a little shove, answered by a counter shove and her "I think you're ticklish," by my "No, you are." Raucous giggling erupted as we attacked each other's ticklish zones, pushing and shoving until we tripped on the edge of my bed and collapsed on it. By then her skirt had crept up her thigh, her hair had come loose, my hand had cupped a breast and my pants were bulging.

"Titsian, no," she moaned and we rolled away from each other panting.

"I'm sorry," I whispered.

"Don't be sorry," she said to my surprise. "It was fun, but I don't think we should continue."

"Where to this summer?" I asked my parents one evening in May.

"Nowhere," answered my father. "The seashores are black with oil and the hills infested with guerillas. We stay right here in our nice, comfortable house."

Rumors had been going around about the fighting in the mountains. It was known that most guerillas were leftists — a sore subject for my father.

"Now all of a sudden that rabble is taking up arms pretending to fight for liberation, for the national cause." His favorite refrain. "Nonsense," he continued, "all they want is to take over after the war, bring us Communism, turn us into Slavs."

*The Greek Communist Party, (Kommunistiko Komma Elladhas
or KKE, or, popularly, Ku-Ku-Eh,) persecuted during the Metaxas
dictatorship had lain dormant until Hitler had attacked the Soviet*

Union the previous year. Throughout the fall and winter, a gradual resistance build-up began with the creation of EAM, the National Liberation Front, a declared umbrella organization of diverse political groups but in fact dominated by the KKE. An important offshoot entered the scene soon thereafter, the ELAS, the National Liberation Army. (The acronym cleverly resembled Ellas or Hellas, the name Greeks give to their country.) ELAS took to the mountains to fight the Germans and Italians, referred to as "Fascists" by the Communists. They also gave that name, correctly, to the followers of the pre-war Metaxas dictatorship which had outlawed Communism and eventually to any group or individual that opposed them. Later, and following a tradition that reached at least as far back as the Peloponnesian War, ELAS ended up battling other Greeks, among them the so-called "Nationalist", non-Communist resistance groups like EDES (National Democratic Hellenic League) and later, the ultra right wing band Orghanosis X. All these guerillas were called andartes, regardless of political affiliation.

"So we stay here and suffer the heat?" I complained.

"You could go to Ekali," suggested my father. "Bebe would like your company, and it's cool there. They sleep under blankets at night."

"Achileas has already asked me," I said, knowing that my uncle would prefer to abduct Kaiti on the back of his bicycle in the manner of Zeus, that prototypical lecher. But maybe Kaiti wouldn't mind being ravished if, in exchange, she could have a continent named after her. Vassilakis had told me that women would do anything for fame and money.

Nestled on the western slopes of Mount Pendeli, Ekali was an up-and-coming suburb a few kilometers beyond Kifissia. Its forested slopes offered stunning views of the fertile Tatoi valley, where the royal family had a summer palace and of Mount Parnis beyond with its golden sunsets. Before the war, rich Athenians, tired of the hotels and crowded housing in Kifissia, began to seek the more exclusive charms of Ekali with its cool fresh air, quiet shady streets and elegant villas. Toula and Bebe lived in one such house built out of fieldstone, with green Provencal shutters, in a grove of tall pines behind an iron gateway. It belonged to Achileas' more accomplished brother Kyriakos who was out of the country. A prominent economist and professor at the University, he had followed the King and the Government into exile in Cairo. Bebe and her mother lived in Ekali in relative luxury, (there was an electric refrigerator instead of an ice box and an upright piano) with occasional visits from the wayward father. Little Tassia, a local village teenager, cleaned the house for them, happy to have some food and a roof over her head. The villa across the street had been expropriated by the Wehrmacht to house a platoon of Bavarians who bustled about half naked and tanned, shouting unintelligibly, forerunners of post-war Nordic tourist invasions.

"Nice boys," said Toula. "They're so polite, bring us chocolates, hard to think of them as the enemy." Bebe had a different view. "Barbarians," she mumbled.

"The girls next door have invited us for some freshly made *vissinadha*," Bebe said one day. "Are you coming?" The three sisters, aged 13, 17 and 19, were her closest friends. Walking past the vegetable garden in the back we slipped through a cut in the fence to reach the neighbors' terrace. The fence had to be cut, explained Bebe, to allow access from one house to the other even after the 9 o'clock curfew. In the shade of the big sycamore a table had been set, decked with a white cloth. On it stood tall glasses, a pitcher containing a dark crimson liquid and a plate of ripe figs. A flock of white canvas chairs surrounded the table. The air was perfumed with the scent of jasmine and pine sap. A chorus of cicadas was practicing its lazy rhythm. An afternoon in a languid summer day. War was far away.

Tina, the youngest, came bounding out of the house, her arm in a sling. "You're here!" She kissed Bebe and shook my hand. Her broad smile ran across a pert, round face under a mop of black hair.

"What happened?" asked Bebe.

"Stupid me. I climbed to pick some grapes. Not serious."

Lana, the oldest, walked majestically toward me, aware of her good looks, and shook my hand with a touch of hauteur. Rini, was already bustling about pouring drinks.

"So Titsian, are you still consorting with the enemy at that school?"

"Please, be kind. One more year and then I go."

"How is my good colleague Nikos?" asked Andhros who came out with his wife to greet their two guests. Some years older than my father, he made his name when Prime Minister Venizelos awarded him an architectural dream commission.

In the late twenties, the crafty Prime Minister and head of the anti-monarchist Liberal Party wanted to cast the fledgling Republic in stone – literally. For this he needed a large, visually symbolic structure. What could be better than one that was already in place, albeit one which heretofore was dedicated to the wrong and diametrically opposite institution? Why, of course! The Royal Palace! Designed by a German architect for Otto, the young Bavarian prince who became the first King of Greece after Independence, it was erected in the center of the newly planned city and, since Otto's expulsion after a nearly thirty-year reign, had been inhabited by some of the royals from the Danish Glucksburg family who succeeded him. It still has all the attributes of an important monument: massive, authoritative, dignified, emblematic of power. Built of light yellowish-gray stone, with white marble trim and a small Doric colonnade, its rather boring blandness was thought to speak of restrained majesty. Hints of classicism seemed to relate well with the nation's glorious ancient history. Its location, furthermore, was perfect. On top of a massive retaining wall, it loomed over two important urban spaces on two successive levels below it. The upper, an elegant, formal piazza next to the retaining wall, still serves as the Monument to the Unknown Soldier. The lower, the main central square of Athens, was known as

Syntaghma, in celebration of the nation's hard-won Constitution.
An actual geometric square defined by four busy streets, paved with
blindingly white marble and appointed with a central fountain and palm
trees, it was bound on three sides by undistinguished buildings — hotels,
banks, shops, outdoor cafes, and disturbed by a ceaseless flow of noisy
motor traffic. Like other public spaces the world over, Syntaghgma has
been the site of important events. Speeches were given here by famous
people, parades were viewed, wreaths were placed, and the blood of
demonstrators spilled on its pavements.

Andhros' architectural assignment had been simply to convert the old royal Palace into the new *Vouli*, the Parliament of the nascent, still struggling and seriously endangered Hellenic Republic.

Days in Ekali passed in pleasant indolence. War and suffering were absent from our daily consciousness. There were no newspapers, no radio. Even the frolicking Germans across the street could not restore the grim reality of events that raged near and far. Enthroned in a large wicker chair under the pines, I spent much of my time reading books from Bebe's collection. She and I enjoyed long conversations in the shade. Thin and frail, she sat wrapped in a shawl, even on hot days, her neck and legs covered to hide ugly sores. Barely 17, she had the touching vanity of a young woman, although her illness had deprived her of a teenager's vigorous sexual appeal. But she was endowed with her own kind of attraction. I found a particular charm in her pale, blue-veined, diaphanous skin, bright brown eyes and thin envelope of hair. She reminded me of my mother's delicate porcelain figurines, those Rococo ladies straight out of a Mozart opera which she displayed in her dining room vitrine. The three sisters next door were important company. Bebe loved them and they loved her. Still, it seemed that she was missing the presence of boys, the parties she heard about, the bantering and teenage flirtations. "Tell me about the girls in your school," she asked, eager for some contact with the world out there. One day she interrupted the Chopin she was playing on the piano and started fingering a jazzy tune I didn't recognize.

"Don't tell me you don't know it," she said. "I hear that it's all the rage in Athens."

She played it again. Still no response. "It's American they tell me, everyone dances to it. Glen Miller."

Achileas arrived one day, his bicycle laden with goodies. Bebe was happy to see him but a bit wary. I was delighted. Toula barely greeted him. He kissed his daughter, unloaded the bicycle and gave little Tassia an appraising once over. In the evening the four of us sat around the dining table under a bare bulb. Moths circled the ceiling. Achileas had brought fresh creamy yogurt in a flat, glazed red pottery bowl. He peeled off the skin on top and spooned out a portion on his daughter's plate.

"That's too much, Baba," she complained.

"No, no," he said. "You need fattening up. Besides it will give you nice little farts, ha, ha, ha."

"You are disgusting!" Toula exploded. Bebe was close to tears.

A day or two later my parents came to stay the weekend. The neighbors invited us for a wartime supper under a black summer starry sky. In one corner, Niko and Andhros reminisced over their youth as students in Germany. Niko knew that his colleague was a Venizelist – one step away from Communism according to my father.

"These *prosfighes*, these refugees," he said, "they're all Communists now. We took that riffraff in after '22 and now they want to sell us to the Russians. Look what they did to that theater, our pride and joy."

Architects and other 'indigenous' Athenians were shocked when they learned that the majestic new National Theater on Athenas Street in the center of Athens had been wasted by refugees from Asia Minor who had been sheltered there following the 1922 debacle. Thousands of people,

whole families, stayed there cooking, eating, drinking, defecating, sleeping.
They tore up the velvet seating, used the curtains as blankets, built
fires out of parts of the stage, blackened the walls with smoke. Pretty
soon, the interior was stripped down to the bare walls, the building was
condemned and had to be demolished, leaving a big void, a monument
to human folly.

That night I was awakened by loud shouting.

"Monster! Filthy swine! Get off her!" It was Toula's voice. "How dare you, she's only a child!"

Sobs and shrieks reverberated. Another voice entered the fray.

"Disgusting little whore! Is this how you show your gratitude? Wait 'til I tell your mother. Slut! Get out of this house!"

To my dismay I recognized my father's baritone. As I came out of my room I saw little Tassia, sobbing and half naked, running down the stair. Toula stood in the hall, wild eyed, her black hair hanging in streaks around a mask of anguish, her nightdress clinging to her bony limbs – a heroine in a Sophoclean tragedy.

"I heard her whimpering. That bastard …he was pumping away on that small creature… shameless…animal." Her voice was barely audible now.

"I was right to chase that scum out of here," Niko said. Was he embarrassed?

Achileas was nowhere to be seen. Had Bebe heard any of this? Lotte?

We gathered around the table next morning. Achileas and Tassia were gone. The others picked at their breakfast in silence. I tried to sum up the experience in my mind. There were four actors in last night's one-act play. Who had committed the greatest *amartia*, the biggest sin? Toula, for cursing her husband? Hysteria, outrage, jealousy, foul language, yes, even hatred, but no sin. Tassia, for seducing her master? She was sleeping in her room and he came to her. Had they made an appointment? Unlikely. Had she provoked his lust by some act, signal, flirtation? I had seen no evidence of that since he came. Tassia was a child, still unfamiliar with the art of seduction. Tassia was clearly a victim, innocent. Achileas? There was no doubt of his guilt. Achileas, with the long reputation of an addicted womanizer, was not beyond being a child molester, even a rapist. Clearly a major sinner but was he the worst of them? That left Niko, my beloved Pappi. He too was indignant, furious, abusive in his language. But he did not direct his fury at the rapist, as Toula did. *He turned against the victim!* Against the little girl. The way it would have been done in some remote village up north or among Arab tribes along the Euphrates. But Pappi? The man who studied in a major European University? Who loved to recite Goethe's romantic poem Mignon? Who whistled Rodolfo's sweet, sentimental *Raconto*?

My parents left later that day. I stayed to console Toula and Bebe.

The incident with Tassia had a perverse effect on me. I couldn't stop thinking of Achileas in bed with her. I was confused, adrift in a sea of erotic fantasy. Images of Kaiti kept pushing in. I saw her walking around the house in her thin dress, bare knees teasing its hem, the row of buttons in front rising and falling, brown hair pulled back to reveal the moon of her face. In bed at night, the figure of the Ingres girl came to life before me, her face soon to be replaced by Kaiti's. It was that simple and unbearably real. Kaiti now stood before me stark naked holding the pitcher over her shoulder, water running down her breasts, past her belly button, along her thighs, glistening in the dim light about her. With her like this before me I could give myself exquisite relief moaning and whispering her name. I marveled at my ability to bring her before me with such ease. But then I remembered the thrill of touching her during our brief tangle on the bed last spring, hearing her moan, smelling her sweat. Seeing her as I did now with my eyes closed was not enough. My powerful imagination was beginning to lose its magic. My senses, all my senses, demanded full attention. There had to be more.

Back in Athens Rudi ran up to me with his usual enthusiasm.

I hugged and kissed my parents. "Is something wrong?" my father asked after a while. I had been staring at him. The whole sordid scene with Tassia had been haunting me. Seeing Niko now had brought it all back. Was he aware of what he had said? Should I have talked to him about it? But I couldn't bring myself to do it and soon other events would distract me.

"I hear you had a good time," teased Kaiti. "What did you do with all those girls?"

"We played a lot of backgammon."

Suddenly I felt vulnerable. Her irony was disturbing. Could she have guessed? Maybe my secret showed on my face. Would she tell Mutti? Oh my God! I told myself that I had to concentrate on school, had to avoid her. I was entering *Unter Secunda* that fall – four more years to go. It seemed forever.

"Next year I'm getting out of here. Can't stand them," hissed Vassilis as we huddled in the schoolyard. "They're losing the war and still strutting around."

"But Rommel is about to take Alexandria…in Russia they've reached the Volga," I said, having heard the BBC the night before.

"You're forgetting America, my boy. Wait till they get organized. You'll see."

By early December he was gloating.

"What did I tell you? I should have made a bet with you, dammit!"

December, 1942 and Christmas was approaching once again. In history class, Herr Schmeiz was lecturing on the rapid spread of Islam in the seventh century. He rolled down the big map on the wall and started to trace the Arab movement from east to west — across Egypt and Libya, on to Tunis, Algeria and Morocco. Suddenly he stopped, still looking at the map, holding the long pointer over the right side of North Africa. "And this is where the Americans are now," he blurted out. It must have just occurred to him that, centuries before, Arab armies had advanced in the same direction as

General Rommel and his dreaded Africa Corps were now retreating chased by General Montgomery after the battle of El Alamein. He also knew – as we all did, having heard it on the BBC - that in November a certain General Eisenhower had landed the first Americans in Algiers and Casablanca. The Greek announcer on the BBC had barely been able to contain himself when, in addition to these victories, he proclaimed the defeat of the German armies in Stalingrad that same winter. Herr Schmeiz turned around trying to stare down his snickering students. He still wore his NSDAP button. But we knew that his days with us were numbered

"Could you imagine a year ago in our misery that things would change like this, so quickly?"

It was the end of another evening broadcast, and my father was excited.

"The attack on Pearl Harbor passed us by almost unnoticed. Think of it. It brought the Americans into the war. They'll change the outcome the way they did back then."

Kaiti chimed in with her ironic smile.

"Shouldn't we give some credit to the Russians?"

My father coughed and looked at the ceiling.

"Of course, of course. But let me tell you, my dear. Stalin cares nothing for human life. He's pushing thousands, millions to their deaths, all for the glory of Communism, just the way he slaughtered his people before the war."

"And Hitler is sacrificing millions of his own people for Aryan conquest." Kaiti dared to say.

"The Russian people are not fighting for Communism, Kaiti, they're fighting for their country, the survival of their homeland. They have become Nationalists, like me, right under the nose of that butcher."

And what about that other butcher? I thought. The one we all admired only two years ago?

———

Early evening, after the BBC and dinner. My parents were out. I had just finished my Latin homework and was propped up on my old bed in the saloni leafing through *Die Baukunst des Siebzehnten Jahrhundert's*, one of my father's heavy tomes on the history of architecture. From time to time I dipped a spoon into a dish of raisin and sesame paste, a gooey but nourishing wartime concoction. Kaiti came in and stretched out next to me. She had just taken her weekly bath and was wearing my mother's bathrobe. She had a fresh soapy smell.

"Don't tell your mother I'm wearing her robe," she whispered in my ear.

"I don't think she'd mind," I said, turning another page.

"May I look at the book with you?"

"Sure."

As I was trying to describe pictures of palaces and churches, I could feel her moist hair against my cheek. I shifted a bit to relieve the rising tension.

"Don't squirm so much," she murmured, lifting one knee to adjust her own position. The robe slipped, exposing a freshly washed, smooth thigh.

"Oops," she giggled and covered up.

I tried to concentrate on the floor plan of a Baroque chapel but the book was shaking.

"What's the matter, are you feeling all right?" I closed my eyes. This was unbearable.

"Remember our tickling match?" I finally asked. "I feel like that now. Thought about it all summer."

"I know…I know how you feel," she whispered and slowly turned toward me resting on an elbow. One side of the robe dropped.

"You're…you're uncovered," I stuttered.

"Yes I am and you like it."

She leaned over, her face above me. I was feeling the weight of her body. The robe had become undone. The book had landed on the floor. I felt her lips pressing hard, heard her moans as in a dream – repeating the sounds I made last summer. And with this memory, my body went into spasms. I joined her moans and cried out "Kaiti!" while my hands turned the image of the water nymph into tangible, exquisite reality.

"Silly boy," she groaned, out of breath. "Look what you've done. You soiled your pants and we haven't even started."

She rose and helped me take my clothes off.

"Mmm, it smells so good," she said, happier now. "I'd like some more of it."

She had removed her robe and was sitting on her knees across from me. Calmer now, I could see her as I had imagined her. She looked even better without that cumbersome jug over her shoulder. Her cheeks were flushed, her breasts were rising and falling, she was rubbing her hands on her thighs looking at me intently. She was beautiful. Under that merciless stare I felt life rising again between my legs.

"Good boy," she crooned as she crawled toward me on hands and knees. Her hair had dropped hiding her face. Through half closed eyes I saw her buttocks rising high behind her. I heard slurps, smacks and growls as her lips and tongue worked their way up my legs, my crotch, my belly. I began to shake and tremble, afraid that I might erupt again and disappoint her. But she was determined – sat up again, tossed her hair back and began to walk her body on her knees until she had reached me. Slowly she eased herself down on me.

"There darling…I finally have you…have you inside of me," she panted. Her movements were languid, smooth.

"Not too soon…please, Titsian darling. Let's move together for a while. Slowly. Up and down…up and down…see? Isn't it…isn't it wonderful?"

Everything now was down there.

"Yes…up and down," I croaked. In a blur, I saw her flushed

cheeks, her hair tossed about, her breasts bouncing – felt myself enveloped by liquid heat.

"That's good…sweetie…keep it up," she coaxed. But as I lifted my hands and touched her nipples, I lost myself.

"I can't…I can't…Kaiti…Kaitiii!" I shouted now. It was all over. She moved a bit longer, catching her breath.

"Oh…oh - you bad, bad boy," she sighed, let go of me. "We have to slow you down." She put on her robe and lay next to me.

"Have you done this before?"

"It's not easy to talk about."

"Why?"

"My father."

"What do you mean?"

"I was fourteen. He came to my room at night."

"No!"

"Only a few times. I stopped him."

"Your mother?"

"I never told her. Stopped him myself. Later he went after my sisters."

"Horrible."

"He was not a bad man. Worked hard, poor, too many children, ignorant. Other men were like him."

"Did you enjoy it?"

"No, Titsian. Later, with a boy, it was not much better."

"A boy?"

"I was sixteen. He was a year older. Big and strong, clumsy, stupid. Not much there for me. Some time around then I decided to take things into my own hands. Make my own decisions. That's what brought me here."

"I'm sorry I didn't give you…what you gave me."

"Oh, my darling. I did have a good time." Then later, "I read somewhere that women can have as good a time as men, even better. Who knows, some day…But now I'd better go up to my room before your parents get back."

In the *Deutsche Schule* Herr Kumpf was telling us about German medieval emperors - Otto the Great crowned by the Pope, starting the endless Holy Roman Empire; Heinrich's humiliation by Pope Gregory in Canossa; Friedrich, dubbed Barbarossa by the Italians and drowned during one of the crusades - and the fall of Konstantinople to a band of looters from the West posing as crusaders.

"Why do we have to waste time with these barbarians?" fumed Vassilis during recess.

"They were supposed to restore Christianity in the Holy Land. Instead they conquered and looted Byzantium - another Christian country."

"Pretty much what they're doing now," I said.

"And you know why they all kept crossing the Alps, running down to Rome?" Vassilis was on a tear. "I'll tell you why: to enjoy the nice warm Mediterranean climate, that's why. They've been in Africa all this time and here now − for the same reason. History repeats itself."

"Then what are they doing in Russia?" I laughed. "History is repeating itself there too. Look at Napoleon. He too went to Egypt, and look what happened to him in Russia."

I noticed that Vassilis was not listening any more. He was sucking in air and shaking one hand up and down.

"Po, po, po!"

"What is it?"

"Look at her," he groans. "She's devastating."

I turned in time to see a tall girl saunter by - long legs, short skirt, full lips, an abundance of blond tresses. There was a movement to her hips.

"Who is she?"

"Erika," whispered Vassilis reverentially. "She just came from Germany. Her mother is a secretary at the SS headquarters on

Vassilisis Sofias, you know, the building with the black banner and the two steely guards in front."

"Good looking girl," I said.

"I want her," said Vassilis.

On my way home, down Arachovis Street and through the Exarchia district near the Polytechnic, I noticed again the new graffiti painted overnight on buildings and walls. Large red letters spelled ELAS, EAM, KKE together with slogans like DEATH TO FASCISM. Here and there appeared the letters EDES in blue, standing for the main "nationalist" guerilla group. It was common knowledge that the Communists dominated the resistance, limiting EDES to the north west corner of Greece and that the two groups fought each other more than they fought the Germans. The writing on the walls looked hurried, slapdash. Paint ran off the letters down to the sidewalk. The Germans, we learned, had shot several graffiti writers on the spot in recent nights. Daily rumors of brutality abounded. The latest was of one eight-year-old found stealing bread from an army truck. The German soldier who caught him put the kid's arm over his knee and snapped it like a twig.

My mother had brought a typewriter from somewhere. Installed on a little table next to the desk in my room, it had become the center of some new activity. Letters were typed, stuffed in envelopes and taken away. I peered over my mother's shoulder one day and read the word Angebot on top of the page.

"*Angebot?*" I asked.

"Yes, it's a bid, an offer."

"In German?" I turned to my father.

"Your mother is representing some vegetable and meat merchants in the *Aghora*, you know, the central market on Athenas street."

"Why the German?"

Niko coughed. "They sell wholesale meat and produce to some German units. Mutti helps out as a translator. No big deal."

"So she is a kind of middleman between the Greeks and the German army."

"You could say that. But it's better not to talk about it."

Since returning from Ekali I had noticed that meals in the house had improved. There was plenty of fresh fruit and vegetables and we frequently enjoyed lamb and chicken. I had a boiled egg every morning, Lotte her coffee with milk and Niko his tea. Most Athenians however were suffering under the heavy burden of the occupation. Although last year's famine had abated, essentials like food and clothing were still scarce and fear ruled the streets. Our family, on the contrary, was doing rather well. We seemed to have money in spite of the accelerating inflation. My father quickly converted paper Drachmas into British Pounds Sterling before his Drachmas devalued. Costs of any significance were now quoted in *Lires*, little heavy gold coins bearing the goateed profile of King George V or his son George VI, turning gold into the real, although not quite legal, currency. The Government was printing new paper money at frequent intervals, its nominal value rising, zeroes being steadily added to the numbers. "Just like Berlin in the twenties when your mother and I were living there," said my father. "They kept printing handkerchief-sized bills engraved with heroic figures symbolizing Commerce and Labor on worthless paper. Just like the Drachma bills your uncle Achileas is turning out today for the Bank of Greece, and equally worthless. We'll soon be reaching billions and trillions, carting the money around in wheel barrows." As many others did, Niko hoarded his gold coins in small cylindrical tubes which became considerably heavier once the cough drops in them had been replaced by gold.

"I heard that Kaufman on Stadhiou is having a sale," I told my father one day. "It seems that they're closing." Kaufman was a small bookstore specializing in foreign language books, mostly art and architecture. Its window displays had always been tempting, drawing the passer-by to go in and browse. But Kaufman was an expensive, elegant store. People mostly leafed through the beautifully printed and bound volumes and slowly worked their way out again. But now suddenly there was a sell-out. Prices had come down and we were able to afford them – an irresistible opportunity. Together or separately my father and I made forays to Kaufman's to enrich the shelves of our two bookcases with world art, printed for a change in full color instead of the smudgy, dreary, black and white reproductions of yore I had confronted in the British and French history volumes. Motivated now and greedy for more, we extended our peregrinations to Eleftheroudhakis, the venerable bookseller and publisher near by on Syntaghma Square. The money seemed to be there.

"Kaufman's has finally closed," I told my father one day. "I went by after school. It's all boarded up. I peeked in. The shelves are empty and there's trash on the floor."

"How sad," said Niko. What do you think happened?"

"My teacher, Mrs. Poumboura, knew Kaufman. He was a Jew, she says. Saw the handwriting on the wall and decided to clear out while there was still time."

"Where did he go?"

"She has no idea."

"Like the Myllers, the Mordos. I wonder what happened to them."

"And what about Jackie Saltiel?"

"He's not as prominent as the others. He can hide more easily."

At about this time I was introduced to grand opera. Thinking back on it, I find it odd that in the midst of oppression, fear and want, opera was alive and well in Athens and that my father was eager to rekindle his youthful enthusiasm for the grand spectacle and infuse his son with it. For years, of course, I had been hearing him and my grandfather whistling and humming bits of opera – overtures, arias, choruses. It must have been the proximity of Italy that stimulated this particular affinity since there seemed to be little interest in music from further north – except perhaps for Bizet and Gounod, but not for Mozart or Wagner. "Classical" orchestral music was not often performed in Athens. In those days however opera had a home in what was known as the National Lyric Stage, where one could hear and see reasonably good performances. Located downtown, near the University, its undistinguished façade and dumpy interior equipped with uncomfortable wooden seats and poor lighting posed no threat to La Scala. Fortunately I knew of no alternatives. The acoustics were no apparent problem and the stage could accommodate the second act of Aida without much embarrassment. Here I was introduced to the operatic war-horses – *La Boheme, Carmen, Rigoletto* among them. All parts were sung in Greek, except once, when some Italian soloists came to perform *Lucia* and sang in Italian, while the chorus sang in Greek. I was enchanted. For me, the productions were brilliant, the voices splendid, the music unforgettable. On the way home I would impress my father by whistling back some of the tunes. "The boy has an ear," he told my mother who had little interest in opera and never came with us.

"They're doing *Tosca* at the opera," said my father in late summer. "The lead is played by a seventeen-year old girl – Maria Kalogheropoulou, an up-and-coming talent."

I remember her as a dark-complexioned, slightly pudgy soprano with a convincing voice and an assured presence on stage. It was hard to think of her as a teenager while she was leaning over Scarpia's body growling *"Muori dannato! Muori!"* Maria continued performing at the Athens opera through the remaining years of the occupation to increasing critical acclaim from the Greek press as well as German and Italian culture mavens. No one however could have guessed that out of the misery of war- ravaged Athens a voice would rise that soon would be heard and idolized the world over.

At 61 Patission Street, near Green Park, stands a handsome five-story apartment house. Maria Callas lived here with her mother and sister between 1938 and 1945 when she left Greece to return to America. Two doors away, at number 63, my mother spent the last twenty years of her life. On my visits to Athens I would frequently walk past 61. A brass plaque next to the front door commemorates Maria's residence there.

There were few opportunities for me to be alone with Kaiti. On such occasions she proved to be a good teacher. I was mad for her. But I sensed that something was missing. "Don't worry about me, Titsian," she said, nibbling on my ear. "I love to see you have your *orghasmi*, and you have so many!"

One day, up in her cubbyhole above the kitchen, she said, "let's try some new things I've read about."

"Oh? Show me, show me."

We're lying naked on her bed. "Look at this little fellow," she said. "He's had his fun and now he's resting. Let's see if we can wake him up."

On her hands and knees she took me in her mouth.

"What are you doing Kaiti? I could…"

"Lie still," she mumbles, her mouth full, working her lips up and down. "Ish delishous."

"No, stop…I'm…I can't…"

She let's go of me just I squirted all over her face.

"Aah," she says after a while. "How was it?"

Still out of breath, I smiled. "I can't…I can't believe it. Where did you learn this?'

"It's a secret," she teased. "But it's only half of it. Here comes part two – your job."

She sat up and moved herself on her knees until she reached my mouth, her thighs on either side of my face.

"Now little boy, put that lovely tongue to work," she whispered.

"Slowly, sweetly."

I felt a pang of panic. The sudden close proximity of the hairy crotch, the hidden red orifice beyond, were intimidating. The first lick though was rather pleasing and I found the tickle of her curls exciting. Soon I was in full swing and the whimpers from above were encouraging.

"Titsian…Titsian my darling…what are you doing to me? I'm going crazy. Never…never before…" My tongue was now inside exploring terra incognita.

"Ach, ach, ach…" Her rhythmic cries were growing louder until a big scream made me retract.

"Are you all right?"

"No, I'm not. I'm going crazy…out of my mind."

"Can I do something?"

"You've done it already, sweet boy, you've done it!"

She fell on the bed next to me.

"I can't believe it," she was hoarse now. *"Me ghamisses me tin ghlossa sou!* You fucked me with your tongue!

We lay there, half asleep.

"Titsian, we're home!"

Was I dreaming? Oh my God! They're back! Kaiti was already up pulling a dress over her naked body.

"Quick darling, here are your pants, your shirt," she whispered, helping me. I stumbled down the wooden steps.

"What are you doing up there?" my mother asked.

"Kaiti…ah…we were talking."

"Talking? Up there?"

I had a sudden déjà vu. Two years ago - in Aghia Paraskevi, the girl, the bicycles, my mother's fury.

"You should be in bed, it's late. You too Kaiti."

But I was already in bed, *meine liebe Mutti,* I thought, breathing a sigh of relief.

In the wake of that incident, my mother's behavior toward Kaiti began to change. She spoke to her sharply, treating her more like a maid, assuming the role of mistress. Did she suspect something? You never know with Mutti, I thought. I belonged to her. She would look at me adoringly, tell me that I had beautiful eyes, stroke my hair, touch my lips. There were times when I thought she confused me with her husband when she called me Nienchen - as she frequently called him, in the way a woman might call her lover. That was fine when I was still a little boy in love with his mother. But lately I had begun to find such demonstrations strange, almost embarrassing. And this sentiment coincided with her strait-laced, disapproving attitude toward relations between men and women. Until recently I had found myself blushing when a girl entered our company, and my mother would always notice, as if an indecent act was about to take place. And now, fearing discovery and exposure, I began to shy away from Kaiti. Suddenly I was afraid to be left alone with her. "What's going on?" she whispered as we passed in the hall. All I could do was shrug and move on. But I was in agony.

One day I overheard my mother ask my father,

"Do you think Kaiti is attractive?"

"She's a pretty girl. Why do you ask?"

"I noticed you look at her legs a lot."

"She has nice legs."

"I think she needs a boyfriend."

"A boyfriend?"

"She needs to go out and meet other people. A young girl should not be cooped up like this."

"Why? Did she complain?"

"She never complains. She probably suppresses her frustration."

"Frustration? I don't know what you mean. She seems perfectly happy to me. As a matter of fact, I think that she is happier lately. I heard her sing to herself while dusting the other day."

"Oh Niko," Lotte said impatiently. "You just don't know what a young woman is like. I'm going to do something about this."

I was in a panic. What will she do? Find her a boyfriend? She already has a lover and she's happy, satisfied. Why is she meddling?

Meantime the typewriter next to the desk was kept busy. My mother, who was a fast typist, produced several letters a day, in German. One particular caught my attention one day. It differed from the others which dealt mostly with crates of vegetables, chickens and sides of beef. It read ANGEBOT on top and was addressed to the Athens *Kommandantur* – a construction bid for the conversion of an old downtown house into an officers' club. "To the attention of Major Heinrich Klopf, Contract Officer," it read. At the bottom was my father's signature over the title *Architekt, Diplom Ingenieur, Technische Hochschule, Berlin.*

One day Kaiti came down from her room all dressed up – new skirt and blouse, new winter coat, high heels, hair done up, lipstick. She looked terrific. I couldn't keep my eyes off her.

"Where did you get all this?"

"Your mother and I went shopping downtown yesterday. You like?"

"What's the occasion?"

"She has a date tonight," piped in my mother looking pleased with herself.

"A date?" My mouth was dry.

"Yes, with a nice man we know, an officer. They're going to the movies and out to dinner."

I put an arm on the wall to steady myself. When the bell rang I rushed to the door. Rudy barked as a stocky man in uniform with gold leaves on his collar came in.

"Major Klopf," said my mother extending her arm.

"Gruess Gott," said the Major and shook hands with everybody. Rudi sniffed his polished boots.

"May we offer you a liqueur?" asked my mother with her most endearing smile, her head tilted a bit to the side.

"Thank you but we are late already." And turning to Kaiti with soldierly vigor, he added, "shall we go, young lady?"

Out of the window I saw them crossing the street. Klopf had his hand under her arm.

"Now you're both working for the Germans," I said during breakfast the next morning.

"What do you mean?" said my father frowning.

"I saw those letters to the *Kommandantur*."

"I see …" His eyes were cast down for a while. He then looked up at the ceiling with a sigh and continued with a low voice.

"Working with the Germans, as you say, is putting it the wrong way. On the contrary, you could say that by doing what we're doing is helping people, helping Greece … at a time when help is needed."

We were both silent for a while. He took out a cigarette, tapped it on the box.

"Somebody has to do it," he finally added. "Besides … you know that we need the money – I had to close the office … and the pension is practically worthless."

"But they are the enemy."

"Of course, Titsian. But we have to separate politics from survival. What Mutti and I are doing is harmless work. It helps us lead a decent life, brings food to the table, pays for your education." He looked out the window and added as an afterthought. "And it gives work to people. People who need it badly."

And who am I to criticize him, I thought. I go to their school, tolerate their views, play along, while others up in the mountains, in the villages, in the poor neighborhoods live in danger and deprivation – struggling to survive, fighting the enemy. He is weak and dishonest but so am I.

My parents were looking at me with admiration.

"You're growing so fast," said my mother. "You must be the

tallest in your class."

"Dennis is a little taller."

"Anyway, I think the time has come for you to wear long pants like a grown man. We have to cover those hairy legs." I was thrilled.

"Still too skinny though," said my father, true to himself.

"Oh, Nienchen. Except for those pimples he's perfectly fine. Stop it."

I relished my new status in school.

"You're becoming irresistible," proclaimed Vassilis. "Careful, Erika may want to have her way with you."

Erika was a year behind us, but she might as well be two years ahead. I smiled at her the other day as we passed in the hall but she ignored me and looked straight ahead. My heart beat faster anyway. I must be in love with her, I thought. Was I in love with Kaiti? It seemed different somehow. Anyway, I was not in love with Kaiti anymore, if that's what it was. Ever since Klopf came into the picture, things had changed. First she started to avoid me, as I had briefly avoided her. Then she told me that we could not continue, that she was very sad, etc., etc. I was devastated, angry, jealous, cried in my pillow at night.

"This has nothing to do with Heinrich," she'd said to comfort me. "He is kind, polite, even amusing at times, but — he's not for me."

"Well then, why …"

"I think it's best that we remain friends, that's all."

"But it was so wonderful!"

"Yes, Titsian, it was and I will never forget."

"Oh Kaiti, Kaiti."

We remained silent for a while, our heads bent down. Then she said slowly,

"Don't tell your mother, but I'm not staying here much longer."

"Kaiti!"

"Yes," her eyes were shining now. "You can't really tell with the war on, but I know that there is a beautiful world out there. And I want it."

⎯⎯

Great news from the BBC. The German Sixth Army finally surrendered in Stalingrad and 90,000 prisoners were taken. Montgomery and the Americans were squeezing the remnants of the *Afrika Korps* in Tunisia. Rommel was returned to Germany. The tide was turning. We cheered at the news. My father now thought that the Allies would win. But there was also much unsettling news that we didn't hear on the radio or read in the papers. By the grapevine we learned of raging battles up in the mountains, where Communists and Nationalists were battling Germans and Italians, but also each other; or about the destruction of villages, the massacres of innocent civilians by the Germans.

Meantime the Germans in the *Deutsche Schule* remained defiant. They still wore their NSDAP buttons and spoke of ultimate victory with baffling conviction. One day in class, mild-mannered Herr Meine stood up as the bell rang, chin raised, and proclaimed: *"Fuer Fuehrer und Vaterland ist kein Opfer zu gross. Heil Hitler."* (No sacrifice is too great for Fuehrer and fatherland.) Do they really believe this? We asked ourselves. If they do, the war was far from over. As it turned out, we were right. More than two years of slaughter lay ahead. The worst was still to come.

With the latest news, the Greeks in school became emboldened. Gradually the old schoolboy pranks known as *kazoura* were revived. *Kazoura* was basically any act, perpetrated by students individually or collectively, that would cause disruption in class and/or annoy a teacher. It became particularly enjoyable when the teacher was unable to identify the culprit(s) and could not impose punishment unless he or she did so arbitrarily or en masse. Favorite *kazoura* tricks included drumming with two fingers under the desk; various individuals serially requesting permission to go to the bathroom;

various individuals standing up to ask stupid questions; making strange animal or indecent noises in various parts of the classroom and so on. An experienced master like Vassilis could raise *Kazoura* to a state of high art.

We derived particular pleasure one day in German poetry class with Fraeulein Schmitz, a young woman who did not wear an NSDAP button and was thought to be particularly vulnerable. The episode began when Vassilis asked to go to the toilet. Upon his return he winked at us and sat down. Soon the finger drumming began, while some boys stood up to ask stupid questions. (Girls generally did not get involved in *kazoura* although they made a willing audience.) Fraeulein Schmitz gradually became upset and committed the tactical error of raising her voice. This of course only served to fuel the riot, forcing Schmitz to declare that she was going to call Herr Romain, the Director. She strode to the door and pressed down the handle, only to find that the handle had come off. The door could not be opened. Beside herself now, a wild look in her eyes, she started to bang on the door with her fists, screaming *Hilfe, Hilfe* until someone finally opened it from the other side. By then we realized that we had gone too far and took pity on her. We sat her down and patted her on the back and Vassilis, feeling guilty for having undone the door handle, ran out to fetch the sobbing young woman a glass of water.

"Poor girl," whispered Dennis. "We shouldn't have done it. She's not even a Nazi."

Diran, the bright Armenian boy whose calligraphy was the envy of the class, took me aside in the school corridor.

"Did you hear about Erika?"

I felt a thump in my chest. "Tell me."

Diran came closer and whispered, "They saw her on the balcony of her apartment in Kolonaki."

"Go on."

"With a soldier."

My mouth was getting dry. "So?"

"Well…you understand. They were smooching. He had his hand up her skirt."

"So?"

"Come on. Stop looking so cool. She's only fourteen years old, for God's sake."

"That's old enough."

"They say she does more."

"More?"

"Well, you know, that sort of thing."

"She's old enough for that too."

"Oh come on, Titsian, don't tell me you're not impressed. It's great news. If she does it with one guy … you know …"

"Diran, that's just cheap gossip. I don't want to hear any more of it." I started to walk away.

"Everybody knows that you are in love with her," Diran shouted after me. "Vassilis has been telling us."

For weeks now I had been tormented by her. She was taller than Kaiti, almost as tall as I. Fully confident of her power, she walked the school corridors with long leggy strides, her curls bobbing, looking straight ahead, seemingly unaware of the turned heads and whispers she left behind. Her presence was relentless even when she wasn't standing before me. This had not happened with Kaiti even before our affair was consummated. Erika became a continuing disturbance – shook my concentration in class, got into bed with me at night, crawled into my head at unforeseen moments. And I was plagued by jealousy, hated that soldier with his hand up her skirt. And then there was Hans Juergen, *"HaJue"*, the perfect Aryan specimen, with the body of an Olympian God. Hitler would have been proud of him. I detested him. A rumor had been going around the school that he and Erika were lovers. The thought was unbearable. I had even seen a lascivious drawing of them humping on top of each other on the wall of the boys' toilet. Below it was written *Ha-Jue und Erika*.

Today I was looking forward to the annual school track meet, held in the old white marble stadium nestled on the Ardhitos Hill, built in 1896 of Pentelic marble for the first modern Olympic games. "Focus on winning," I told myself, eager to shake her out of my mind and beat Dennis in the 50-meter dash. The loudspeakers played rousing music. Just as we were getting ready to line up for the race, a new song came on: *Auf der Heide bluehmt ein kleines Bluehmelein, und das heist…ERIKA.* (A small flower blooms in the heath and its name is Erika.) I groaned, even here she wouldn't leave me alone. We lined up, crouched, the gun was fired and off we went. Dennis, unhampered by lust, won the race. I came in second.

I tried to imagine walking up to her, standing very close, intimate. *"Ich will Dir etwas sagen."* I want to tell you something, I would say. She looked at me, made a face and walked on. Or, I would use the old *"Willst Du ficken?"* approach. I could almost feel the slap on my face and hear Romain's assault in the Director's office. "I have to get out of this obsession," I told myself. "It's hopeless. I should know by now how they feel about us. We are an inferior race. Not as bad as the Jews or the Gypsies, but still alien, dark, undesirable." But then I would remember that I had a German mother, that I too was an Aryan and that Greeks too were supposed to be Aryans. So, why not? Seeing myself in the mirror at another time, I thought "I may be Aryan but not a HaJue kind of Aryan. I look more like an Arab, a Turk or even a Jew. Big nose, black hair, dark skin. (But wait a minute, aren't the Myllers blond and blue eyed?) There is no way, they, she, would accept me as an equal." On another day:" But don't opposites attract each other? How boring that she and HaJue are lovers. How much more interesting for her to find a swarthy fellow like me irresistible instead of that bland, blond Aryan. And remember old boy, your mother fell in love with your father and his nose was even bigger – and he's shorter. She must have thought him gorgeous, certainly good enough to father her child!"

I never got to speak to Erika. "I've experienced two kinds of love – requited and unrequited," I told myself. "How romantic." When school ended in June, most German civilians were shipped back to Germany. I went down to Larissa station to see them leave. I thought I saw her in the distance but I wasn't sure.

In October Kaiti announced her decision to leave.

For the last two years the Germans had been recruiting, even forcing people from their occupied territories in Europe to come to Germany and work in the war industry. Although the pressure to go North had been great, Greeks had been reluctant to join. But with the war going badly for the Wehrmacht, the need for outside labor was growing. Inducements were offered and many weary Greeks were tempted.

"Oh, Titsian, I have to do it," Kaiti told me. "It's an opportunity to see another world. I'm in a rut here."

"It's that fellow Klotz, I know it." I was fighting tears. "Are you running after him?"

"Nonsense, dear boy." She took my hand. "I haven't seen him in weeks. Besides, he has a wife and two kids and he's already been sent to Russia, poor man. No, it's me. My dream for a better life."

"Oh, Kaiti, Kaiti."

"Titsian, you're wonderful. I'll never forget you."

My mother had found her a little suitcase. She was wearing her new coat. Tears flowed, hugs were exchanged, promises were made.

"I'll write you the minute I get to Duesseldorf."

We wished her *kalo taxidhi*. My father would take her to the station. My mother and I waved from the balcony. Rudi barked.

I never saw Kaiti again. Years later my father wrote to me that she had married a Greek man, a fellow laborer in Germany. They emigrated to Venezuela, had children. She seemed to be happy.

The Water Nymph
by Jean-Auguste-Dominique Ingres.

Kaiti

Kaiti and Rudi

Aunt Toula with my poor sick cousin Bebe.

My mother working the phone during the occupation, ca. 1943.

My parents and I with handsome Achileas and unhappy Toula.

Rudi

LESSONS

"**I** THINK THE time has come," said my father one day. "We have to take you out of there."

It was spring of 1943 and the news from BBC supported the decision to leave the German school. The Russians were moving west, beyond Stalingrad and Moscow, and Leningrad was soon relieved of its long siege. British and American planes were bombing Italy in preparation for an invasion. The Greeks in school finally decided that it was safe to jump ship.

My father insisted that it be to a private school.

"None of these is near here," I complained. "I'll still have to walk clear across town twice a day. Why do we have to live so far away? In Siberian exile?"

"Stop it Titsian," said my father, guilt for dragging us here still taunting him. "We're just fine where we are. Besides, the exercise is good for you." (From one who never showed the slightest interest in it.)

"Why do you think all these fancy schools are in Kolonaki or Psychiko?"

"Tell us."

"Because that's where all the rich live – the ship owners, the merchants."

"So?"

"You always tell me how terrible they are – profiteers, thieves, philistines."

"Well…"

"So I go to their schools to grow up and be like them?"

"You go to those schools to get a better education," said my father who really meant it.

I enrolled at Makri, a private school with "a good name" located a short block from Kolonaki Square, not too far from Evzonon Street and Marasleion, our old neighborhood and my first school. I would be there for three more years.

The school occupied a prominent corner on Vasilissis Sofias Avenue, across from the closed American Embassy and the National Gardens and not too far from the "new" Royal Palace. Once a rich man's mansion, the school building and its meager grounds were guarded by a tall black iron fence. A couple of tired palms in front along the avenue stood as a reminder of an elegant past. A dusty flat rectangle in the back made up the schoolyard, empty and quiet between recesses unless a gym class came out to kick a ball or hop around doing its version of calisthenics. The interior was attired in the manner of a Parisian hotel *particulier* - marble floors, high ceilings, classical moldings and a grand staircase meant for nobility - except that here girls wore blue school smocks and bobby socks instead of crinolines. Quite a change from the no-nonsense Bauhaus architecture of the *Deutsche Schule* and the vision of luscious Erika sashaying her hips down its long corridors.

I was happy that Vassilis and Dennis were here with me and none of the German boys, especially the odious HaJue, though the SS headquarters down the avenue with its sinister black banner and the two granite-faced and steel-helmeted troopers standing guard outside was a nervous reminder of continuing German presence. Here every one spoke Greek in a refreshingly benign, unthreatening "we're-in-this-together" atmosphere. No more Romain, no more Kaspar, no more *Heil Hitlers,* no more ramrod, crew-cut, tow-headed, heel-clickers. Just us dark-skinned, big-nosed, unruly, lecherous, athletically deficient, borderline Aryans.

⌁

One morning, as I was coming out the front door on Kodringtonos, the old lady in the small house across the street called me from behind her iron gate.

"Young man, can I talk to you for a minute?"

We had only exchanged an occasional *Kalimera* before this. I crossed over, intrigued. Since moving to the neighborhood, all we learned was that Soso Kandhili was once a well known operetta singer of belle époque vintage. My father recalled her name. A small woman with puffy white hair and pert but cunning features, reclusive, an air of mystery about her, she made me think of Mrs. Haversham in *Great Expectations.*

"Come in, come in," she prompted.

Through the gate and the narrow courtyard we entered the parlor in darkness. She turned on the light to reveal a landscape I had only seen in pictures, from a time I knew belonged to my grandparents. I recognized the overstuffed chairs, their arms and backs protected with embroidered antimacassars; the doilies on shelves and side tables crowded with bibelots; the heavy velvet drapery over the two windows. I noticed the many framed sepia photographs of a ripe, curly haired young woman, an ample bosom swelling out of her décolletage.

"Is that you?"

"Oh, yes. I was a star in those days, young, beautiful. Everybody loved me."

I sat at the heavy oak dining table. The air in the room smelled stale. She disappeared for a while to return with a plate and a glass of water.

"Here is some *ghlyko nerantzaki* to sweeten your mouth," she said. "I made it myself."

She sat next to me as I raised a spoonful of the syrupy, green orange preserve to my mouth.

"I heard that your mother is German," she started. "You speak German?"

"Yes, of course."

"Would you be interested in teaching it to me?"

"You want to learn German?"

"You're surprised? An old woman like me?" She laughed.

"But I don't really have any experience … teaching, I mean."

"That's perfectly all right my boy," she said with a sweet smile. "I don't need a professor. Just a few words of conversation. I'll pay you well."

I was delighted. My first job.

"It's agreed then. We start tomorrow. Five o'clock?"

As I was leaving she said, "I want to show you something. Come with me."

Down a dark corridor she opened a door and we entered a room. She turned on the light and I let out a long whistle. Before me stood rows and rows of racks, the kind I had seen in clothing stores. The clothes hanging there were not new, and the musty odor I met in the front room was heavier here.

"If you've been to the theater or the opera, you probably have seen some of these."

"You mean …?"

"Yes, costumes. Theatrical costumes."

"Amazing."

"On these racks for example is a full set for *Rigoletto*. Look, right here, this is the tunic the duke wears when he appears before the heroine, Gilda, pretending to be a poor student. Have you seen the opera? One of Verdi's best."

"I'm afraid not. But I know some of the music. I love Gilda's 'Caro Nome'"

"Good for you. Anyway, when I need some money and a good offer comes along, I will rent a set out to a production."

"To the Lyric Stage?"

"Oh yes, many times"

"Then I must have seen your costumes. I go with my father."

She walked me back through the courtyard to the front gate.

"I live here all alone," she said casually.

I brought some of my beginner's grammar books to our first session in the sweltering front parlor under the pale light of the chandelier.

"We won't need these," she said pushing them aside. "I'm not good with books. We have to talk to each other – that's what I need. I need to be able to talk."

"All right, but you should learn to speak correctly, grammatically. People have to understand you, *Kyria Soso*."

"You'll speak to me and when I reply, you'll correct me."

And so we proceeded. She was interested, eager, almost impatient. But she made endless mistakes and her accent was terrible.

"The word is *schnell*, not 'snell', *Kyria Soso*. I know some of these sounds don't exist in Greek, but they're important if you want to be understood."

"I know, I know. You're right my boy. But I just can't do it. And then there're those …what you call them … *umlauts*, those you tell me have two little dots above them. Impossible."

Still, we made progress, and there were days when she started the lesson with a little smile on her face, as if remembering something.

Weeks passed and Soso was making very good progress. She could now pronounce the 'sch's' and the 'tsch's', had almost mastered the umlauts and built up a respectable vocabulary.

"Bravo *Kyria Soso*," I praised her one day and the little smile lit up her face.

"I'm well motivated … by you. A good teacher makes a good student. *Nicht wahr?*"

"Pretty soon you won't need me any more." She laughed, pleased.

Just then a clatter was heard in the kitchen. "Oh, that foolish …"she blurted. Then, quickly, "it's probably the cat."

"The cat? I didn't know you had a cat, *Kyria Soso.*"

"Yes, yes. She lives in the back. Catches mice."

Almost immediately she looked up, stared at something behind me, her face a mask of terror.

"Nein, Hans … nein," she stammered. I turned to face a figure standing in the dark. It now stepped forward, and the light caught strands of blond hair, a timid grin on a boyish face. He must have been a couple of years older than me.

"Entschuldige, Soso. Ich wollte nur etwas Wasser." (Sorry, I just wanted some water.) Soso put her elbows on the table and sank her face in her hands. After a while she looked up and faced me.

"I might as well tell you the whole story. But, for God's sake, keep it secret. If you tell your parents, beg them not to tell anyone. Not another soul must know. You understand? You promise? You swear?"

I hesitated for a moment trying to recover.

"Don't worry *Kyria Soso.* We are good people. No one else will know."

"So then – meet Hans. He's a German soldier, nineteen years old, a deserter. Doesn't speak a word of Greek. A friend brought him to me. He decided to hide after he learned that he was being sent to Russia. He knew that he would die there. Better to risk a firing squad here. And the weather is better than the frozen steppes up there." Her stare was fixed on me. "Now you know – the only one … beside my friend who brought Hans to me. But I had to bring you in. I had to learn his language."

"Don't worry *Kyria Soso.* I hope you'll want to continue our lessons. You were doing so well. And from now on Hans can join us. I can translate for both of you, it'll speed things up. You two must have been having good conversations even without me. You've made amazing progress in such a short time."

"Motivation, my boy, motivation. I've been helped by two handsome young men. What a treat for an old woman."

So the lessons continued, now with Hans as the third participant. And what fun we had. We sipped tea, consumed Soso's sweets, laughed a lot. Soso was happy, relieved.

"You boys take me back to my youth," she said coquettishly. "I was on the stage, a beautiful girl, full of life. Men were crazy about me. I had lovers. But after a while, when the wrinkles appeared, the lovers began to disappear, and I was alone. Until I found Hans."

My parents were intrigued. Lotte wanted to meet Hans, invite him over for *Roladen.*

"He must be sick and tired of this oily Greek food," she said. "It's time the poor boy had a real meal, with people who spoke his language."

"Mutti, something tells me that he doesn't want to have anything to do with his people."

Anyway, Soso wouldn't let Hans out of the house. "And your mother can't come visit." she looked fierce. "Too many people are in this already."

But fate was cruel.

One day we looked down from our window on a gray army vehicle parked outside Soso's house. We stood there frozen. Soon, two helmeted soldiers came out, Hans in shackles between them. He looked resigned, the grin on his face almost defiant. He knew that he had escaped the Russian front. The soldiers pushed him into the car and drove off. Soso was nowhere to be seen.

As the days went by, I wondered who could have betrayed Hans. Who knew about this?

Let's see…Soso and I, of course. My parents. Her friend — unnamed. I couldn't think of anyone else. Soso had been so careful, so protective of Hans. She was worried about my parents knowing. Her friend? A patriot who wanted revenge? That didn't make sense. And so the matter gradually joined the ranks of unsolved mysteries.

As the years passed, an unwelcome, subversive thought began to germinate in my mind. In the course of her business dealings with the Wehrmacht, my mother, a friendly, chatty woman, especially in her native tongue, must have had many casual conversations - conversations not always related to business. Could it be? I wanted to dismiss the thought. Whatever Lotte may have been, she didn't have it in her to be a fanatic. Had she been living in Germany she probably would have been among the millions who went along - out of inertia, out of fear. But she would have been incapable of betraying anyone, a German at that. She surely would have felt sympathy for his plight. But then again … in casual conversation … All it takes is a careless word, a quick attentive ear …

Since modern Greek is spoken by few people, learning a foreign language – especially a European one - was critical. My German, already gave me a leg up. But German had not been a preferred language in Greece, and less now when it was the voice of the Enemy.

Even before liberation, French had been the language of choice and a required component in the education of young bourgeois Athenians. My father and his sisters had been taught it and used it in conversation to impress society or to pass on information unsuitable for the ears of children. It was the language of the *beau monde*.

"Would you like to learn French?" my father had asked me the year before.

"I'd love to read some of your novels," I said, "and Verne and Dumas in the original. I like the sound of it on the radio."

I had been in the middle of a bad Greek translation of *Twenty Years After*, the last of the *Three Musketeers* trilogy and I was curious about the French authors my father had been reading in those soft cover books with pages he had to cut with a kitchen knife.

A teacher was found and was to come to the house three times a week after school. Madame de Lorme's piled-up white coiffure, abundant chest and imperious demeanor defined her as a grande dame from another era. *"Il faut que nous parlons seulement en Francais,"* (we must only speak in French) she commanded before we even sat down in the dining room with the heavy blue chairs. Kaiti winked at me when she came in with coffee and cake. The low winter sun reached deep into the room illuminating dust particles in the air. My eyes felt heavy. *"Faites attention!"* (pay attention) Mme. snapped, forcing me back to reality. Madame de Lorme believed that you learn best by acting out. So I went through the motions repeating *"Je me leve, je vais a la porte, je ouvre la porte." ("Faites la liaison!"* make the connection, she ordered,) *"pardon Madame - j'ouvre la porte, je ferme la porte, je vais a la chaise, je m'assieds."* (I open the door, I close the door, I go to the chair, I sit down.) I felt foolish going back and forth to the door. Once when I opened it I found Rudi on the other side eager to come in and fool around. *"Plus tard,"* later, I whispered to him pleased with myself, looking back at Madame for approval.

A year later, I knew that beautiful as it was, French was not enough.
"I have to learn English," I said to my father.
"English…?"
He had to swallow hard. For years he had ridiculed the language of Shakespeare, pretending to be speaking with gravel in his mouth, making guttural sounds. It went with his political inclinations, just as Russian did, a language he detested. Although the English were not Communists, they still were Capitalists, Colonialists, naïve Parliamentarians, exploiters, snobs, and they had repeatedly betrayed Greece. But Dora Saltiel, a bit of a snob herself and a resolute Anglophile, would always give him a hard time. He never dared challenge her too much. Unlike Lotte, she knew her cultural facts. She would counter his Goethe with her Byron, ("and a hero of the Greek revolution at that!") He would bring up Leibniz and she'd throw Newton back at him. But now things were different. The Brits and the Americans, the Australians and New Zealanders, all "Anglo Saxons," were winning the War. And they all spoke English, millions of them. Even the Indians, dark as they were, spoke

excellent English. Faced with this force, my father was doing a slow, expedient linguistic about-face, accepting English to fit his recent political adjustments, although he had no interest whatsoever in learning the language himself. He was satisfied; German, French and Greek were all he needed. I, on the other hand, having already made good progress in those three, was convinced that English was not just another language but one that would replace the failed Esperanto to become the undisputed highway of world-wide communication and unlock the gates to a brilliant future ...

"I found a teacher for you," announced my father a few days later. "She's Greek, but she has lived in England and speaks very well, I'm told."

Fotini Karavou, a prim thirtyish spinster, spoke with a mild British accent. We sat side-by-side at a small table, a proper distance between us. I had brought a notebook and she produced a dog-eared reader. Having two and a half languages under my belt, I was surprised to be confronted by something akin to Chinese. What is this capital 'I'? And why does one address everybody, even children and servants, with the plural, polite, 'You'?

"But it makes things easier," explained Miss Fotini. "You don't have to worry about whether or not to use the polite form as you do in Greek. It's very democratic."

"Not always," I said. "When the American President Jefferson said 'You' to one of his slaves did he really mean that they were created equal?"

"Let's talk about some interesting irregular verbs," answered Miss Fotini.

Spelling was another area of frustration. In my three other languages the pronunciation of syllables was relatively consistent. Not here. I couldn't understand why words like 'though', 'through' and 'enough', all ending in 'ough', could produce the sounds of three different vowels, with the 'gh' turning into an 'f' sound in one word and remaining silent in the other two.

"That's just the way it is, Mr. Titsian," said Miss Fotini rather annoyed.

"I guess I have to memorize the spelling of every word."

"You have to do that in Greek too."

"But you know it's not the same," I said, exasperated.

—————

In those years, when schools were closed during one crisis or another, parents would step in as teachers. Schooling in our house however was not what you could call rigorous. That was not my father's style. Learning came about less through direct instruction, more sideways I might say, through conversation, a bit like a Platonic dialogue. With coffee in the afternoon, or fruit in late morning, a subject would pop up and pretty soon we'd be looking up a reference in a book, read a passage or pore over a map. Niko loved to elaborate on what he had read in print; what he had heard from others or the radio; what he had seen recently or on his youthful travels in the twenties; what thoughts had come to his mind when he saw the moon rise yesterday or the sunset an hour ago or when he woke up from a dream in the night.

He spouted facts at the slightest opportunity. "Did you know that the Nile is the longest river in the world," he'd say, "but the Amazon carries the most water?" adding that one Francisco de Orellana, a Spanish conquistador, traversed the entire equatorial width of the continent on that immense river, all the way from the mountains of Peru to the Atlantic Ocean, a voyage of 6,420 kilometers through huge rain forests, fending off poisoned arrow attacks from naked aborigines, threatened by deadly little piranhas and giant Anaconda constrictors. Or that Everest is the highest point on earth and the Dead Sea the lowest. Or that Amundsen beat poor Scott by just a few days to be the first to reach the South Pole.

Niko turned geography and the whole animal, vegetable and mineral world into romance. History received similar treatment - narrated by him as stories alive with adventure and drama. His words were stimulants, made me want more, drove me to books. Before first grade I had already visited the land of the Lotus

Eaters with Odysseus and his hapless companions. Before the subject came up in school I knew about Marat and Robespierre, the guillotine and the names of most Napoleonic generals and battlefields. It took a while to find out that there was more to history than Niko was willing to concede. Like a little boy, he too preferred the glitter of warfare.

My father was a conversationalist and a raconteur. I remember him during the occupation, when social gatherings were mostly at home. He would be expounding on some topic within a small circle of visitors – young, unemployed architects, (one a professed Communist, his presence barely tolerated, offering an easy target), retired army buddies (ardent royalists), some relatives, (among them uncle Achileas whose left, populist leanings Niko ridiculed), and assorted friends like the Saltiels. My mother usually stayed respectfully in the background or whispered on the side with one of the women. Enthralled, I followed the frequently animated discussions, occasionally putting a word of my own into the fray. In later years my wife was impressed by Niko's love of prolonged discussion, of old-fashioned conversation in the manner of Madame de Stael's salons. As usual, a random word or sentence would trigger a topic to be dissected and dwelled on at a leisurely pace. Not exactly a Platonic dialogue, but enough to engage Judy's interest. He was a bit pedantic, she thought, but she still enjoyed the sport. I would put in a word now and then but mostly I translated.

I have mentioned my father's other preferences - for nineteenth century opera (but not Wagner), for German poetry before Rilke, for fleshy Renaissance allegories and gooey seventeenth-century sunsets, for French prose in the realm of Loti, Daudet, Maupassant and Dumas. Niko was an unabashed romantic. A natural teacher, he easily imbued me with his knowledge and his preferences, and, inevitably, his own dogmas and prejudices. Gratefully and enthusiastically I took it all in, at least early on. In return I was happy to show him what I had learned in school, in books, seeking validation, more depth, correlation, expansion. It didn't take much for me to engage his interest. He was eager to mold me and I was willing to be his clay. Once I overheard him say to somebody: "You know, I have made that boy what he is. I have given him his *morphosi*, his education, his culture." I was pleased to overhear this boast, but then again, what about my schools, my teachers? What about *me*? Was I just a vessel to be filled? At other times his partisanship would push him to superlatives. "He may grow up to be a genius," he told Lotte, who saw me from a different angle. This hyperbole came to haunt me later when, thinking that I was destined for greatness, I tormented myself trying in vain to live up to that prophesy. Ultimately though, my father's deep devotion, even his naïve prejudice about me, combined with his high regard for cultural achievement and his essential character – all contributed to his supporting and promoting my voyage to America. He did this knowing that I might never return, that he might never see me again.

DOG DAYS

O CTOBER 1943. THE bell rang one night. We looked at each other. No one was expected. Should we open? I went to the top of the stair and yelled down. "Who is it?"

"It's Dora and I." The Saltiels came up.

"Can you put us up for a few nights?" Jackie asked.

The Saltiels were frightened. Earlier in the year Jews in Thessaloniki had been deported to what was said to be forced labor in Poland. This couldn't happen in Athens they thought; unlike the large, prominent Jewish population in Thessaloniki, the few Athenian Jews would get by, integrated as they were within the Gentile majority. That illusion was quickly dispelled. Alerted by the news from the north, the Grand Rabbi of Athens warned the community and fled to the mountains. The great majority either went into hiding, as the Saltiels did, or fled.

Surprisingly, Jackie and Dora's stay with us turned out to be good fun with much laughing and bantering, card playing, BBC listening, sharing meager meals. You wouldn't know a war was raging outside, that we might be awakened by sudden knocks on the door in the middle of the night, that we might all be arrested. Instead, the news kept our spirits high. The Allies had invaded Sicily forcing Italy to surrender. Mussolini was jailed. After Stalingrad the Russians were now reaching Kiev. Huge air strikes were turning German cities into rubble. Hitler and the mighty Wehrmacht, after so many years of arrogant, oppressive dominance, were finally losing the war.

Fortitude, we told ourselves, hold on a bit longer, good days are just around the corner.

Little did we know that the worst was still to come…

"I ran into Spyros today," Niko said one day. "I could hardly recognize him."

He and his cousins Spyros and Nikos Dhamaskinos grew up together and joined the military at about the same time. Spyros became an Air Force officer, his brother joined the Navy. Both distinguished themselves during the war, Spyros flying missions over Albania, Nikos on a destroyer in the Aegean. After the Germans came in, Spyros, along with other officers, fled to Egypt to continue fighting there. Not much later though, it was rumored that he had returned to Athens to join the underground as a spy for British Intelligence.

"The SS caught him, took him to Xhaidhari and tortured him," my father continued, shaken. "He has no fingernails left. They pulled them all out, one by one … over several days. And he has lost all his hair."

Lotte put her hand over her mouth.

Xhaidhari was a detention camp the SS had opened a few months ago, along the road to Elefsis, near the Dhafni church. Spyros had described it as an abandoned army barracks without beds, sanitary facilities or heat. Emaciated, infested with lice, prisoners had to suffer the stench of their own excrement. Pathological sadists, the SS guards carried whips, shouted abuse, took pleasure in beating and torturing. Every day during roll call in the main yard, one or more prisoners were pulled out and shot, without apparent provocation. Prisoners lived in constant terror of torture or execution.

Stories from the country side were even worse.

Kalavryta was a historic village in the mountains of northern Peloponnisos. On March 25, 1821, in a small church nearby, the Orthodox Metropolitan Germanos had declared Greece's independence after four hundred years of Turkish occupation. That date has since become the Greek national holiday. In late October 1943, outside Kalavryta, Greek guerillas killed 78 German soldiers in an ambush. In retaliation, German army units rounded up the entire male population above the age of 14. They were herded up a hill above the village and executed – more than 1,000 souls. Many years later my wife and I visited the memorial that had been built on top of that hill. From there we could see Kalavryta in the valley below, a peaceful village today nestled among blue peaks, smoke rising from chimneys, sheep grazing in the meadows. On that fateful day, babies, children, women and old men were able to look up from the village and witness the atrocity on the hillside. They must have heard the rat-tat-tat of the machineguns as their boys and men were felled. Today, Kalavrita, its mountains and its bustling ski resort are a known tourist destination attracting many Europeans, Germans among them.

A column of soldiers was marching down Septemvriou Street.

"Look, *tsoliadhes!*" I said to my father who was standing next to me on the balcony.

They wore khaki Evzone uniforms – short skirted *foustanelles*, tasseled skullcaps, thigh- and calf-hugging tights and *tsarouchia*, the rugged Balkan peasant footwear, a jaunty pompom on each upturned pointed toe. They carried a gun over the shoulder, marching more or less in unison, the free left arm swinging back and forth.

"It must be the new Security Battalions," said my father.

"They don't look very sharp," I said. "Nothing like the Germans."

"Yes, but they're good enough to fight the Communists. Here or up in the mountains."

Ioannis Rallis, the third and last Quisling Prime Minister under the Germans, had founded the Security Battalions earlier in the year. But they did not become an active force until fall of 1943, after the collapse of Italy when they were deployed across the countryside to help the Germans fight the guerillas. For over a year, they and some of the xhorofilaki, *the gray-suited, traditional gendarmerie, would spread bloodshed and terror across the Greek landscape.*

In late 1943, the German-controlled news outlets announced that all radios had to be taken to designated locations to be sealed, their dials fixed on the Athens station.

Anyone disobeying was to be arrested and was subject to the death penalty.

"That's the end of the BBC," said my father. "From now on we live in rumor."

The blast threw me out of the narrow cot. The two window panels had blown open, but the hinges held and the glass stayed in the frames, braced by the diagonal tapes we had glued on last year. A gust of frigid February air rushed in. I picked myself up and wrapped the bedclothes over my shoulders. My parents sat up on their beds, dazed. *"Was… was war das?"* stammered my mother, shivering. Out the window a bright light cut into the darkness.

"Look … oh my God …" my father was shouting. " Huge explosion …" He rushed to close the window. "It's Peireas … aflame!"

We cowered in the dark waiting. With the allied bombings accelerating, my father had insisted that I sleep in their room. I resented being treated like a child, but secretly liked the idea. The next day we learned that a cargo ship loaded with explosives had been hit in the harbor, presumably by Allied bombing. The blast had leveled several city blocks along the waterfront, and once again the schools were closed. The Makri faculty, unlike most others, decided to continue classes, but not in the school building. Mr. Margharitis, our 'humanities' teacher, had us seated around the dining table of his apartment in peaceful, contemplative discussion – he, standing in for Socrates and we, his rapt disciples, in some Platonic dialogue.

June 1944. The German controlled Radio Athens announced that the Allies had staged an invasion on the coast of Normandy. "The armies of Fortress Europe," it said, "are containing the small beachhead and are inflicting heavy losses on the invaders," etc., etc.

"At long last," exulted my father. "This'll keep the Russians in their place. Ha! Stalin thought he had Europe to himself – and with Roosevelt's help!" But celebrations were muted. The city was preoccupied with its own problems, and the Germans were still with us. Marauding gangs of self-styled nationalists, royalist youths, were combing the streets looking for Communists to kill. A couple of days before I had seen an open truck race by with a machinegun mounted on it. The men wore makeshift uniforms and their helmets had the letter X painted on them. They belonged to *Orghanosis Xhi,* an armed, virulently anti-communist group commanded by a certain Colonel Ghrivas much admired by my father.

In late June my father decided that our neighborhood was unsafe.

"Uncle Dino and Aunt Stella have invited us to stay with them," he said. "They think it's safer there, we can pool our resources."

My father's older sister Stella, her husband Dino and son Tsanos lived in a one-story house with a small garden on the outskirts, a half hour's walk from our house, in a modest new neighborhood called Sepolia, adjacent to open farmland. There was little love between Stella and her brother. She had sided with her mother Aspasia when my parents came from Berlin, spreading venom among the relatives. My mother could not hide her dislike of her.

"This place reminds me of Maroussi," my mother whispered

as the three of us sat in the room we shared. "It's like a village, all these little, low houses. At least we don't have to go outside to pump water, and the toilet flushes." And then, turning to me, she recounted one of her favorite litanies of woe. "You don't know how much I suffered there, all alone, no one to help me, your father away." Her eyes turned red, she reached for a handkerchief. "And this after that horrible experience in the hospital, when you were born. I thought I would die. Never again, I said to myself, never again."

"Come now, Lotte," said my father. "It could be worse. At least we're together."

"And then there is your sister," she continued, unstoppable. "I can't stand that woman. Such a hypocrite." Her face was getting redder. "That sly, honeyed voice, that smarmy smile painted on her pasty face – what a façade! She'll stab us in the back at the slightest opportunity. Remember the things she said about you back then?"

"Now, now. That all belongs in the past. We have to get along with them."

But Lotte wouldn't let go. "And you went and got him that job up there. He, a governor! Ha! What a fat airbag, he's been so full of himself since he wore those medals and that sash across his bloated chest."

"Now stop it Lotte, stop!" Niko was getting angry.

She finally broke down, put her head on his shoulder. "I'm sorry Nienchen. I'm so anxious, I say silly things." He kissed her head and patted her back.

Days went by in unbearable heat and boredom undermined by bouts of raw anxiety. We shivered as fiery slogans, shouted over megaphones, slashed through the night, peppered by the crackle of gunshots. PRODHOTES! FASISTES! DHOLOFONI! O LAOS! – words that resounded in threatening cadence, terrifying. Traitors, Fascists, Murderers, the People … My father and my uncle went into town a couple of times, only to return exhausted with reports of more horrors. Nothing functions any more, they said. No buses, no cars, only a few stores open, streets empty. Gangs of armed men, some in uniform, some not, were performing in a street theater acting out civil war, anarchy. Where were the Germans in all this?

We managed to keep ourselves busy with endless backgammon and poker games and I quickly devoured the few books in the house. With the absence of radio and newspapers, we found ourselves willing to believe any rumor that came along. And of course, food was a major problem. Forays into the neighborhood produced meager results, and we had to make do with dry beans and raisin paste just as we had during the first winter of the occupation.

But when August 15 came along, the day of the Virgin Mary's *dormition*, we decided to celebrate. The chicken that had been kept in the yard had stopped laying eggs and everyone agreed that its time had come. No one however was willing to perform the dastardly act – except me. Somehow I found the idea captivating, perhaps because death and dying were becoming common encounters, permeating the air around us like a toxic cloud. Everyone gathered in the yard to watch the execution. Surprised at my own sang-froid, I applied the long kitchen knife on the unsuspecting neck and moved it forcefully back and forth while thinking of poor Louis and Marie Antoinette, of Charles the First, of Anne Boleyn. I imagined myself wearing one of those sinister, black hangman's hoods. And just as in Paris and London, the crowd here seemed to enjoy the atrocity, cheering loudly as the headless fowl flew around the yard spurting blood.

Dino's brother Kostas and his family lived nearby and came to visit often. Lotte could barely tolerate them. Velos was Tsanos' age and chubby, budding Loula, a year younger. At sixteen, I was the oldest. Tsanos, who was sexually precocious, organized zesty bed games with Loula as the centerpiece, when we all tumbled around grabbing, biting, giggling and screeching, in a still innocent orgy, while outside a different kind of theater was playing itself out.

"Just beyond that cornfield lies Peristeri and beyond that Kokkinia," said Uncle Dino, stuffing his pipe. "Refugee neighborhoods, all red. Panos Stathis is making life miserable for them. Bastards, murderers all."

Stathis, a captain in the *Idhiki Asfaleia*, the notorious Special Security Police, was making a name for himself killing ELAS insurgents and terrorizing civilians in the western refugee slums. Other Special Security groups were active elsewhere in the *gheitonies*, the "neighborhoods," as the sprawling settlements surrounding Athens were known. They worked together with the rural police gendarmes, the Evzones of the new Security Battalions and, some said, the Gestapo and the SS. I frequently passed by their headquarters off Tritis Septemvriou Avenue, just two blocks from our house. It took a long time – much of it after the war - before I was fully aware of the ruthlessness and brutality with which they pursued their targets.

"I've met Stathis," Uncle Dino boasted. "A great man, a real hero. The other day he walked by, pistol in hand. Waved at me."

My father and Dino had much in common. Both retired officers, both longtime Monarchists, both besotted with hatred of Communism, they fit well in the Metaxas autocratic, royalist establishment. The outlawed Left would call them Fascists – or worse. Niko, through his connections in *Ethniki Etairia*, managed to secure a plum job for his brother-in-law as Governor of Western Thrace, up north. Stella, living in style, forgot her quarrels and sent loving letters to her brother. An official picture shows her husband in tails, a red sash across his starched shirt, shiny bald head over a haughty countenance, looking, significantly, like Francisco Franco, the recently triumphant Fascist dictator of Spain.

Eventually it occurred to my father that staying in his sister's house was no safer than staying in his own. At the end of August we packed our belongings, tied a leash on Rudi and, like refugees ourselves, trudged through the hot, desolate streets back to Kodringtonos. It was to be a fateful decision.

During our exile at Aunt Stella's we had heard of von Stauffenberg's aborted attempt on Hitler's life, resulting in the execution of some 5,000 conspirators and the insane prolongation of the war. Once back home, eager to get real news, my father mustered the courage to defy the ban and break the seal on the radio. The first news from London celebrated the liberation of Paris. "It should be our turn next," said my father. "But I doubt it. Not with ELAS pounding at the gates."

With so much violence in the streets, school and language lessons were not resumed. Broadcasts on the restored radio announced rapidly changing events. Russian armies had entered the Balkans, forcing German allies Rumania and Bulgaria to capitulate. Yugoslavia, with its strong Tito-led Communist resistance was about to collapse. We cheered when we heard that the British had landed in the Peloponnesean port of Patra, returning after so many years. Word had it that the Germans were preparing to leave. But there was still no rejoicing. We heard shooting day and night, punctuated by occasional explosions. From the roof I could see columns of black smoke rising here and there, dissolving into a gray scrim, the September sun behind it blanched to a pale yellow disk. A sense of foreboding hung over the city like some noxious vapor.

Paul Radomski SS Commandant of the Chaidhari camp where my father's cousin Spiros was tortured.

Young Greek Jews. All except one perished.

Jewish men are forced to do calisthenics in Thessalonika, 1942. Most perished in Auschwitz.

DELIVERANCE AND TRAGEDY

WHEN GREEKS DESCRIBE autumn, they speak of *ghlyka*, sweetness. Liberated from the haze of summer, the air has a special, magic quality. Everywhere the warm light etches sharp incisive images. It is this light, they say, that led the Greeks of antiquity to fashion out of white marble the dentils, flutings, triglyphs, capitals, volutes, entases, cornices and the relief sculptures on the metopes, friezes and pediments of their temples. *Ghlyka*. The morning of October 12, 1944 was just such a day.

For some time now, the sounds and smells of violence were permeating the city. Open trucks festooned with armed men dressed in looted military regalia had been racing up and down Septemvriou in pursuit of the Enemy – Xhi, ELAS, EDES, gendarmes, Security Battalions, police – not Germans anymore, not Italians - only Greeks. From the right, from the left, from the center; Communists, Socialists, Monarchists, Republicans, Nationalists, Venizelists, Fascists; freedom fighters, collaborators, traitors. One of these names would describe somebody out there – but not the thousands who stood by watching helplessly, scared, as the hatred spread. The city lit up at night with the macabre fireworks of combat, the glimmer of stars in the black, tranquil sky above unable to compete with the mayhem below – a spectacle that had all the makings for the celebration of a peaceful national holiday… or trench warfare in the Great War.

Everybody knew that the Germans were planning to leave. The handwriting was on the wall after von Stauffenberg's attempt on Hitler's life. A failed venture, but still a sign that the end was approaching. And with the news of the fall of Paris, spirits began to soar; it looked as if Athens, so far away from the big battles up north, was surely to be next.

On the balcony that morning, Rudi at my feet welcoming the day with rested lungs, I surveyed the cityscape. The Acropolis, as usual, looked unfazed by the turmoil around it, secure in its eternity. A little to the left, old Lykavittos, dressed in its green skirt, billowing gray blouse and party hat, rose as a steady reminder of my happy childhood at its slopes. On the horizon to the right, the blue Saronic beckoned to faraway places, to a future of peace and happiness – my future, I thought. And above it all, the vast smiling sky proclaimed that all would turn out well, that there was nothing to worry about. I took a deep breath and shook my head. Was this brilliant morning a good omen or just another cruel hoax?

A steady mechanical hum coming from the left drew my attention away from my reverie. Much more traffic than usual, I thought. A continuous flow of gray vehicles was moving from right to left on Patission a block away. And suddenly I understood. "My God," I whispered. "It's happening, it's finally happening!" One after another, army trucks, packed with neat rows of helmeted soldiers, their guns held upright next to them, kept moving to the north. Then more soldiers on motorcycles flocked behind them, leading the way for the artillery and the tanks mounted on heavy carriers. Then more trucks. No flags, no martial music, no marching, no triumph. They looked harmless somehow, like the plastic toy soldiers my mother bought for me in Berlin. Now I was looking at an army in retreat. I ran into the house. "Mutti, Pappi, come out, look! They're leaving!" Rudi barked, shaking his stubby tail. We held unto the balcony rail, awed, speechless.

"*Zurueck nach Deutschland*," my mother finally said, wistfully.

"No such luck," answered my father. "No way are they going home, not with three huge battlefronts pressing on the *Vaterland*."

"Remember three and a half years ago? Kaiti was with us, remember? Now they're going the other way, tails between the legs."

"Sic transit gloria mundis," concluded my father. I wondered what was on his mind.

I just had to say "Amen".

As we stood watching, people began to appear on their balconies, others stood outside their doors; still others walked slowly toward Patission to savor the humiliation at close range. The two women across the street above the casket maker's shop, still in their bras and panties, leaned out their window craning their necks for a better view. Soso Kandhyli stood outside her iron gate wearing a frilly robe under a honeycomb of wild hair, her lovely young soldier long gone – a Greek Colette. *"Fevghoune!"* They're leaving! shouted somebody. *"Fevghoune!"* came the echo, multiplying, ricocheting across the walls, as more windows and doors opened and more people poured out. Down the street a man had unfurled a flag and was attaching it to the balcony rail. Inspired, I ran in to climb up to the storage loft above the bathroom and brought out our long forgotten blue-and-white flag with the little yellow crown in the middle of the cross. The memory of that day four years ago came back to us now: when we had last hung the flag and the whining sirens had announced the beginning of the war for us; when Ioannis Metaxas, the Greek Fascist dictator, dared to defy the Duce, rejecting surrender with a single word: *Oxhi*, No.

After a while, church bells joined in the celebration. First Aghios Dhimitrios in the west, echoed by Aghios Onoufrios on the other side. Soon all of Athens had turned into a giant concert hall. In a chaotic, delirious performance, small falsetto bells, their clappers striking rapidly, tried to keep up with the slower but louder and deeper boom of their bigger brothers. In an unusual burst of unity, a spontaneous chorus of altos, tenors, baritones and Russian basso profundos heralded liberation. But wait, not so fast, warned another sound, we're not there yet. Ominous crackling staccatos suddenly disrupted the celebration. Toward the south we saw little puffs of gray and occasional large black balls of smoke with bright yellow centers. "They're still fighting down there," said my mother clasping her husband's arm. "And I thought we were safe at last."

As it turned out, the Germans had not quite left. Eager to preserve their reputation for gratuitous evil, they made a last-minute foray into Peireas to destroy the harbor with explosives. Elsewhere, in a senseless act against the civilian population, they attacked the city's power plant in Keratsini in an attempt to sink all of Attika into darkness. Happily their plan was frustrated by the unlikely collaboration of ELAS and city police, aided by a handful of brave workers at the plant, saving Athens from yet another trauma. And in a bizarre show of utter hypocrisy, the Germans staged another ostentatious performance before leaving. They marched a platoon to Syntaghma dressed up for honor duty in steel helmets and shiny black boots, where they lined up, presented arms and shouted commands while a lieutenant stepped forward to deposit a wreath beneath the supine body of the ancient Greek hoplite carved in marble, still wearing his helmet and holding his shield — the monument of the Unknown Soldier. However, as soon as the Germans left, a large crowd of liberated celebrants ran across the plaza, grabbed the wreath and trampled it to shreds. By mid afternoon the Germans had left and an eerie silence fell upon the city. But not for long.

"What is that noise?" I asked. "Sounds like thousands of bees."
We walked out on the balcony again. The sun had just set, leaving a rosy glow over Mount Aighaleo. A gentle breeze carried with it the salty scent of the sea. Aphrodite was beginning to twinkle in the western sky, forecasting another cool autumnal night. The buzz I had first heard was getting closer, louder, cutting into the peaceful evening, building up to an ominous roar. And then we saw them.

Up past Patission where the Germans had retreated a few hours ago, a mass of humanity was pouring down toward us. The buzz we had heard was turning into wordless, rhythmic chanting, its beat reflected in a picture of bouncing objects above the marchers. In the fading light we began to discern the placards, the flags and the long banners stretched across the rows of people. Soon we could recognize the words – "KAPPA, KAPPA, EPSILON… KAPPA, KAPPA, EPSILON…KAPPA, KAPPA, EPSILON…" repeated relentlessly.

"My God," whispered my father. "It's the KKE, it's the Communists! Look at those red flags, the hammer and sickle!" I turned to look at him. He was holding onto the railing with both hands, his jaws tightened, his lips pulled in. I hadn't seen him like this before. "Prosfighes," he continued. "Refugees. From the neighborhoods up there. The red districts."

"*Nienchen*, I'm scared," said my mother, under her breath. "What will happen to us?"

"Nothing will happen to us." He was defiant. "It's going to be all right. The British will be here in no time … and the government from Egypt."

"But there are so many of them, so angry."

"Yes, many …"

We didn't sleep until late that night listening to the fierce jubilation. "LAOKRATIA … LAOKRATIA, they were chanting somewhere. People Rule.

The light of the morning sun was reaching the wall opposite my bed as I woke up. There was clamor outside, unusual sounds this early. I leaned out the window. There were people out there, many people. I ran to the eastern balcony from where, looking in both directions, I could see all of Septemvriou Street, brimming with populace.

"They must have been up all night," I said sotto voce – afraid they might hear me. My father had joined me, still in his pajamas. They looked like the mob we had seen a few hours before. Many more kept pouring in from side streets, filling the ranks, assembling for action. The flags were there and the banners and placards. In the bright daylight individual faces stood out of the crowd – men, women, boys and girls, children, even babies. Some looked angry, shook their fists, bounced their signs, waved flags. Most milled around convivially, chatting, laughing, joking, as if attending a party.

There was a self-assured air about them – it was their day after all, their time to stand up, to finally raise their flag after so many years. Their banners proclaimed their passions and grievances in large letters: DOWN WITH … LONG LIVE … GET OUT OF … and the names until now seen only as graffiti painted on walls during the cold nights of occupation: KKE, EAM, EPON, ELAS. Other signs identified participants as TEACHERS FOR… WORKERS AGAINST… Civil Servants, Pensioners, Students, Artists, Women, Lawyers, Officers, Resistance Fighters, Professors and so on.

"Where have all these people been hiding?" I asked. "When did they make all these signs?"

"They must have been preparing for years," said my father. "So damn well organized, amazing."

The demonstrations went on for days. There was fear of a Communist takeover as had happened in Bulgaria and Rumania. Armed ELAS soldiers, red bandanas around their necks, patrolled the streets. We heard rumors of arrests, vendettas, executions of "traitors". In speeches before large crowds, "Fascists," "collaborators," "reactionaries" were condemned. The mob demanded *Laokratia*, the rule of the people – no longer *Dhemokratia*. For a while it looked as if the guerillas had complete control. But my father's prediction was fulfilled a few days later, when platoons of British soldiers disembarked in the Bay of Faliron under the command of a certain General Scobie, a man whose name would soon become legend. He set up headquarters in a new prewar office block just off Syntaghma Square, around the corner from the Grande Bretagne hotel and above the chic Zonar's and Floka cafes where my mother until recently met her friends for coffee and aperitifs. "Tommies" in khaki uniforms, ankle spats, berets and pink cheeks walked the streets trying to fend off kisses and bear hugs from adoring Greeks who greeted them with *"Bravo paidhia"* (bravo boys) and shouts of *"Tsortsil good, Xhitler bad."* (Churchill good, Hitler bad). My parents and their friends breathed a sigh of relief.

Not so the Left who looked at the new intruders warily, their feelings mixed. Sure, the English were allies. During the occupation they sent men up to the mountains to help the guerillas. Supplied them with money, weapons, uniforms, tactical training. They were friends, for God's sake, fighting the common enemy side by side with our boys and girls. But now? Why are they here now? We don't need them any more. It's our country. We are its liberators … finally in charge. All they can do now is mess up our plans by helping *them* – the Fascists, the traitors, the collaborators.

The Right on the other hand, encouraged by the arrival of the British forces and fed up by the relentless display of red power, decided one day to stage its own demonstration.

"Don't go," my mother begged as my father and I were putting on our coats. "You know how those people are, they'll hurt you, they have guns!" For days now students from the University had been promoting the parade with leaflets and megaphones.

"We'll see about that," said my father, trying to look determined. "Let's go Titsian." He was wearing his suit and tie and his fedora as if he were going to the office. "Take a scarf along and the umbrella. It looks like it's going to rain."

Crowds were walking down Septemvriou toward the center. Some of the people smiled at us and we smiled back. We understood each other. Nice folk, kind, friendly, well dressed – like us – and they carried only blue and white flags. I felt included, secure. In Omonia Square we joined a noisy, gathering multitude waiting for the march up Panepistmiou to Syntaghma Square where we would hear the speeches. Omonia was a large polygonal square with an island in the center, the convergence of several streets and avenues. The axis of Septemvriou extended across the square to become Athenas Street running past the central market and the old Mosque on Monastiraki Square all the way to the foot of the Acropolis. From where we stood, above the heads and through the flags and signs, I could see the Ionic colonnade of the Erechtheion. For a while we milled around the closed flower stalls that encircled the island. My father recognized some friends, there was talk.

"I'm amazed they haven't declared that Greece is now a Soviet Republic," one of them said. "They seem to own the country."

"They're afraid of the British," said another.

"But the British are only a handful. ELAS has a huge army, they can do as they please."

"It's not over yet, that's clear."

"The Germans were tame compared with what lies ahead."

The dominant colors around us were blue and white with a few British and American flags interspersed among them. A group was practicing the slogan I was seeing on many signs. "MEGHALI … ELLADHA … MEGHALI … ELLADHA …" went the chant, the accent on each second syllable –"Large Greece," the offspring of the old *Meghali Idhea*, the Great Idea fantasy. In the mood of the moment, I joined in the chant, although I wasn't quite sure why *Meghali Elladha*, a cause so discredited during the 1922 debacle, was again worth resurrecting, when so many other problems needed attention. Compared to the Reds, the Right seemed to have no other message.

By now Omonia was teaming with fellow travelers eager to move on. Slowly the mass ambled up Panepistimiou, past the Library, the University and the Academy. Thousands filled the avenue – shouting, waving, chanting, laughing, happy to see that their numbers were as impressive as those of the Communists. MEGHALI … ELADHA …MEGHALI … ELLADHA … they screamed, elated, gaining confidence as they looked at each other, feeling the power of their voices. At the Metoxhikon building, above the cafes, British soldiers were perched on windowsills, enjoying the show, smiling and waving. The demonstrators in the street were delirious by now. The march came to a halt as the crowd screamed "SCOBIE … SCOBIE … SCOBIE." A sea of flags and placards danced to the rhythm, my father and I joining the bedlam. The *Englezi* are here, we told ourselves, and there are so many of us. We have nothing to fear, we're safe.

Suddenly, out of nowhere, men came charging into the crowd. "Fascist pigs!" one shouted. "Collaborators!" yelled another. There was shoving and pummeling. What was going on? Who are these people? One wearing a red bandana grabbed my father by the collar and shook him, knocking the fedora off his head. "You stinking swine," he bellowed, "the people are starving and you want *Meghali Elladha?*" My father's frail body crumbled and he sprawled on the pavement. "Leave my father alone!" I screamed, pulling at the red bandana. He was a big man. The backward swing of his arm hit me squarely in the face and knocked my glasses off. But I still managed to bend down to reach my shaken father. People rushed in to help, others scuffled with the attackers, cursing and shouting. A policeman appeared. As they hauled Niko to his feet and replaced the fedora on his head, he looked at me and shouted, "Titsian, you're bleeding!"

"He hit my nose, I'll be fine," I said, but it hurt. Somebody handed me my glasses.

"We've got to get you to a doctor!" Niko was in true form.

"I'm all right, Pappi. Let's go home."

By now the crowd was moving again. *Meghali Elladha* still filled the air. They had little else to say.

My father's second prediction came true a day or two later when Prime Minister George Papandhreou and his cabinet finally arrived from exile in Egypt. The cabinet, put together some months before, was to represent

all political factions including Communists and Socialists who had been excluded from government during the Metaxas dictatorship. As a result, KKE and EAM now held several cabinet positions. Nonetheless, the arrival of Papandhreou was seen by the Right as yet another favorable development, while suspicion, doubt and irritation was building up on the other side. My father and his friends were baffled. Why did the Communists and their leftist allies agree to join the Government as a minority when they have almost total control of the country? He didn't trust them. They must have something up their sleeve …

Papandhreou and his cabinet disembarked in Peireas from the ancient battleship 'Averof', greeted, of all things, by an honor guard of ELAS soldiers. Crowds cheered their motorcade along the road to the Acropolis where Papandhreou ceremoniously raised a huge Greek flag, replacing the Swastika that had hung there for three and a half years. After the obligatory dhoxologhia at the Cathedral, Papandhreou moved a few blocks north to a balcony overlooking Syntaghma Square – the venue for passionate political speeches to this day. Before him he saw a vast sea of undulating, pulsating red, dancing to the beat of the by now well worn 'Laokratia' emerging at full volume from one hundred thousand throats. He was taken aback. He hesitated. But like any practiced politician he gathered his wits and began to speak. Using the language of his tormentors, he declared that "in free 'Laokratic' governments the majority rules, the minority checks, but the public functions of the State belong to neither. They belong to the idea of the Fatherland and are meant to serve all people. In a government of justice, the Law is the ruler."

The Right later attacked him for concluding his speech by shouting "We believe in Laokratia" just to please the mob.

There was more good news for the Right a few days later. "The Rimini Brigade has landed!" rejoiced my father. "They are parading downtown tomorrow."

We had been reading in the papers about the heroic Greeks who had fought with the Eighth Army in Italy only a few months ago and raised the blue-and-white flag on the City Hall of Rimini along the Adriatic coast. The next day, perched on a wall armed with my little Kodak Retina, I joined thousands of enthusiastic Athenians lined up along Panepistimiou to greet the new arrivals. Dressed in British uniforms but led by Greek flags, they marched smartly up the avenue. Directly opposite from me stood Papandhreou with his ministers and the Archbishop. Were the Communists among them? I wondered. Would they helplessly salute a rival army when no such honor had been conferred to their equally, if not more, heroic ELAS?

During November, in a cat and mouse game, Scobie and Papandhreou were negotiating the disarmament of the guerilla forces in order to start the formation of a National Army. The Left, obviously reluctant to give up its military superiority, made unacceptable demands, among them the condition to disarm the Rimini brigade. But there were also disagreements and a strange air of indecision within the powerful Left. Siantos, Ioanidhis, Zevghos and other Communist "political" leaders delayed or negated proposals made by "military" chieftains like Sarafis, Velouchiotis and Bardziotas, some of whom had advocated immediate attack for a quick takeover of Athens. With a force of some 18,000 strong, battle tested, well-armed (by the British,) ELAS veterans poised in and around the capital, one could only ask: what held them back? Some said that it was a certain agreement made in Moscow in early October. The story went like this: Churchill and Stalin are sitting at a table opposite each other in the Kremlin bickering over the future of Eastern Europe and the Balkans.

The question is: who will influence the future of these countries, the USSR or the West? Leaving Poland and Czechoslovakia aside,

Churchill takes a piece of paper and writes:

Rumania USSR 90% West 10%

Greece USSR 10% Britain 90%

Yugoslavia USSR 50% West 50%

Hungary USSR 50% West 50%

Bulgaria USSR 75% West 25%

Churchill then pushes the note toward Stalin who reads it and after a brief pause takes a pencil, scratches a simple check mark on it and pushes it back toward the Prime Minister. There is silence. Churchill finally asks whether they should destroy the note. Stalin shakes his head, smiles and says "keep it." Although the story has been disputed it has contributed to Churchill's reputation as the savior of Greece.

Anyway, in Athens negotiations for disbanding both Left and Right guerilla armies broke down, resulting in the resignation of all EAM ministers in the cabinet on the last day of November. Two days later, EAM and KKE proclaimed a mass demonstration for Sunday, December 3 and a general strike for Monday, December 4, 1944.

All through the night of Saturday and into the early morning of Sunday we heard blaring megaphones urging the People to join the big demonstration. On Sunday morning I went down to buy a newspaper. Among the many dailies usually on display at the neighborhood kiosk I saw the big headlines of the leftist press. "EVERYONE TODAY AT 11:00 TO THE EAM DEMONSTRATION IN SYNTAGHMA SQUARE!" read Rizospastis, the official newspaper of the Communist Party. "DOWN WITH THE GOVERNMENT OF CIVIL WAR! FORWARD TO THE GOVERNMENT OF NATIONAL UNITY!"

"We are in deep trouble," said my father after he put down the papers I'd brought up. "These people will stop at nothing now."

Papandhreou was faltering. After first approving the rally, he decided at the last moment to ban it and directed the police to block the entrances to the Square. But it was too late. By now thousands of incensed demonstrators waving the usual flags and banners, shaking their fists and shouting, their voices a terrifying roar, pushed on and overwhelmed the police lines. At some point in the morning the mob came before the Police Headquarters at the corner of Vassilisis Sofias and Panepistimiou, across the street from the Grande Bretagne hotel on one side and the Old Palace and the Monument of the Unknown Soldier on the other. For one reason or another (and there were conflicting reports,) the police started shooting and it was said that as many as 27 civilians were killed and many more wounded. Soon stories of the "slaughter" spread through the city and were expanded on in newspapers together with photographs.

We of course had stayed home as did everybody we knew. By afternoon stories began to reach us – several versions, the degree of horror depending on the narrator's point of view. Hundreds were killed, we were told. Blood was running down the gutters in front of the Grande Bretagne. Women had dipped their skirts in it to show the world the enormity of the Government's treason, to expose the crimes of the fascist police that served it, to dramatize the suffering of the people under its yoke. Foreign correspondents staying in the Grande Bretagne were shocked and put the blame on the police for being trigger-happy. My father on the other hand thought that the Communists had it coming.

Ta Dhekemvriana, the December 1944 Communist uprising, was launched on this day.

❦

The Evzones walked single file down Kodringtonos staying close to the walls on both sides of the street, rifle held with both hands. Their movements were circumspect, wary. Something serious is going on, I thought as I looked down on them. They must be going toward Sepolia, Tsanos's neighborhood. Hard to believe that we were staying there just a few weeks ago, that we thought it would be safer than here.

I had seen the Evzones marching while the Germans were still here a year ago. They had formed the so-called *taghmata*, the dreaded Security Battalions, to help the Germans fight the guerillas, both Communist and Nationalist, in the countryside. Briefly detained after liberation, they were recently rearmed to join existing urban and country police groups, the Rimini Brigade, and the British in opposition to the rising Communist threat.

"They seem to need every man they can get," my father had said.

"Even collaborators, Pappi?"

It was early December, a day after the bloody Syntaghma demonstration, known as the Massacre. The city had been relatively quiet since liberation but today we were hearing shots and explosions again. Uncle Dino had just come up the stairs, pale and out of breath. Back in July, when we were staying at his house, he was bursting with confidence. He would puff at his pipe and stand erect, his bald head shining in the sun, prominent nose protruding under a tall, square forehead. He was the man of the house, ordered Stella around. "Bring me some water, wife," he would command when returning from somewhere, sweaty and tired, plopping into a chair. "I'm thirsty." An official picture of him as governor hung on the wall. He held his head high affecting dignity, the gravitas of public office.

Today Uncle Dino looked subdued. Was he scared?

"They're attacking police stations all over the city," he announced. "ELAS is moving toward the center. It's been their goal all along. We knew it, didn't we? Now they're exploiting the Syntaghma mess to move in for the final blow."

"Nonsense, Dino. Scobie and the Rimini boys will chase them back into the mountains. The Brits have tanks, and those Spitfires, for God's sake."

Dino shook his head, seemed to have lost his fortitude. He'd come up from Sepolia to shop for supplies before holing up in his little house with his wife and son and his brother's family. He was worried. The neighborhood was infested with Communists, he said. "There are hordes of them out there, infuriated by that stupid event in Syntaghma. If our local gendarme station falls …" The sentence hung in the air. On the way out he turned. "By the way, Niko. Did you hear what they've done to the Xhites in Theseio?"

The day before, a large force of ELAS guerillas had attacked the headquarters of Orghanosis Xhi in Theseion under the Acropolis where Colonel Ghrivas and his men had barricaded themselves. Ghrivas had managed to escape, but those remaining, mostly young men from bourgeois families, were "slaughtered."

"Hadn't Rallis and the Germans worked with Ghrivas?" I asked. My father gave me a long stare. "Ghrivas is a patriot, a nationalist. No wonder those thugs hate him."

Ghrivas' band of right-wing guerillas had been openly fighting ELAS in Athens during the waning days of the occupation. He had expected that Scobie and the British would replace the Germans. But Scobie let him down. No one came to help.

But the attack was not limited to Ghrivas' small band. As early as the evening following the bloody Syntaghma demonstration, the First Army Corps of ELAS under the leadership of Kapetan Nestor was ordered by the KKE First Secretary and self-appointed ELAS Commander-in-Chief George Siantos to launch an all-out attack on the police and gendarme stations in Athens. Among them was the hated Gheniki Asfaleia, the General Security headquarters, near Omonia Square and the even more odious Idhiki Asfaleia, the Special Security, just off Septemvriou, only two blocks from our house.

From my window I could see the roof of *Idhiki Asfaleia*. The Acropolis in the distance seemed to hang on top of it. The largely undercover unit housed here, a kind of Greek Gestapo, was active even before the war, during the Metaxas dictatorship, under the aegis of a man named Maniadhakis, Minister of Public Safety, who gained notoriety for his brutal persecution of Communists and others opposed to the Fascist takeover. During the occupation, *Idhiki Asfaleia* managed to enhance this reputation by brazen murder and torture and, some said, by collaboration with the Gestapo and German army. Having heard my father mention Maniadhakis in past conversations but having paid little attention, I began to realize that terrible things might be happening down the street. I now recalled conversations with my father, who apparently knew that *Idhiki Asfaleia* had been formed to pursue Communists on the rise before Metaxas came to power. Niko would get annoyed when I suggested that Metaxas was a dictator. He was a patriot, Niko said, a Nationalist, protected us from the Slavs, said OXHI to Mussolini. As it turned out, my father knew Maniadhakis and probably approved of the happenings inside the building down the street.

The attack came the night after the Syntaghma killings.

We had finished our dinner of boiled white beans and gone to bed. I had insisted on sleeping in my own room wrapped in the heavy red flokato rug. My bed was pushed against the icy outside wall. I must have been dreaming. People were shouting at me, their voices cutting through the frigid gloom, in drawn out, harrowing cadence.

"YOU ARE SURROUNDED BY THE PEOPLE'S ARMY!" thundered the megaphones. "SURRENDER NOW AND YOU WILL BE SPARED THE HORRIBLE DEATH AWAITING FASCIST TRAITORS!"

The message was repeated several times. Then minutes passed in silence. The fusillade erupted suddenly – spontaneous, deafening, breathtaking. A window pane shattered, the shards crashing onto the floor next to the bed. I grabbed the flokato, slung it over my shoulder and fled into the narrow hall where I cowered with my parents, shivering, sleepless as the pandemonium outside went on relentlessly. Rudi whimpered, huddled next to us. Hours passed in agony. Toward the morning it stopped and we managed some sleep.

"Just two or three panes are broken," said my mother as she swept the shards off the floor. "You can't walk around in bare feet, Titsian."

"We have to cover the holes," said my father. "It's freezing in here."

"What's that on the ceiling? And on the wall over there?"

"My God! It's bullet holes!"

"You can't sleep in here any more," said my mother.

"And what about you? "

Just then, I remembered something.

"Do you know what day this is, Pappi?"

"What?"

"It's the sixth of December! Your name day, Saint Nicholas day! *Xhronia polla!*"

"Oh yes! *Xhronia polla,* Nienchen," exclaimed my mother. Many years. We kissed him and the three of us held each other for a while.

"First time with no presents, Pappi. No gooey *tourtes*, no *kourabiedhes*, no chocolates, no well-wishers."

"I have my well-wishers right here. That's all I need."

"I wouldn't mind some of those sweets now. What are we going to eat?"

"We're alive, that's what matters."

"What's that noise?" I asked later that morning. It sounded like tin cans being dragged on the pavement. My father and I were playing backgammon in the entrance hall wrapped in our overcoats, rolling the dice with frozen knuckles. I rushed into the dining room to peer through the shutters, ignoring my father's warnings.

"Some big heavy machine moving slowly, come see," I said.

"I can't believe it," my father whispered, as if afraid to be overheard in the din. "It's a tank! A British tank! We're saved!"

The tank rumbled on, leaving chewed-up asphalt in its wake, and came to a stop at the intersection just below us. Horizontal slivers of it were visible through the shutter slats. The massive chains, wrapped over a cluster of little wheels, the restless turret on top with its long proboscis, gave it the look of a giant lethal insect. Now and then the turret turned 90 degrees guided by invisible eyes to point down one deserted street or another. Something seemed to be moving on the left. The turret turned slowly in that direction just as a head and a red bandana pulled back from the corner of the coal yard across the street. Then, in a flash, the barrel of a gun poked out, and a shot was fired. "Dumb idiot," I blurted as a burst of light flashed from somewhere in the tank. Minutes passed. The sniper had disappeared. The lid on top of the turret opened slowly and a head wearing a red beret emerged. An English soldier! Deftly he lifted himself out, jumped onto the deck of the tank and hopped down to the pavement. "Watch out!" I wanted to shout in my new English, but I was speechless, as in a dream. The soldier was surprisingly nonchalant. He walked around holding a rifle in one hand, now and then shouting something to his invisible comrades, exploring, as if looking for hidden playmates in a game of hide and seek. Eventually he returned to the tank and disappeared down the turret. The tank then turned itself around, spewing globs of asphalt from its chains, and slowly rumbled back in the direction of the police station.

"The soldier didn't seem to be afraid," I said. "He knew there was a sniper out there and a whole army behind him."

"It could be that ELAS is under orders not to shoot at the *Englezi*," said my father. "After all it was the Brits who supported them through the occupation, sent them arms, trained them. It certainly wasn't the Russians."

"That means that Scobie could just push them out of Athens without a shot being fired."

"Wish that were so. But they won't give up. They're on the

verge of success, they control most of the country." He paused for a minute, then added ominously.

"If the Brits resist there's going to be a fight. A bloody, ugly fight."

As we sat down for another game, there went the rumble again. We rushed to the window. This time the tank was carrying some passengers – a dozen or so gendarmes from the *Asfaleia* station were piled on the flat deck, holding their heads and bodies down, an easy target for the guerillas, but no shots were fired. The tank reached the intersection in front of the house, slowly swiveled to the right, gouging the pavement, and then moved up Kodringtonos, to disappear around the corner of Patission. An hour or so passed and the tank returned with another load of men, some in civilian clothes. The maneuver was repeated a few more times followed by an uneasy silence. We looked at each other in amazed shock.

"I can't believe it," shouted my father, his face darkening as reality crept in. "The English are not staying. They've evacuated the station. They've abandoned us!"

My mother burst into tears. "Oh Nienchen, what's going to happen to us? What are we going to do?"

My father was looking around, as if expecting an answer from the walls, the ceiling.

"We …we just stay put for now. See what comes next." We hugged each other as we had done in the morning and stood there helplessly.

"The revolver," said my father suddenly. "The revolver! We can't just leave it in the drawer. They may come in and find it."

"But don't we need it? To defend ourselves? Isn't that why you got it?"

"Yes, yes. But this is different. If any of them come up … they're vicious … you heard them."

I took the gun and the box of bullets out of the desk drawer.

"Where?" I asked holding the weapon with two fingers – it could have been a dead rat. "Under a mattress?"

"Too obvious."

"But are they going to ransack the place? Do they have time for that sort of thing?"

"If they suspect you of something …why take a chance?"

Suddenly in a panic, we ran around the apartment looking for likely hiding places. All options were rejected by my father as too obvious.

"What if we buried it?" said my mother.

"Bury? You mean in the ground? You'd think we had a garden."

"But we do. A very small one – just outside this door."

Gun and bullets were finally interred in the big pot with the big leaf ficus outside the front door, at the top of the stairs.

"They'll never look outside the apartment," concluded my mother with some satisfaction. In our misery, we felt that the act had somehow brought us closer to salvation.

Sometime during the night I peered out from under my red blanket to see a festive looking pattern of flickering yellow on the ceiling. "What now?" I mumbled as I staggered to the window to open the shutters. The sudden burst of burning light forced my eyes shut. I heard my own convulsive gasp as they blinked open again and I saw the spectacle. Huge orange flames fringed in green and blue were leaping into the black sky. My nostrils took in the powerful stench as the wind fanned the bonfire, propelling the acrid smoke toward me; I could taste the cinder dust on my lips. In a Faustian *Walpurgisnacht*, the last of my senses was attacked by the staccato of crackling, crashing timbers as the roof of the hated building finally collapsed.

My mother rushed in, a blanket over her shoulders.

"Come inside, for God's sake. Close the window, you'll freeze!"

"Like watching a volcano." I was mesmerized. "No danger of freezing."

Later we huddled on the floor trying to ignore the triumphant, terrifying roar outside - to seek relief in stupor, in dreams.

The morning was overcast, gloomy, deceptively quiet. The blackened stone walls of the police station stood as a silent reminder of the night's orgy. Wisps of gray smoke curled out of the carcass. The heavy, toxic smell hung in the air. "Where are they?" I asked looking out the window. The streets were empty. Later we heard gunfire, occasional explosions. "They must be fighting down near the Polytechnic, at the *Gheniki Asfaleia*," said my father. The day passed. There was nothing to do except wait, play backgammon, leaf through books and try to remain calm, to concentrate on something.

We went to bed early that night, trying to save our candles. I must have been asleep when the explosion came. Still wrapped in my red blanket, I felt myself propelled through the air landing on the floor in a mess of broken glass. My ears hurt. For a few seconds I heard nothing. Not again, I thought. When will it stop? My parents rushed in.

"Are you hurt? No cuts? Bruises? Quick, come inside. No more sleeping in here."

"What? ...Where? ..." I was still dazed.

"They blew up the police station."

"Three nights in a row." I was alert now. "How they must hate those people."

The blast had shattered the remaining windows and icy air was moving through the house. We found refuge again in the entrance hall. Rudi was whimpering.

"Oh no!" exclaimed my mother. "He's done his pipi on the floor!"

"I don't blame him," chuckled my father. "I almost peed myself."

Dawn found us on the floor piled against each other, breathing quietly, limbs entangled, Rudi in the middle – a wreckage washed ashore, survivors in a storm.

A couple of days before, the ELAS Second Division of Attiki was advancing on Athens in defiance of General Scobie's directive banning guerilla forces from the capital. The goal was to attack the Rimini brigade billeted in the old Ghoudhi barracks in the vicinity of today's Hilton hotel. The Second Regiment of the Division, under the leadership of Kapetan Nikiforos, a well-armed, battle-tested unit, had already reached Filothei, not too far from its target, and set up camp there for the night. While Nikiforos was attending a meeting elsewhere, a detachment of British tanks and infantry came up in the dark, encircled the sleeping men and ordered them to surrender their weapons, which they did quite willingly. They were then loaded on trucks and driven out of Athens. When Nikiforos returned later that night he found an empty camp and was unable to explain to his commander George Siantos how one of the best ELAS units was eliminated without a single shot being fired.

Two days after, the bell rang. We looked at each other. "Let's not answer it," said my mother grabbing her husband's arm. We waited. The bell rang again, more persistent.

"We'll have to open it," said my father.

"No, Niko, no!"

I got up and pressed the buzzer. We heard steps. A man with a rifle was coming up the stair. He was wearing civilian clothes and a worker's cap. Not bad looking.

"Could you show me the way to the roof?" he asked, politely.

"Through this door," said my father. "Could we offer you some water? We have little else." The last with a little laugh.

"No thanks."

He went up the spiral stair. Standing in the kitchen, we held Rudi who wanted to follow, and listened. Bang, bang went his gun a few times. There was a lot of other shooting.

"He must be a sniper," said my father. "The whole building has now become a target. Stay away from the windows."

Suddenly a roar approached overhead, follower by a rapid staccato like the sound of a giant sewing machine.

"An airplane!" I shouted. "Strafing us. Must be British. How exciting!"

Minutes later the roar returned – more rapid fire. Hurried steps bounced down the spiral stair.

"Thank you," he blurted. *"Fevgho."* I'm going.

"Good luck," shouted my mother maternally, happy to see him go.

The empty shells from the RAF plane's machine gun I found on the roof the next day, were large and deadly looking. A prized possession.

In the early hours of December 5, Winston Churchill sent a telegram to General Scobie, excerpts of which appear below. (The emphases are Churchill's.) "You are responsible for maintaining order in Athens and for neutralizing or destroying all EAM-ELAS bands approaching the city…do not hesitate to fire at any armed male in Athens who assails the British authority or Greek authority with which we are working… Do not hesitate to act as if you were in a conquered city where a local rebellion is in progress…With regard to ELAS bands approaching from outside you should surely be able with your armor to give some of these a lesson which will make others unlikely to try… We have to hold and dominate Athens. It would be a great thing for you to succeed in this without bloodshed if possible, but also with bloodshed if necessary."

Unbeknownst to Winston and my father, Scobie was in serious trouble. He was short of supplies, the roads between Athens, the harbors and the airport were threatened, and he felt undermanned. At one time he seriously considered withdrawing his troops to the seashore, surrendering all of Athens to ELAS in defiance of Churchill's orders. Surprisingly, he didn't seem to realize that, until mid December, George Siantos, First Secretary of KKE and leader of ELAS, was reluctant to attack the British even as his army was fighting Greek gendarmes and soldiers. And then – additional reinforcements from Italy began to turn the tide in favor of the Greek Right.

Unaware of such developments, we and most Athenians had to face the hard fact that most of the city, including our neighborhood and almost all of Greece, was now under Communist control. This realization weighed heavily on us. We felt deeply threatened – anxious, insecure. We had lost all contact with friends and relatives. Were Toula and Bebe still in Ekali? Was Achileas with them? No word from the Saltiels – and they lived on Patission, just a few streets away. And what about Stella, Dino and Tsanos in their little house in Sepolia? In our condition, the war outside – in France, in Russia, in Italy, the Pacific – was of no consequence. Still, we longed for news, any news. We felt alone, abandoned.

The neighbor from the floor below knocked on the door.

"There are some people here who wish to talk to you."

"Who? What? Who are they?" My father was pale, trembling.

A man and a woman came up the stair.

"We are neighbors of *Kyria* Stella, in Sepolia. She asked us to stop by. We left our house, going to cross to the British side."

"Why? What happened?"

"They've arrested your brother-in-law. And his brother Kostas."

"What do you mean arrested? Who?"

"The ELAS people, three or four of them, with guns. Took them away."

My father leaned on the wall, his hand on his chest. We were crowding behind him.

"The women? The children?"

"They're in the house. Scared, worried. The *Elasites* are going around knocking on doors. They've taken away others. We've got to get out of here, I said to my wife. Left everything behind. It's not safe there."

"We've got to leave Lotte."

"Out there? They're fighting. We'll get killed."

"These people said there's a kind of cease-fire between twelve and one. We'll have to risk it. It's already eleven o'clock."

"But where do we go?"

"I don't know yet. First we have to get out of here."

We stuffed a few things in two bags.

"What about Rudi?" I asked. "We can't leave him."

"We must. Mrs. Vafiadhis below will look after him. He'll be all right. ELAS is not interested in him."

"Shall we take the revolver?"

"Don't be ridiculous."

We stepped out of the front door, downstairs. The shutters in Soso's house across the street were closed. So was the casket maker's shop and the corner store. I peered up and down Septemvriou as we reached the corner. Just a few days ago the long avenue was brimming with humanity – shouting, waving their flags, their angry placards. No one was there now. The shooting seemed to have abated. An icy wind was pushing dark clouds across the sky, kicking up dead leaves and sheets of yellowed newsprint. All the way down to Omonia, the street was flanked by lifeless grey walls, empty balconies, shuttered windows. Smoke was still curling out of the pile of rubble that once was the dreaded secret police headquarters. Where are they? I asked myself. Where are the fighters hiding? The man who shot at the British tank, the sniper who climbed up on our roof? I could hear the sound of our own footsteps on the pavement as we rushed on.

"Hurry," my father prodded. "Hurry!"

We knew that fighting around the other major police station at the end of Patission Avenue had been raging for days. Our challenge was to cross Patission as quickly as possible and hope that the noon cease-fire was observed. By now it was twelve thirty. We gasped as we reached the corner. Before us on the pavement, like a giant dead insect, lay a yellow streetcar on its side, overturned to make a barricade, its windows shattered, its wheels and underside exposed, its long power rod flung across the tracks. Behind it, in an incongruous counterpoint, stood the classic façade of the Archeological Museum tucked in among its rows of tall palms – a serene reminder of timeless values. But we were in the grip of the present. Oppressed by stifling terror, we could only feel the urgent yearning to be saved. We took a deep breath and charged across the deserted avenue.

Staying close to the walls, we hurried on looking for the next opening to get us out of the line of fire. Coils of smoke rose down the street. "The *Gheniki Asfaleia*," said my father. "Still holding on." Passing the Polytechnic, we turned left on Tositsa. Narrower streets now. More secure? The British-held zone was uphill, ahead of us. That would be Kolonaki, our old neighborhood. We had to get there before the shooting resumed. At Exarcheia Square, we turned left, then right. Piles of rubble here and there. Smoke. Acrid smell. No people. "I think it's just around that corner." Niko looked disoriented. As we turned, my mother gave a little shriek. Before us stood a man – tall, his red bandana barely visible under a black, bushy beard. He held a shiny Sten automatic. A pair of bandoliers crossed his chest.

"Pou pate?" Where are you going? A deep, surprisingly melodious voice. My father raised his arms as in surrender.

"My brother…" he stuttered, "very sick … sent for us … please." The man looked at us, let time pass. His beard parted around his mouth, he looked amused.

"Ande pighenete," he finally said. Go on.

"Thank you, thank you," we croaked. We rounded another corner and faced a miraculous sight. A long street ran straight up an incline toward a gray sky. At its base, just ahead of us, big coils of barbed wire, as tall as a man, stretched across the street. On one side behind it stood what looked like a lone British soldier. He must have been one, since he wore a beret, gaiters and a khaki uniform, and carried an automatic. We hesitated, the figure looked unreal. The soldier raised a beckoning arm. I turned back to see if the ELAS man had followed us. But no one was there. As we approached, the soldier reached to part the wire and we walked through. "Thank you, Sir," I crooned, testing my new English. "Like the gates of heaven," grinned my father as we slowly advanced up Skoufa Street toward Kolonaki Square. "Like Moses at the Red Sea."

"Where are we going?" asked my mother, stopping to catch her breath. We had raced up the street, eager to get away from the battle line.

"I was thinking …" said my father, looking this way and that. "The Krietis have a house near here, on Omirou. They may have room for us, it's a big apartment."

"What a good idea Pappi!" I was thinking of those glorious summers in Ekali and the fun I had there with the girls.

When we reached Omirou Street, my father pointed downhill at a large house.

"That's it I think. Let's hope they're here and not stuck in Ekali."

He pushed the top button next to the front door. We waited. He raised his hand again then let it slap on his forehead with a chuckle.

"How stupid. No electricity, no bell."

We pounded on the door with our fists. From above a voice shouted *"Pios einai?"* (who's there?) We looked up and heard a pleasantly surprised "Aaah!" followed by "I'm coming down to open!" When finally the door was opened, we came face to face with Tina and her father Andhros.

"Excuse us," my father smiled, uncomfortable. "We had to leave our house. Our neighborhood is in Communist hands. Just crossed the barbed wire down there. Ah …" he blurted," can we stay with you?"

"Of course, of course," said Andhros.

"Just a few days … we won't be in the way."

"We just can't offer much food …"

"We'll share, naturally …"

"Don't worry, we'll manage. It's good you got away. We hear rumors …"

"How can we thank you," said my mother. "We'll contribute whatever we can. You're wonderful to take us in like this without warning."

"It'll be only three or four days, I'm sure," added my father.

We stayed for three weeks.

During the first week fighting still raged nearby. Confined in the house, we had no idea which way the battle was going. We heard gunfire, explosions, saw smoke. ELAS could be only a few houses away. They might soon be pounding on the door below. What then? Resist? Out of the question. Hide? But where? We told our hosts about Dino's abduction. It could happen here too, we said. After all we had seen, we had heard them – right outside our house! Andhros however stayed calm. The Brits won't let us down, he assured us. He trusted Churchill's determination. After all, he stood alone against Hitler back then, and now he's winning. And he brought around Roosevelt and the Americans.

"And what about the Russians?" My father was returning to his old refrain. "Surely they'll support the Communists. They've been doing so all along, through the Comintern."

"Stalin still has his hands full up there. This is a side-show. The fact is that the British are here – here, fighting ELAS."

We felt besieged. Food supplies, already meager, were rationed. Water was hoarded in buckets, watering cans, kitchen pots, for fear that it might suddenly be cut off. At night we used a single communal candle planted on the big dining table around which we ate, conversed, played games, read. Food was heated on a *kamineto*, a small contraption fired by rubbing alcohol or benzene, with prayers that matches and fuel would last.

"Robinson Crusoe had to make do," Tina said. "How romantic that sounded. But he was stranded on a warm, fertile, island paradise. And look at us. At least we're not alone."

One day we made an amazing discovery. We found that the

phone worked, but only in a particular way: when the receiver was picked up at certain hours it "broadcast" news! That is, a male voice would read a brief bulletin of the day's events. It was a comforting surprise after days when only rumors, some quite outrageous, had reached us, fuelling our angst. But the "phone man," as we called him, raised our spirits with news that ELAS was failing in its efforts to take the city, that the British were holding on. Then one day Andhros picked up the receiver and immediately raised his hand to silence the room, bending forward to hear better.

"My God," he whispered.

"What, what?" we practically shouted, expecting some local disaster.

"It's not here …wait a minute …be quiet." He finally hung up, shaken.

"In Europe … the western front … a huge German counterattack." He sat down. "They broke through the lines in Belgium … the Americans are retreating!"

"I can't believe it," said my father. "Just yesterday it was the Germans retreating."

"It can't be more than an act of desperation. Their last breath, a death rattle."

"The Americans have been careless, too confident. It's that posturing general, Patton."

The spacious Krietis apartment could accommodate all eight of us with little discomfort. My parents and I slept fully clothed under oriental carpets on two daybeds in the large *saloni*. Although the fighting had stayed far enough away to leave the windows intact it was still unusually cold. We could see our breaths and had to rub our hands and noses to wipe away the frost. My father and I were impressed by Andhros' studio office, lined with bookshelves and dark paneling, a large desk in the middle. A number of other rooms seemed to exist further back, enough, I thought, for a separate chamber for each of the girls and their parents. "What luxury," mumbled my mother, the memory of her Maroussi hovel deeply engrained in her mind. In this milieu we whiled our days away trying to fend off boredom, seemingly safe from imminent danger, with growing optimism for the outcome. "I'd so much rather be bored than live through those days again," I told Tina. Being here was actually fun – what with three cheerful intelligent girls to keep me company, the card and backgammon games, the lively conversations and the occasional flirtatious bantering. Youth brushed away all fears – most of the time. In our cozy confinement we missed Bebe, worried about her and Toula, how they were surviving in that remote house, surrounded by snow up in Ekali in this harsh winter. And what about Stella and Tsanos alone in the little house we had shared with them, thinking it would be safer there? It was painful to imagine their crushing fear and anxiety. Happy at our own situation, we put such thoughts aside quickly.

ELAS had been making a big push to take the city but Siantos, the KKE party chief, appeared reluctant to attack the British directly. Instead he and his kapetans focused on two principal targets: the Rimini Brigade in their Ghoudhi barracks and the gendarmes in Makriyanni near the Acropolis. For reasons still unexplained though, they committed too small a force against a better trained and better armed opponent. After several days of bitter fighting, ELAS was forced to pull back. They had reached their high water mark. Soon the Rimini Brigade and others staged counter attacks, gaining ground and initiative. By then ELAS had begun to engage the British, but it was too late.

On a sunny day we decided to venture out. The girls and I bundled up and walked to nearby Kolonaki Square curious to see how the neighborhood had fared during the siege. The oblique glare of a winter solstice sun barely rose above the apartment houses around the square. My old beloved neighborhood. We wouldn't be refugees today, I thought, running from a neighborhood plagued by war and infested with vengeful mobs, had we not moved away from here five years ago, because my father feared Kolonaki was unsafe!

A small crowd was milling about, letting the warm rays penetrate their heavy clothing, breathing the open air, happy for a brief reprieve. The war was still too close for café tables and chairs to appear - essential components of Greek public life. But we knew that soon enough, as long as the sun shone and the shooting stayed safely away, the inevitable would happen: one after the other the *kafeneia* would reopen, tables and chairs would appear on the sidewalks, and blissful Athenians would once more take their seats, light up, sip their drinks, gossip and ogle each other.

Christmas would have passed like any other day except that my mother's dauntless devotion to *Weinachten* had to be vented somehow. The essential components of course were absent - the tree, the music, the food, the presents. But we had a candle, and it was reverently placed on the center of the dining table together with some pine twigs while some of the German speakers among us attempted a rendition of *"Oh Du Froehlicher."* Lotte had done it again!

"It looks like the worst is over in the Ardennes," said Andhros holding the phone to his ear. "The Germans are being pushed back."

"That's a relief."

A brief silence as his eyebrows rose. "Unbelievable," he murmured.

"What, what? Tell us."

"Are you ready for this?"

"Come on tell us!"

"You won't believe it. Winston Churchill is here ... here in Athens! Arrived last night ... with Eden and some generals. Absolutely amazing!"

On Christmas Eve in London, Churchill decided to "go see for myself." A family and children's party had been planned for that day. "After having been much reproached by the family for deserting the party," he recounts, "I motored to meet (Foreign Secretary) Eden," whose

Christmas he "also spoilt," to board the airplane that took them to Athens. On December 26 he wrote to his wife:

"We have had a fruitful day, and so far there is no need to give up hope of some important results. HMS Ajax (he spent the first night on a war ship,) is very comfortable, and one can get a view of the fighting in North Piraeus at quite short range…I went into the Embassy up that long road from Piraeus to Athens in an armored car with strong escort, (he was carrying his own gun,) and I addressed all the plucky women on Embassy staff, who have been in continued danger and discomfort for so many weeks, but are in the finest of moods. Mrs. Leeper (the Ambassador's wife) is an inspiration to them.

2. You will have read about the plot to blow up H.Q. in the Hotel Grande Bretagne. I do not think that it was for my benefit. Still, a ton of dynamite was put in sewers by extremely skilled hands and with German mechanism between the time my arrival was known and daylight. I have made friends with Archbishop, (Archbishop Dhamaskinos, who later became Regent,) and think it has been very clever to work with him as we have done, leaving the constitutional question for further treatment later.

3. The conference at Greek Foreign Office was intensely dramatic. All those haggard Greek faces round the table, and the Archbishop with his enormous hat, making him, I should think, seven feet high, whom we got to preside. The American, Russian and French Ambassadors were all very glad to be invited.

You will hear speeches on radio no doubt, or see them printed in Wednesday's papers. ELAS arrived late, three in all. Thanks were proposed, with many compliments to us for coming, by the Greek Government, and supported by ELAS representative, who added reference to Great Britain, 'our great ally' – all this with guns firing at each other not so far away.

4. After some consideration I shook ELAS delegate's hand, and it was clear from their response that they were gratified. They are the very top ones. We have now left them together, as it was a Greek show. It may break up at any moment. We shall wait for a day or two if necessary to see. At least we have done our best."

Two days later Churchill returned to London. Then in quick succession: Papandhreou resigned; the King, from his exile, reluctantly appointed the Archbishop as his regent, and in early January, General Plastiras, the vehement antimonarchist, the "Black Horseman," who in the 1922 debacle formed a Revolutionary Committee, took over the Government and had members of the previous cabinet shot, in what was clearly anticonstitutional behavior, to put it mildly, became the new Prime Minister. And all along the fighting continued until mid January, when an armistice was finally agreed upon.

⟐

"What do you think?" my mother asked my father. "Shall we try to go back? I'm suddenly worried about the house. And poor Rudi, so many days alone up there."

"I'm not sure we should go yet … there may be snipers …"

"They announced that all of Athens and Peiraias is clear," said Andhros, who probably was eager to reclaim his house. I would rather we stayed. I liked the girls, the big house, the old Kolonaki neighborhood. If only we could live here, I thought, just around the corner from school. All my friends were here. We kissed the family goodbye, thanked them for their most generous hospitality, and all promised to see each other again soon.

"Will you be going up to Ekali once this mess is over?"

"God knows what they've done to the house," replied Andhros. "There are rumors of vandalism and theft."

"I'm worried about our own house," said my father. "We left in such a hurry. Anyone could have smashed the door and gone in."

"Rudi wouldn't let them."

"He'd roll over and lick their feet."

We walked down Omirou Street carrying our little bags. I lowered my cap and raised my collar.

"Zeus must be angry at us," I complained. "Here it is mid January and no *Alkyonidhes* to warm us up."

We reached Panepistimiou and turned right toward Omonia square. A few people scurried around leaning into the wind. On our right, miraculously undamaged, stood the familiar trio of facades - Academy, University, Library – incongruous reminders of optimistic young Athens, when it was being reborn a century before, now reduced to lifeless cultural icons. As we approached Omonia the landscape quickly changed. When we came to Patission and turned right, we knew we had entered a battle zone – the scene of recent fierce combat. Puffs of grey smoke still curled up windowless, bullet-pocked, charred walls. Pavement and sidewalks were littered with debris; an evil looking foam rose out of the sewers and spread along the gutter; what seemed to be an arm lay limp on a windowsill, the body, if any, hidden inside. The stench was unbearable. Covering our noses and mouths, we proceeded, careful not to stumble on fallen masonry, blown-out doors and windows, jagged shards of glass and plaster. On the corner of Stournara Street, next to the Polytechnic, a ravaged office block was smoldering.

"That's what it was all about," said my father. "The *Gheniki Asfaleia*, the Security Police headquarters. We passed by here during the noon lull, remember?"

"The second most-hated building," I added. "Too bad they didn't blow it up too."

"Don't say that. These men saved us. They're heroes."

Further on the overturned streetcar was still lying across the avenue. We reached Kodringtonos and turned left. One look down the block and I shouted, "It's still there!"

Our steps accelerated. "I have the key, Pappi, I'm running ahead." I bounded up the stair, unlocked the door and stepped in, greeted with howls of ecstasy. I picked up the little bundle of fur, pressed him to my chest and let the long tongue slobber all over my face. "Rudi, dear boy, you're well, you survived!" By then my parents were at the door, fending off leaps of joy. "It stinks in here!" said my mother twisting her nose. "My God! Look! It's everywhere. Watch where you're stepping. At least we don't have to open windows. Plenty of icy air in here."

Mrs. Vafiadhis below told us about the marauding bands that went through the neighborhood stealing radios, refrigerators, jewelry, rugs — anything that looked precious.

"And what they couldn't take they destroyed," she said. "When they came here I held them back, told them no one here has a *Frigidaire*, just plain old ice boxes, no radios. Not worth the effort, I said. So they went next door. No one was there. Ransacked all three floors. Others went on down the street. You should see them loading horse carts, wagons, motorcycle trucks. It was an orgy for two or three days."

"I don't know how we can thank you Mrs. Vafiadhi," said my mother with her most engaging smile. "You saved our home and our little Rudi."

"Sweet fellow. Howled and whimpered the first few days, but then he gave up and we became friends. We shared whatever food I had. We managed."

Two days later my cousin Tsanos came over. "Mother asked me to come. We're desperate. No word from Father and Uncle Kostas."

His lips quivered. "We hear stories … mass graves in Peristeri … you know, near us. Mother thinks you and I should go there and see … I can't imagine … he's a good man, Uncle Niko. Never hurt anybody."

"Of course, Tsano. I'll pick you up tomorrow morning."

"I wish we had left … the way you did."

My father hugged him. "Everything will be all right," he said.

Next day my mother and I had a long wait. Usually, when someone was late, she would stand on the balcony or lean out of a window trying to coax the appearance around a street-corner of the person she was waiting for. (Whenever I was late, I would see her at the railing shaking her arm reproachfully. When both my parents stood there I knew I was in real trouble.) Today was particularly bad. We found early on that reading didn't work, at least not for long. So we tormented each other with banal conversation and trips to the balcony until we heard the key on the door. One look at my father's face and we knew that what we had feared was true.

"I need to drink something," he mumbled, going for a chair, not even taking his coat off.

"I'll make you some tea."

"No please. Do we still have some wine or that old bottle of cognac?" We sat next to him as he took a sip. She held his hand.

"They killed them, they killed them both. They were executed, at close range." He put his glass down and covered his eyes. His chest heaved as he tried to stem a sob.

"Horrible … the poor boy saw it all … his father right there … in front of him." No one spoke for a while.

"You know what?" my mother finally said between sobs.

"Yes, I know, I know …"

"If we had stayed there …"

"Or if we had stayed here …Oh my God!"

We held each other for some time, our relief almost unbearable. For a while, grief was overcome by joy.

It was a bleak morning. Tsanos and my father walked, asking directions on the way. "Oh yes, the exhumations. Down that way. You'll tell when you see the crowds." In a large open field, rows of excavated soil lay next to long shallow trenches. Men were still digging at the far end. The corpses were neatly arranged in a line parallel to the trenches. Men with notebooks were walking up and down the rows helping relatives identify victims. There were cries, sobs, screaming. Some women had thrown themselves on a body shouting, pulling at their clothes. A putrid smell filled the air. Tsanos pulled at his uncle's sleeve.

"I don't think I can do this, Uncle Niko. I feel sick."

"We have to Tsano. We came all this way. It's important. Put your handkerchief over your nose."

They walked slowly down the rows bending down each time looking for familiar features. Many of the victims had bare feet, none wore an overcoat. "They stole the overcoats and shoes," said a policeman. "And all the watches and some gold teeth." Some men still wore suits, vests and neckties. There were some women, their long hair disheveled, their skirts hoisted up, their stockings wrinkled. Tsanos suddenly moaned, "oh, oh, oh."

"Where, what?"

"I see him … over there."

He stumbled ahead, my father after him. He too recognized the broad forehead, the aquiline nose, the brown house jacket. Kostas lay next to him. One of the notebook men wrote down the names. "Shot at close range," he said. "You can see the tiny holes on the side of the head. They were executed. Only a few days ago. Just as ELAS was retreating."

Tsanos walked back with his uncle to give the news to the two widows and the children. On the way he remained silent, staring ahead. His eyes were dry.

As the days went by they learned more about the executions. Many of the victims were predictable targets: policemen, gendarmes, members of the Security Battalions and right wing gangs like Xhi, men who had overtly fought, persecuted, killed or tortured perceived Communists. But there were others. Academics. politicians, businessmen, people thought to have collaborated with the Germans or the Quisling governments or those who just opposed EAM/ELAS. Among the most wanted were retired monarchist officers and those who may have had ties with the

Metaxas dictatorship – men like Dino and my father. Some were said to have been the victims of personal grudge.

The hostages were another story. In a desperate move, as ELAS insurgents were retreating from Attica in January, they took civilian hostages with them. It is said that as many as 65,000 people were led away, among them children and the elderly. They were taken to the new ELAS headquarters in Thessaly, several hundred miles from Athens. Most hostages had no affiliation that marked them as enemies. Members of some level of the bourgeoisie, they were simply not identified with the militant Left. Seized helter-skelter, they were dragged out of their houses or picked up in the street and forced to march after surrendering their shoes and much of their clothing. In this condition, they walked for miles in freezing weather along a barren landscape with hardly any sustenance. Those who fell behind, mostly the sick and the elderly, were pulled out and shot or abandoned. Others simply succumbed from illness, hunger and exhaustion. Those who survived were eventually freed.

On February 12, a treaty between the warring parties was signed at the seaside resort of Varkiza that stipulated, among other conditions, the surrender by ELAS of all its arms. Although the Communists appeared to have done so, they actually managed to hide their best weapons and establish military camps in neighboring Yugoslavia, preparing for the second phase of the civil war that lasted from 1947 until 1949. By then the Brits had turned Greece over to the Americans who, together with the Greek Right, continued to fight the Communists in what turned out to be the first conflict of the new Cold War.

On the day of his father's funeral, Tsanos gathered some of the neighbor kids in his parents' bedroom, among them two or three teenage girls. They lay on the matrimonial bed under the cover of a large blanket. Only their heads stuck out. The movement of the blanket suggested considerable activity under it – mostly hands moving here and there, legs and torsos wiggling with abandon. I was watching from across the room wishing I could join the bacchanal. Their delirious giggles blended with the wailing sounds from the *saloni* where the rest of the family had gathered with friends and neighbors while gobbling down freshly baked sweets and cherry liqueur.

(Years later this scene came back to me as I watched a movie of a peasant funeral in the Carpathian Mountains. The body lay on a cot on the ground floor of a house surrounded by mourning, tearful relatives. They ate and drank wine. One by one they sneaked up to the second floor where there was music and laughter. The film ended with everyone dancing with abandon while downstairs the body was bouncing on the cot in rhythm with the dancers.)

Tsanos however was not indifferent and would never forget. The pain he suffered on that cold January day remained with him for the rest of his life. An avid anti-Communist, he joined the Greek Navy as an officer, choosing to serve as a doctor, a surgeon, instead of a warrior.

Toula and Bebe had been trapped in Ekali during the December uprising.

"We had no idea where Varvaressos was," said my aunt. By now she called Achileas by his surname, spit out like poison. "He abandoned us there. Probably stayed at his *studio* with God knows which floozy."

"Stop it, Mama."

"Anyway," she continued. "It was a nightmare. If it weren't for the vegetable garden, some dry beans and a jug of rancid oil left over from the summer, we would have starved. And it was brutally cold, freezing, much colder up there than Athens."

She reached for a small white box with the red numeral 'one' on it, her Papastratos cigarettes; took one out, tapped it on the table, put it to her lips, struck a match, lit it, and took a deep breath. She held the cigarette between thumb and forefinger as the smoke curled out of her nostrils and her eyes closed with pleasure. A handsome woman, black strands of unruly hair falling on her shoulders, straight out of some Greek tragedy.

"We had no idea what was happening in Athens. One day we would see British soldiers going somewhere on the highway; another day *Elasites* in open trucks and red bandanas would be rushing in the opposite direction. There was gunfire somewhere around Tatoi. Some Brits apparently were holed up in the King's palace there. Most of the time though, we would sit in the house alone, hungry, shivering, scared, dying for some news."

"It was later, in early January, when the real trouble began," said Bebe. "First there were the hostages. They were herded by here on the way to Thessaly. Hundreds, thousands of them - women and children, old people. Most of them had no shoes, no coats, no hats. Some could barely walk, would stumble, fall down, get shot. We never knew such cruelty could exist. The Germans…of course. We were an inferior race to them, like the Jews, the Gypsies, the Slavs. But Greek against Greek?!"

"After this, came the mob," continued Toula. "All that riffraff from Erithrea down the road, you know, the refugee village between Ekali and Kyfissia – misery planted in the midst of affluence. In the 'thirties they used to work as waiters, washerwomen, gardeners, toilet cleaners, pot scrubbers in the fancy hotels – the Cecil, the Aperghi and the villas of the nouveau-riche profiteers and lackeys of the Metaxas dictatorship. They would scrape and bow, while all along black bile built up inside, unbearable hatred, relieved only by the long-nurtured prospect that some day … come the revolution …"

A long drag on the cigarette produced a satisfied hiss as Toula exhaled.

"And sure enough the revolution came," she went on. "At first they restrained themselves or were restrained by EAM. That was still the early period when only the detested gendarmes and security battalions were attacked and the *Englezi* were seen as friends and allies – more or less. But then things went sour and everybody became an enemy, and the time for revenge and looting set in. They swarmed around like locusts, hordes of them. Every house, hotel, pension was invaded. They broke down doors, smashed windows, ripped curtains, overturned furniture. Back and forth on the highway they would carry whatever their arms could bear – men, women and children loaded with paintings, tablecloths, pots and pans, candle holders, toasters, china dolls, silver platters, radios, phonographs, chairs, carpets, even toilet seats. And what they could not carry by hand was loaded on carts, bicycles and those little motorcycle trucks that were everywhere during the occupation. What they couldn't take they would smash to bits. A few poor souls were found in their houses badly beaten."

"You should have seen Mama when they came to our house," interrupted Bebe. "Superb, like a Greek Goddess, like *Athena Promachos*, like a lioness defending her cubs. How dare you come in here, she bellowed. And you know Mama can out-curse any stevedore in Peireas. For a moment they hesitated – this sounded like one of their own. But then they pushed her aside and proceeded to strip the house bare. The Frigidaire was the first thing to go. We camped out in the empty house for a couple of days and then slowly walked back to Athens. The fighting was over by then."

On February 12, 1945, Winston Churchill was in Yalta conferring with Stalin and Roosevelt. He sent a telegram congratulating the parties on the signing of the Varkiza Agreement adding that he regretted not being able to stop by on his way back to England. But the Archbishop and Macmillan pressed hard, and Winston reluctantly made a detour, arriving in Athens on the 14th.

Athens was in an uproar. Churchill had come back! I rushed to Syntaghma Square along with thousands of my compatriots. Soon the plaza in front of the Monument to the Unknown Soldier was brimming with Athenians. The lovely light of a setting winter sun cast a golden glow on the old Palace rising majestically against a dark grey sky. Suddenly a loud cheer erupted as several men appeared before the columns high above the image of the fallen soldier on the wall below. There was the Archbishop, an imposing, bearded giant, his stovepipe hat and shimmering silver cross centered on the black robes. And there stood the new Prime Minister, General Plastiras, the fiery Republican revolutionary of 1922, my father's favorite nemesis, just as tall in his dark suit, his deep-set, fierce black eyes and dauntless mustache projecting the image of the unforgiving, proud soldier/statesman. Between those two, dwarfed by them, peered a roly-poly man almost comically dressed in a blue RAF uniform, looking quite pleased with himself, his right hand raised, making his familiar V sign. The crowd could barely contain itself. If they could have climbed the wall to smother him with love, they would have been up there. "Chur chill … Chur chill … Chur chill …" we all kept chanting. Faced with such enthusiasm, Winston finally decided that he had to do more. As the words came slowly out of his mouth I strained to understand. Churchill seemed to be speaking with his mouth full, in his peculiar upper class English, and I could catch only fragments of his oration. "Let no one stray from one's duty to the fatherland," he seemed to be saying. And later …"From the bottom of my heart I wish you every happiness …" Then again, "From the bottom of my heart comes the hope that Greece will take the place it deserves among the victors, the nations that suffered the most in this war … let justice prevail … let there be unity and forever reconciliation among you." He concluded with a rousing "Greece forever …Greece for all!" Whether they understood this rather hackneyed crowd-pleaser or not, Winston's exultant audience made it seem as if they did.

"He has a way with words, that old fox," my father said with grudging admiration when I recounted the event. It was only a few years ago that he spoke of the British as arrogant, snobbish, thieving Imperialists, exploiters of little countries, enemies of King Konstantin, friends of the loathsome Venizelos, guilty of having ruthlessly lured Greece into the debacle of '22 …

Communist guerrillas marching in Athens, November 1944.

ELAS andartes, Communist guerrillas in the countryside.

Napoleon Zervas, guerrilla leader.

*Winston Churchill and Archbishop Damaskinos
during the December 1944 Communist uprising in Athens.*

PICKING UP THE PIECES

S PRING 1945. THE Germans had left, and in May the war
in Europe was over. It was time to pick up the pieces and look
to the future.

Closed for almost a year, school opened again. The walk there
from my house across Athens now had a history of its own. As an
eleven year old, wearing short pants even in the coldest weather,
I crossed the deserted park in the early morning on my way to
the Deutsche Schule on Arachovis street. The War had not reached
Athens yet and the Germans were still the good ones – or so my
father kept saying, and I believed him. That tune changed when
the Wehrmacht marched in, but I stayed in the German school. I
was wearing full-fledged long pants then and thinking of lovely
Erika as I made my way through the city. When I defected to the
Makri school, the walk became longer – and more dangerous. The
Germans were still in Athens, and Greeks were openly fighting each
other in the streets.

Walking to school this spring day, I tried to tell myself that all
was well again now that the city was finally "free" - free of Germans,
free of terror, free of partisan hatred. That's what the newspapers
and radio commentators said and people wanted to believe. What I
saw and heard and felt, though, contradicted such happy thoughts.

Athenians, for one, scurried through the streets as if the Enemy's boots were pounding the pavement, the black SS banner still hung on Vassilisis Sofias. People looked drab and oppressed as they did when the *Koukouedhes* and right-wing death squads terrorized the streets and floods of red flags rallied threatening mobs. Sooty, pockmarked facades, decrepit buses and trams, smelly, unkempt streets, the whole depressing cityscape all conspired to extend and reinforce our sense of shock and emptiness. It would take a long time for such open sores to heal - wounds left by successive years of violence, dissension and suffering. Passions seethed as desperate men and women, feeling betrayed, took to the mountains to prepare for another struggle, another round of violence.

I have to leave all this, I told myself, prompted by a rage that had been growing inside me. I had read and traveled enough to know that there were better worlds beckoning. But where? With my four languages, Europe would be a natural choice. But Europe was in shambles, even France and England. That left the only option. "But is my English good enough?" I fretted. "It has to be. I have only two years, I must pick up the pace."

I was surprised to find that the kids in school were quite cheerful, happy to see each other, full of stories from the past year. Most lived in the Kolonaki district within the area that had been protected by British barbed wire and were astonished to hear of our flight and the murder of our relatives. Interesting, I thought, that the British ended up defending the neighborhoods of the wealthy, most of them supporters of the Right, while other decent people saw their houses vandalized, or were taken hostage, or ended up in a mass grave.

Back in the big classroom, the Principal, Mr. Ioanidhis, who taught ancient Greek, stood before us, a copy of Plato's Kriton in his left hand while his right hand, index finger raised, moved up and down following the tempo of his recitation. He was a tall elegant man in his sixties. His closely cropped white hair rose straight up above a gaunt, handsome face. Plato flowed out of his mouth in the lilting tones of Cyprus. After reading a sentence, he stopped and addressed a drowsy boy in the fourth row.

"Psoriadhis, please identify verb, subject and object in this sentence." Psoriadhis, who had been admiring his fingernails, was startled.

"Syghnomi?" (I beg your pardon?)

"It looks like you're dreaming again, Psoriadhis," said Mr. Ioanidhis. "I want you to parse the syntax of the sentence I've just read to you." Silence. Two female hands came up on the other side of the classroom.

"As usual, some members of the so-called weaker sex seem to be paying attention in this class," concluded Ioanidhis, turning to one of the two girls. "Yes, Miss Panayotopoulou?"

"Excuse me Sir," she said. "A number of us feel that using one of Plato's dialogues this way is, ah…wrong."

A pair of prominent white eyebrows pulled together.

"Wrong? Did I hear you say, wrong?"

"Yes… Sir. Excuse me, but we think that, not only is Plato a great philosopher but also, that his language is beautiful, almost poetic… of great literary value."

"So?" His lower lip began to tremble.

"Forgive us Sir, but we think that his prose should not be used as a platform for grammatical instruction."

There was a long moment of critical silence in the room. I felt my heart thumping.

"Well, well," Ioanidhis finally said, his head now bobbing back and forth. "Aren't we presumptuous! And who are 'we' may I ask?"

"Some of us," she whispered her head bent down.

"Speak up, young lady!" More silence. "Would any of the conspirators have the courage to identify themselves?"

The second girl slowly raised her hand. I realized that I had no choice but do the same.

"Any others?" demanded Ioanidhis. After some moments he said with a wan smile. "So we have a gang of three here. Three who think they know better. Anyone else agree with them?" No response.

"Well, let me tell you. It is because of what you call 'literary value' that we use this text. So, we continue as before and I don't want to hear any more comments. Period. Now, Psoriadhis, you still have the floor."

The new History and Art teacher offered another view. Mr. Margharitis was a small man, nattily dressed, his thin hair meticulously combed back, Fred Astaire style, his voice and gestures gentle, modulated, aristocratic. He carried a cane to assist a limp.

Traditionally, history in Greek schools was taught in shamelessly jingoistic terms - starting from the time the combative Achaians descended from somewhere up north to overrun primitive Neolithic villages and bring Civilization to the Balkan Peninsula, all the way to 1913 when King Konstantine and his father George brought back Christian Culture to lands that had suffered for centuries under the barbaric, Antichrist Ottoman yoke. Greek history was depicted as a continuous string of resplendent events that every boy and girl should salute with pride: that King Konstantine, for example, represented a direct descent from both Alexander the Great who carried Greek Culture all the way to India in the fourth century BC, conquering the barbaric Persian Empire; and that Konstantine Palaiologhos, the last Emperor of Byzantium who, in 1453, abandoned by the deceitful Papists in the West, died at the ramparts of Konstantinople defending Christianity against the rapacious, heathen Turks who originally came from lands that Alexander had conquered many centuries before. Or so it went.

Little, if nothing, was said of the fact that, to the Orthodox Church ancient Greeks were heathens, worshipers of lecherous, partying, violent Gods and Goddesses frolicking up there on Mount Olympus instead of being nailed to crosses, pierced by arrows, or hiding in catacombs to escape the Roman sword. Nor did history teachers underline such embarrassments as the alliances some Greek city states made with the Persians to fight fellow Greeks; or how the triumphs of 1913 went up in flames in Smyrna, after that same King Konstantine led his soldiers to ignominious defeat in a stupid war against the Turks in Asia Minor in the name of the Great Idea.

Who could blame the poor Greeks, vassals for centuries, for wishing to see themselves as direct descendants of Homer, Plato or Sophocles? After all, ancient Greek civilization is the envy of the world to this day, and modern Greeks want a proper share of that glory, even though the only thing connecting them is a common language and the awareness of their common land - that crusty, gnarled earth, the blue of the sea reaching out to eternity…

And what did I, a modern Greek, feel whenever I looked at the Acropolis out of my window? Or when I visited that lovely little temple on Cape Sounion? Are they more "my own," say, than Chartres, Stonehenge, or even Machu Picchu? What really belongs to me, I thought in later life, is of my own time — the books, the art, the music, and of course the architecture - Falling Water, the Salk Center, that delicious chapel in Ronchamps …

Mr. Margharitis had a different approach. "Unlike your parents, I don't want to be the one to take you by the hand to show you the world," he told us. "You should learn to make your own discoveries. Make comparisons, place things side by side and look at them. By recognizing their differences you unfold their uniqueness."

My first "serious" essay, written in meticulous calligraphy, (which came of use later, as you will see,) the finished document presented to Mr. Margharitis with two hands, like jewelry on a silk cushion, and then formally read by me to the class from the teacher's podium, compared the Greek Temple and the Gothic Cathedral — in this case the Parthenon and Notre Dame in Paris.

The tanned, scantily clad Greeks, I wrote, held their religious ceremonies within sight of the Doric peristyle with its robust, fluted columns, their calyx-shaped capitals holding the heavy entablature above. From around the *vomos*, the sacrificial altar, Athenians could look up and admire the sculpted images of the marble metopes between the triglyphs — a movie reel of tableaux depicting heroes, centaurs, maidens, warriors and gods in action - and higher up, the triangular pediment packed with more mythical doings, all in sharp chiaroscuro.

(I can't help but note that many of these stones were carted away, with Turkish complicity and Greek indifference, by the infamous Lord Elgin and are now safely displayed in gloomy light at the British Museum.)

Up North, the poor folks inside their medieval Basilica looked up as well, high up, and their hearts leapt at the sight of His magnificent works. Sheaves of stone formed slender columns that rose past fields of glass resplendent in color to branch out and shape the groin vaults of the ceiling and lead the eye forward toward the Sanctuary, to heaven, to salvation. Outside, high above the city, visible from far beyond, the massive bell towers and soaring buttresses summoned the flock with a myriad of turrets and arches, saintly, safely clad statuettes, grotesque waterspouts, convoluted tracery. "Come to me," they beckoned. "Come to the house of God. I have even more amazing wonders to show you inside."

By contrast, the hefty Mediterranean Temple, solidly rooted to the ground and ruled by quite a different God – or Goddess in this case - contained only two dark rooms inside its windowless cella walls. No service was held there and only a few attendants were allowed to enter. This was the home of Athena *Parthenos*, the virgin Goddess who gave her name to the city. Her splendid gold and ivory statue lived here in privacy, while her worshipers remained outdoors. Seen from there, the Temple stood as a decorated Object, a sculpture – to be looked at, admired and read from outside under blue, sunny skies. To be seen by me every morning from my window as I woke up.

It was spring in twentieth century Athens; the temples lay silent while churches were filled - Easter week was here again. From Palm Sunday on, priests and psaltes, the mellifluous church cantors, exercised their vocal cords for hours on end, in a fog of incense, the glow of thin yellow candles, the mournful peal of bells and the company of restless worshipers who came and went all day, their attention span only long enough to light a candle, make repeated crossing motions, listen for awhile and move on. Outside, nature was hailing spring with its own aroma and an orgy of wildflowers. Scarlet carpets of *paparounes* sprawled on empty lots replacing the *tsouknidhes*, winter's hostile green nettles, and temporarily hiding the debris and garbage dumped there. After that savage winter, spring, sweetly, hesitantly ushered in what might be some kind of normalcy.

—

"Impossible to believe," I said one evening in early May after we had turned off the radio. "They were overwhelmed by huge armies on all sides and yet they continued to fight … on their own soil … to the very end. Didn't they know months ago, even a year ago, that it was hopeless?"

"They were defending their country," said my father. "You can respect that."

"Defending? They were the aggressors, they started those wars. How can we respect that?" I was looking at him. I had to tell him what I should have said a long time ago.

"The country that gave us Schiller and Beethoven lost its bearings Pappi. They cowered under that posturing buffoon … followed him like lemmings, like sheep led to slaughter … down to the last possible day. That's what's unbelievable. A kind of mass suicide."

"They didn't want to give up … as they did in 1918."

"At least then they had the good sense to defy the Kaiser's generals and quit and stop the useless bloodshed."

"Well … it's all over now."

The day before, we had heard that Hitler and Eva Braun had blown their brains out in the bunker under the *Reichskanzlei*, and that Goebels had administered deadly poison to his six lovely children, then killed himself and his wife.

"It was only nine years ago when Mutti and I saw him in Berlin,"

I said. "The crowds were delirious. *'Der Fuehrer'*, they would call this comical man, and shout *'Sieg Heil'*. You liked him then and so did I."

"Let's not talk about it."

"Remember last year, as the Red Armies were pushing into Poland, when Tante Grete wrote to us from the Sudetenland?" She and my grandmother had been shipped there to escape the bombing. " *'Unser Adolf wird es schon schaffen,'* she wrote. Our Adolf will still get it done. Can you believe it?"

Soon the newsreels and the pictures came. The world was in shock. Nothing like this had been seen before. Attila the Hun could not have done worse, people said. In *Sineak*, the news movie theater on Panepistimiou, I got my first view of the horror. Somewhere in Bavaria American soldiers had excavated huge trenches and exhumed thousands of naked human bodies. A bulldozer was digging on one side, pushing corpses around like so many sticks. The voice-over reported that these mass graves had just been found. There were many others, it said. The film then moved on to other news – big floods in Ohio, the United Nations conference in San Francisco …

Back in the late 'thirties, we heard vague reports of so-called concentration camps in Germany, the sinister sounding *Konzentrazionslager*. "For Communists and criminals," I remember my father having said dismissively. "Serves them right." Later, during the occupation, Jackie Saltiel told us that Greek Jews were being shipped north as forced laborers. Eventually we all became preoccupied with ELAS and other internal problems, and forgot about the Jews – until now. Still, it took some time for us to learn that in the spring of 1943, nearly 50,000 Greek Jews – except for a couple of thousand, the entire Jewish population of Thessaloniki, men, women and children - were stuffed into cattle cars, taken to Birkenau and murdered. Unlike the ones I saw in the newsreel, they were incinerated, turned into ashes, disappeared.

Many years later, while traveling in Eastern Europe, Judy and I visited Auschwitz. In nearby Birkenau we came face to face with horror. A single rail-road track ran into an arch way in the center of a long brick building. On the other side – inside the camp – the track branched out into four or five tracks that continued on for about a mile. On either side stood rows of mostly ruined detention barracks. We walked to the end of the tracks where the gas and incineration chambers had been – demolished by the Germans just before the Russians came. Men, women and children, dazed, blinking and staggering after days in airless cattle cars stinking of defecation and death, were herded out toward the "showers", only to realize in the last moments of choking, screaming and piling up at the doors that they were facing death. The men who lived in the detention huts were spared as long as they had the strength to strip the bodies of clothing, jewelry and gold teeth before disposing of them. The Germans ran the camp with ruthless efficiency. Recently found photos show men and comely young women in SS uniforms sunning themselves or singing cheerfully like guests in a country resort. Nice kids, just relaxing after a hard day on the job ...

But what about the Jews my parents had befriended before the war? After hiding in our apartment, the Saltiels lay low for a while. Somehow no one betrayed them to the Gestapo and they resurfaced when the Germans left. The friendship with my parents continued for many years. Jackie survived Dora and my father. He saw my mother frequently and I met him on one of my trips – a shrunken old man, but the spirit was there and he still made Lotte laugh.

We didn't know if the Myllers and the Mordos got away until we learned that they had arrived in America a year or two earlier. A lifetime later, in a brief memoir, Liselotte Myller described their happy years in Nuremberg before the Nazis came to power, their flight to Athens and their brief time there.

"Our wonderful life in Athens came to an end when the Italians attacked Greece in October 1940. When the Germans joined them in April, it was time once again to leave behind everything we so laboriously built up from scratch. We boarded the last ship out of Piraeus and traveled in a convoy for eleven days, crisscrossing the Mediterranean to elude German dive bombers. We were attacked every day, and one of our ships was sunk. After several months in Palestine, we embarked on a freighter sailing through the Red Sea, around Cape Town, across the submarine infested Atlantic to Brazil, finally reaching New York harbor. The trip took seventy days. Here we had to start all over again. Ernst, with characteristic determination, began the tedious process of establishing himself professionally to earn a living. I had to get a job as a nurse giving enemas to a rich lady. We put the boys in a public school. In just three months Ernst passed the required English test and two medical licensing exams. He was fifty, exhausted but exhilarated. His practice grew and soon he became as esteemed as he had been in Nurnberg and Athens. In 1953 he was elected a Fellow of the American Academy of Obstetrics and Gynecology".

For the third time in twenty years, life for the Myllers was reaching a normal stride. Once again they had pulled themselves up by their bootstraps. But fate struck again with shocking cruelty. Uli, serving in Korea as a second lieutenant, was killed in an airplane crash. Four months later, Ernst succumbed, unable to live with the pain of his young son's death. Liselotte eventually remarried and my mother often saw her during her visits to New York. Rolf became an architect and started a family. We revived our friendship.

In the late forties, Peter Mordo, the son of Renato, lived alone in New York trying to make a living as a jazz guitarist. I would join him on trips to the Apollo theater in Harlem to hear the likes of Dizzie Gillespie, Lionel Hampton and Coleman Hawkins. We loved that music. But Peter was unhappy in New York. He was lonely and didn't succeed as a musician. While I was still in school he went back to Europe, to Germany of all places, married a German girl and ended up running the jazz program for the West German radio station. Many years later, I visited him, his wife and little boy in Stuttgart. The Germans were kind to him and he loved his job. He was happy.

Years after the war, when I returned to Greece and introduced my wife and one-year-old son to my father, I asked him: "Are you aware that back at that time, this child, your grandson, would have been taken, along with his mother, to Auschwitz and killed?" My father, who was enchanted with his first grandson, remained silent. Surely that connection must have occurred to him.

I was seventeen and the confusion between carnal and romantic love continued to plague me. After Kaiti, the conjunction of the two remained elusive. My mother may have contributed to this dichotomy. I still remember her covering my eyes in the dark movie theater to protect me from the sight of female nudity - *guck nicht!* - or preventing dangerous proximity to Thalia or Zouzou. There was something Bad there, she meant to tell me, or I thought she did. Eventually I was to learn that lust and love went well together. But first came the awareness that one could exist without the other and that lust had top and urgent priority over love.

In the dark days before the sexual revolution, finding a willing partner like Kaiti was rare. Seduction required special skills and time consuming effort. Masturbation provided immediate, free but incomplete satisfaction. Prostitution had its own problems, but at least there was contact with a real body. I thought I'd give it a try.

During the occupation brothels had been identified with an 'X' inside a circle stenciled on the wall next to the front door – an "out of bounds" sign meant to keep soldiers away or simply to alert the public. Brothels were licensed by the government and supposedly inspected from time to time for hygiene. I walked past one or two such signs every day on the way to and from school. I was curious and tempted. It had been a long time since Kaiti, and the Ingres girl had lost her éclat. So one day I gathered my courage and walked in. A square room was lined with chairs like a dentist's waiting room. One or two men were sitting waiting for something. I too sat down. A scantily dressed girl came out of a door and crossed the room paying no attention to us. Time passed. I began to worry that this indeed might be something other than I had expected. I had been nurturing the image, stimulated by books and movies, of half naked, delectable young women seductively lounging around in an elegant salon, some sitting on the laps of fully dressed men, others guiding their charges up a stair to a paradise of carnal delight. This was sordid by comparison – shabby and smelly. Just as I was getting ready to bolt, two women in brassieres and panties came and sat down across the room. The one with the big breasts, full lips and long hair looked interesting. What to do now? I stood up and slowly walked toward her. She was busy talking to her colleague and paid no attention. I stood in front of her and cleared my throat. She looked up at me as if annoyed by the interruption. "Are you …" I started, and then, as if calling a taxi, "Are you free?" She looked me over, turned to her friend and giggled. "He wants to suck my breasts," she said, "misses his mommy." Loud guffaws this time. I was ready to run again.

"Take your pants off," she commanded later as we sat on the side of a creaky bed. I obeyed, she gave me a condom and fell back on the mattress, her legs spread apart.

"Let's go," she ordered. Halfway through our motions she said, "what happened to you? You turned limp on me."

"I'm sorry. I don't know why …"

"Come on, try again. I haven't got all day."

I finally managed to consummate the act but not without recourse to desperate thoughts of Kaiti, Erika and even the Ingres girl.

I tried the bordello once or twice again before giving up.

Sometime later I approached my father.

"I don't know how to tell you, Pappi …"

"Tell me what?" It didn't take much to agitate my father.

"My… my penis … it feels itchy and sort of sticky."

"Oh my God! How… when … let me see." It was so embarrassing. "Did you by any chance …?"

"Yes. One of those places in Exarcheia."

My father took me to Dr. Papakonstandinou, a specialist in venereal disease, whose office and grubby cot on which I had to lie with my pants down, reminded me of the scene that caused my problem in the first place. To make things worse, or better, depending on one's point of view, Dr. Papakonstandinou was assisted by a gorgeous young nurse who casually handled my genitalia like offal about to be put on the spit for *kokoretsi*. The inevitable of course happened, provoking a girlish giggle and the doctor's admiration. "Now, there is a healthy erection," he said. "You have nothing to worry about, my boy."

And then there was Ellie.

I had resumed French lessons while continuing with English and had struck up a friendship with Ellie who sat next to me at the Academie Francaise. After class one day, I suggested that we stop down at Zonar's for a coffee.

"I can't stay very long ," she said. "My brothers want me home early."

"Your brothers?"

"My father was killed in the resistance, so Yannis and Panayotis are in charge of the house now; my mother is feeling her age."

Her clothes and manner did not suggest a Kolonaki background. Unsophisticated, one would say, a bit awkward, naïve? I found all that quite attractive. *Une fille douce.* "Bright, pretty," I thought. "But there is something in those melancholy eyes …"

We had long conversations – the meaning of life, her plans for the future; she wanted to go to the University, study languages, literature, write books, teach. Children? Not for a while. And it has to be with the right man. A man of integrity, a man who respects her, a man who will fight for the common people. How do you mean? *Oh laos,* the people, have been suppressed for too long – by the rich, the fascists, the corrupt politicians. The people need the support and leadership of honest, educated, visionary men and women. She believed that women have a role in this. Not just as housewives and child raisers. Her mouth became irresistible as the words – earnest, serious, ardent – parted her lips. I wanted to kiss her. The mind, I began to realize, made the body more desirable. Was it not like that with Kaiti? What about Erika? She had never spoken to me. Would I still want her if she opened her mouth and something dumb came out in a squeaky voice?

A few days later I asked Ellie to go to the movies. I thought I might be able to hold her hand in the dark, perhaps more. Halfway through, she let go of my hand, leaned over and whispered "I have to go."

"What? Why?"

"I'll tell you tomorrow." A quick peck on the cheek and she was gone.

"Why did you leave?" I asked the next day.

"I'm sorry. I had forgotten that I had promised my brothers to be home."

"They really keep track of you. I thought you wanted to be a free woman."

"*Touché.* But they take their paternal role seriously. They know that I have a … a friend, that's you. They're suspicious, they interrogate me about who you are, your family, your politics."

"And what do you tell them?"

"That I, ah, like you. That you are smart and serious. That you want to go to America and become a movie director."

"And my politics?"

"I really don't know much about that. You seem to share my concern for the people. Don't you?"

"Of course I do."

After a long pause she continued.

"Let me level with you. This is difficult, given the times we're in, but I have to tell you."

My mouth was getting dry.

"Go on."

"My father, our father, was a colonel in ELAS during the occupation. He was killed in Makriyanni during the December fighting with the Gendarmes. My brothers fought also. They keep a low profile now, although they're still members of EAM, secretly."

Silence. Finally she asked.

"What about you, your parents? It's very important to me."

My reply came slowly.

"Ellie ... I'm sorry... we're on the other side."

"I was afraid of that, I didn't dare think about it."

I told her about my father, his politics, our flight to Kolonaki, the discovery of my uncle's body.

" I don't want all this to come between us, Ellie. I like you very much."

Silence again.

"I like you too," she finally said. "But it is a problem. My brothers would never approve of us seeing each other. They are very angry about what has happened. Like many others they feel betrayed. If it weren't for my mother and me, they would be up in the mountains continuing the fight, as so many others are thinking of doing ... soon."

"I'm having a party on Saturday," said Anna with an enchanting smile, "can you come?"

A dark-haired beauty, her physical attributes were barely contained within the dark blue school tunic held together by a string of white buttons and a demure white collar. She wore bobby socks.

Parties presented a problem. I couldn't dance.

"Nothing to it," said Frosso at the party. "Have you had any whiskey yet?"

"I don't drink."

"Oh, Titsian, shame on you. Whiskey gives you courage and limbers the joints. Here, have some."

I took a sip of the brown liquid and screwed up my face.

"Don't tell me you've never …" taunted Frosso. "Anyway, you hold onto me like this. Not so far, a little closer. Do you know that song *'Cheek to cheek?'*"

My joints were anything but limber. Her hair tickled my nose and I could feel her breasts as she pressed against me. I could also feel the start of an erection.

"You're doing very well Titsian, bravo."

Was she laughing at my predicament? Rather pleased with herself. These well-brought-up girls, pretending to be so pure, so innocent.

"Thanks for the lesson," I told Frosso when the song thankfully ended and I turned to join the boys in the corner. I had seen them whispering and giggling, holding their cigarettes stylishly while I was dancing.

"Quite a dish, that Frosso," said Dhimis with a smirk. He was a pretty boy and a flirt. He came to class dressed to kill: jacket and tie, freshly pressed trousers and laundered white shirt, a dashing handkerchief in his breast pocket, brilliantined pompadour, perfumed and powdered. Girls fell for him, boys envied his easy, nonchalant, seductive charm.

"That was Artie Shaw you were trying to dance to out there," said Dhimis. "Good clarinet but not as good as Benny Goodman's. Have you heard *Sing Sing Sing* yet? Superb. With Gene Krupa on the drums. Goes on for twenty minutes. Makes your blood race."

"There's nothing like Glen Miller," Kratsos butted in. "We went to see *"Sun Valley"* something or other, with Tex Beneke, it was so good, couldn't resist the beat, got up and started jitterbugging in the aisle. People were shouting at us. They almost threw us out. *Meghali plaka*, what a blast."

We were obsessed with America.

Although it was Churchill and the British who kept the Communists from taking Athens, it was the Americans whom the Athenian bourgeoisie admired. The city was inundated with American products, many of which came through CARE and other relief agencies. Overnight it seemed, Greeks discovered delicacies like corned beef (fat-streaked red and white lumps of protein stuffed in slant-sided cans); Hershey bars (milk chocolate studded with almonds); graham crackers (ginger-flavored biscuits); and cellophane-wrapped slices of yellow cheese labeled 'American'. Politeness and gratitude, augmented by novelty, led people to praise these exotic imports. (But not for long. As soon as traditional Greek foodstuffs began to reenter the markets, CARE packages started to lose their attraction and preferences returned to white feta cheese, olives, freshly baked warm bread and bittersweet, dark Pavlidhis chocolate.) Nevertheless, *i Ameriki* was all the rage. To say that something was *Amerikaniko* immediately raised it to a higher level; to liken a woman to an *Amerikanidha* rendered her more desirable; to declare that someday you would like to go *stin Ameriki* was aiming for the unattainable. Jazz and jitterbugging were replacing operetta and fox trot. After the dark years of occupation when Zara Leander's contralto carried through German morale-building propaganda movies with songs like *"Ich weiss es wird noch einmal ein Wunder geschehen,"* (I know that someday a miracle will happen,) Athenians enthusiastically and indiscriminately welcomed Ginger, Betty, Clark and Ronald, Jimmy, Charlie, Groucho, Irene and the rest of the Hollywood firmament of stars, starlets and meteors. We sneaked off in the middle of the day to fall in love with Ingrid in 'Casablanca' and learn from Humphrey how to handle a cigarette, wear a trench coat and a fedora and look cool. In newsreels we saw Douglas MacArthur standing ramrod erect surrounded by soldiers and sailors on the big battleship accepting the Japanese surrender. Incredible, we said, how suddenly all was changed: first the Italians, then the Germans and now the Japanese – defeated, humiliated. The bad guys had lost, the good guys, (the Americans that is) have triumphed. How wonderful.

June 1946

The class has gathered in the Makri courtyard for a graduation photo. Seven girls and eleven boys are lined up in three rows. Artemis, Anna, Frosso and two other girls, all in summer frocks, sit demurely in the front row. Five boys plus Marianna and Zena, Dhimis' current flame, stand behind them. In the top row, on some sort of raised platform, stand the remaining six boys. I occupy the top left corner, arm-in-arm with dapper Dhimis and directly above frizzy-haired Kratsos, on whose shoulders rest my hands. All the boys wear suits and ties except three, I among them. My white, short-sleeved shirt is unbuttoned at the neck. I sport a virginal mustache as do some of the other boys. After Kratsos I seem to be the tallest. There is something opaque about my features, perhaps because you can't see my eyes behind the reflections on my glasses, nor does any particular expression show on my unsmiling face. The rest of the group looks quite cheerful, in a festive mood, as befits the occasion. We'll soon disperse. The boys will go into military service, all except for me – I'll manage to escape. (Years later, my father will pay the required fine that will allow me to return honorably to my mother-country.) Most of the boys will attend university and eventually marry, some more than once. Most girls will just marry, some of them more than once.

High School graduation June 1946. I stand at the upper left corner.

My High School class posing on Syntagma Square. I stand in the back middle.

My dear friends Vassilis and Dennis and I hiking, 1946. I still see them every year when I travel to Greece.

AMERIKI

IN THE SUMMER of 1946, shortly after my graduation, my mother and I ran into Toni Kalomeras. The son of friends of my parents, Toni had disappeared during the occupation.

"I didn't know you were here," said my mother, delighted. "I thought you had gone to America."

"I did, I did. I was there during the entire war. Went to University for a while, got drafted into the army, and now I'm here as a translator waiting to be discharged."

He was wearing a greenish U.S. Army tunic. "I'm staying with my parents up in Kyfissia on weekends. Come see us, we can talk about America." He was looking at me.

We sat in wicker chairs in the shade of a sycamore sipping coffee.

"We understand that your young man here wants to go to America," said Mrs. Kalomeras. "My Toni has so much to tell him about it. He knows it intimately."

"Now, now, Mama," interrupted Toni. "Let's not forget that much of my time was in the Army. Not a good introduction to America. But I can still help."

The best way to get to America quickly, he said, was on a student visa. I should apply immediately to some colleges and universities. Since it was too late for fall and probably spring semester, I would have to lose a year. But that was okay. Even if I went there this winter, I could use the time to improve my English, become acquainted with that wondrous new world. He would give me a list of schools.

"Don't get too excited," he warned. "It's not easy to get in, especially in one of the better schools and … don't forget, you're a distant foreigner, no chance for a personal interview, no way of knowing you other than what you reveal in your writing."

Without a typewriter, I wrote twelve letters by hand to the twelve colleges Toni and I had picked out. Since writing was the only way I could make an impression, I invented a kind of hand-numbing calligraphy that imitated the face of a typewriter, a time-consuming, boring project. But I was flying high. Each paragraph, each page, each letter became wings that lifted me up and forward and across the ocean to the land of wonders, to the rest of my life. When completed and blotted, each letter was carefully folded, stuffed in an airmail envelope that was meticulously addressed, sealed with a greedy, drawn out lick and taken to the central Post Office near Omonia Square, where it received its stamps and was gingerly slipped into the slot after being kissed and silently blessed.

—

End of summer. Most of my friends were in limbo, as I was. We knew that this was the last of youthful, irresponsible freedom. Some were waiting to go into military service, others were weighing their chances for admission to university, and a few of the girls were already engaged to be married, uncertain of the prospects ahead. There were parties as before, except that more alcohol was consumed. A sense of abandon ruled – who cares, the war is over, live it up, whoopee! When I danced with Frosso, who was engaged, she thrust her pelvis and wiggled her behind as her fiancé exchanged jokes with his pals at the bar. Most of my time though, I drifted around, waiting …

The bell rang. I rushed to the top landing. *"Ghramma apo tin Ameriki,"* (letter from America) came the mailman's familiar voice from below. On my way up the stairs I was already tearing the envelope. Elaborate Gothic letters spelled Columbia University on top of the page. "… no openings at this time…" I read, "we wish you …" I sat down on a step.

"It's only the first of twelve," my father's consoling voice came from above. "You didn't expect a yes answer from all of them?"

On Monday two more letters arrived. One put me on a waiting list.

"That's encouraging, don't you think?" said my father valiantly.

"I need a yes, not a maybe." I was despondent. Why would they risk admitting somebody they have never laid eyes on, from so far away? I had better start thinking of the University or the Polytechnic here in Athens. It was hopeless.

Three more days passed in agony. I must get out of here, I thought, I must. Thursday was a dreary day; it had been raining all night, the sidewalks were shiny and a nasty wind was blowing. Not a day for cheer. My father was reading the newspaper in the living room when he heard my screams.

"They're interested! They didn't say no!" I ran in and put the letter on his lap. "Amherst College, in the State of Massachussetts!"

"College? It's not a University?"

"Who cares, Pappi. I'll go anywhere – it's in America, that's what matters."

"Well then, let me kiss you." My father broke out in one of his now rare smiles. "I knew it, I knew you could do it."

My mother came in, put her arms around me, held me tight.

"Mein Kind," she wept, *"mein Kind."*

"No tears, Mutti, I'm not leaving yet. They still have to accept me."

Two more rejections and then …

"Pappi, I have a second possible yes, this one from a University!" I had kissed the mailman on both cheeks. "Princeton University this time, in the State of New Jersey, the one where your friend knows that French professor."

"Bravo, *paidhi mou!*"

"Listen what they say," I was translating … "'your interesting letter indicates that you have an excellent command of the English language and should have no difficulty on that score in doing the caliber of work that we require.' How about that! And there's more. 'Your handwriting indicates that you have a natural talent for Art or Architecture and deserve every consideration…' Can you believe it? Those boring hours of hand-printing every miserable word paid off after all!"

This time it was my father who embraced me. He too was in tears now. He knew that he was sending away his only child, that he would not see me again for a long time – if ever again.

"Get up, boy!"

I opened one eye. In a blur I could see the face of a man very close to my own. I grunted.

"You've got to get up!" Louder now. He shook me.

"No … dowanna." My head was splitting, a heave was coming on.

"I came down to this hellhole to bring you up on deck. You've got to get out of bed. Been here for two days. Nothing left in you anymore."

"Lemme alone."

February, and the Mediterranean was furious. After the first day the storm got to my gut and ear canals. All remnants of black bile had been discharged. Death was becoming an option. The six sailors I had been sharing the cabin with in the bowels of the *SS Puebla* had been helpful, but couldn't remove the sickening smell of engine oil, or silence the deafening, stomach-churning crash of the bow as it hit another surge. I just wanted to go to sleep – forever.

"I've got to get you to walk," said the man, "get some food in you."

What a repulsive thought. Who's this man anyway?

An hour later I was sitting in the ship's mess, my head in my hands, a plateful of something unpleasant before me. Other people seemed to be sitting at the table speaking in subdued voices in what sounded like Greek.

"You've got to put some food in your belly," said somebody. "You can't go back down there on an empty stomach. You'll die."

I remember staggering on deck supported by the same man who was sitting next to me now. Out there, I had to avert my face from the pelting, icy spray, holding onto the railing, struggling to stay on my feet, the boards under me testing my balance. Even up here I was aware of the bow crashing against another mountain of gray, menacing foam. "Keep your feet apart," the man kept shouting. "Let the movement guide your steps." And yet, I felt a strange kind of relief up there, the cold invigorating, good to be away from the stifling gloom below.

The last days in Athens had been frantic. More translations, more documents, more official stamps, more anxiety. The photograph in my new, third passport (the first without my mother) showed a bespectacled, faintly smiling, geeky youth, his black hair neatly combed sideways, his generously endowed nose, poised over an insipient moustache, had now reached its ultimate destination. In the December chill I joined a crowd of shivering hopefuls queuing up outside the American Embassy, opposite the Makri school. The Consul looked over Princeton's letter of admission and nodded. When I finally got back my passport a few days later, I found in it the magical words Student Visa written on a big, official looking United States of America stamp.

We were fortunate to find a boat that set sail the next day – before anyone could change his mind.

The gloomy, frigid air of February 19, 1947, reminded me of the day, two years before, when my parents and I fled our house and braved the ghostly streets of Athens in search of safe shelter. The memory of that time came alive again as I stood on the deck of the *Puebla* looking at Peireas, its waterfront in ruins, monuments to man's insatiable drive to kill and destroy. (But wait, another, happier memory fades in: Was it not in this same harbor that an eight-year-old boy in short pants on a sunny summer day stood on a ship like this with his young mother? They too were about to take a trip, thrilled by the prospect of the adventure that lay before them.)

Down on the quay, stood my past – a little group of dark figures, bundled in their overcoats, waving. Niko and Lotte, Toula, Stella and Tsanos. Friends were also there: Dhimis, out of character in a hat; Vassilis and Dennis, their going-away present still in my hand – a little wooden box with the image of the Parthenon carved on it and the inscription *The Big Two To Their Third*. (On one of our hikes to Mount Parnis we had baptized ourselves *The Big Three*, after the three who met in Yalta in the waning days of the War.) There were tears, hugs, kisses. "Write to us," they all asked. "Yes, yes, of course," I kept saying, impatient to get on board, afraid the ship might leave without me. As the *Puebla* pulled away I raised my arm in a final salute, my mind already elsewhere.

Naples came first, its harbor a cemetery of half-sunken hulls. While a contingent of scruffy Italian families was boarding, some of us took a walk through the once regal capital. The war had ended there three years before, yet its traces were very much in evidence, worse than Athens, I thought, and I was shocked when a group of scrawny girls, children, not older than ten, offered themselves for sex. I'm leaving all this behind, I told myself. I'm going to a world unscathed by war, a truly new world. A day later we stopped briefly in Gibraltar, one of the two pillars Heracles is said to have left behind to commemorate his tenth feat. Beyond them lay the ocean, the mysterious, briny unknown named *Okeanos* by the Greeks after one of the Titans in their mythology. Until Vasco de Gamma and the other Iberians had the courage to challenge it, the mighty Atlantic was thought to be boiling hot or inhabited by lethal monsters. Was it this threatening when they sailed into it with their wooden toy boats, I asked myself, as mountains of gray ocean exploded over the bow and the furies goaded by the God Aiolos howled in my ears.

Most of my fellow passengers were Greek sailors hired to join ships' crews in America. Others were immigrants, Greek and Italian, going for the first time or returning after the war, men and some women in their twenties and thirties. The Greeks got along well together, telling stories, playing backgammon, speculating on what lay ahead, walking back and forth on deck when the weather improved as we detoured toward the Canaries. I had developed sailors' legs waddling around in the rhythm of the ship's movement, feeling cocky. I wore the fetching brown cap I had bought at Lambropoulos' store, just for this trip, and a khaki green American army jacket, a gift from Toni. (My wife still keeps that old photograph of me over her desk. "Titsian on his way to find his beloved," she'll say. "What a poseur - but cute.") It's a sunny day, the vast Atlantic, calm at last, stretches endlessly beyond. I'm looking dreamily westward like Columbus on the Santa Maria.

"You want to take a walk?" asked Vasso one day when we were sitting in the saloon, as we did every day, fighting boredom. Vassiliki, known as Vasso by then, was a teenager from some inland village on her way to join relatives in Chicago. She laughed a lot and enjoyed insipid banter with the men. She made me feel like a snob. But she was a girl, young and rather well built.

"Why not," I said. "Toward the prow or the stern?"

"To the front."

We stopped behind a bulkhead, bracing against the wind, shivering.

"You like me?" she asked, looking at me, very close. I could smell a mixture of perfume and sweat. The girls in Athens would never ask such a question. Frosso perhaps, after a glass of whiskey. But here we were fully dressed, freezing – not the same. Still there were serious stirrings down there.

"Aha!" Vasso exclaimed in triumph, her hands on my crotch, her voice darkening. "I knew it! Yes, yes, I feel it! Let's go!"

"Go?"

"Yes, over there."

She took my gloved hand and guided me to a stack of thick coiled ropes. We climbed on top and over the coils. Inside there was a hollow, empty space, protected from the wind, cozy. She was in a hurry – lifted the army jacket, unbuckled my belt, unbuttoned my fly and, breathing heavily now, reached in and deftly pulled my underpants down.

"Aah," she exclaimed like a connoisseur about to taste an exquisite vintage wine.

"And you?" I panted, having learned about altruism from Kaiti.

"Later," she mumbled, her mouth full.

Great excitement on board. Evening, after dinner, and the *Puebla* was slowing down. Everyone was on deck, leaning over the railing, silent, eyes fixed on a long string of glistening beads suspended between starry sky and velvety ocean. As the ship glided closer, the beads turned into larger, recognizable objects spread in a wide circle around us, their reflections picking up the languid movement of the dark sea. We now began to hear the hum of the vast metropolis. Over to the right I saw some lights moving in opposing directions, in a kind of slow-motion linear ballet.

"What do you think those moving lights are over there?" I asked the man next to me.

"Cars," he said, seeming to know. "The Belt Parkway. Brooklyn."

"Like a dance, and so quiet."

It was early March. We'd been at sea for twenty days.

A polyphony of sounds woke me up the next morning. I recognized the grinding staccato of the anchor's chains, the deep baritone of the ship's horn. But there was more. Shouts, metallic clanking footsteps, other horns. I rushed to the deck to be greeted by a miracle. On a clear, brilliantly sunny morning, the *Puebla* had slid from its overnight hold in the outer bay to drop anchor in the inner harbor's center stage. Waiting for the Immigration people to board, the passengers lined the railings to relish the spectacle all around them. In a flash, the dawn approach to Venice a decade earlier came before me. That had been beautiful, a work of art. This was magnificent. That was chamber music. This was a giddy mass of brass bands on some heavenly parade. The bay was throbbing with boat traffic – ferryboats brimming with morning commuters, tug boats, freighters, ocean liners – whistling, hooting, criss-crossing this way and that. The shores to the right and left were bristling with action – cranes, smokestacks, warehouses, terminals, piers, docks, houses, sheds, shacks, ramps, bulkheads. Cars, buses, trucks, vans were tirelessly on the move, guided by invisible hands.

Seemingly afloat ahead, a bit to the left, rather smaller than expected, stood the grande dame of freedom, her raised arm holding the torch, a crown on her head, her long gown firmly planted on her podium. She was overshadowed by the sight to the right – the cluster of slender towers seeming to rise straight out of the water, reaching to the sky like secular cathedrals – the very picture I had stared at in the Eleftherouthakis encyclopedia – *"Apopsis Neas Yorkis,"* view of New York it said below. Manhattan!

"Juedisch-Kapitalistisch verseuchte Oberschicht" (Jewish-Capitalistic contaminated ruling class) read the caption in the Nazi schoolbook in the *Deutsche Schule* describing New York's population under a similar photograph. Manhattan!

"I finally set foot on American soil," I wrote to my parents two days later, like a pilgrim who had made it to the Holy Land. I missed them, and some day I might miss the country of my birth. But I was here, and for now at least I had no intention of going back. *AMERIKI !*

My passport to America.

I took this picture of devastated Peireas from the ship that took me to America, February 1947. My parents and many of my friends are among the well wishers on the quay.

To America on board the SS Puebla.

NIKO AND LOTTE

A POSTSCRIPT

I HAD BEEN hearing muffled voices behind closed doors. Once I heard my father shout, "But I haven't done anything wrong!" My mother came out wiping her eyes.

"Mutti, what's going on?"

"Nothing, nothing."

I went in. Sitting at the dining table in his familiar old house jacket, his hunched back turned to me, my father was staring at a stack of gold coins before him, his black-maned head resting on his hands. I had seen those coins before. He and my mother had been collecting them since that business with the Germans a couple of years ago. *Lires* were the real currency then and would be for many years to come. That gold had allowed us to live with some comfort during those tough years, paying for decent food, clothing, my little Kodak Retina, my new watch and, of course, my private language lessons and private schools.

"I heard you and Mutti talking … " "Something terrible is happening, Titsian,"

"Can you tell me?"

"I don't know how to say it. I'm so ashamed." I put my hand on his shoulder.

"Tell me, Pappi."

"You remember when we did that little work for the Germans. Mutti had those wholesalers in the *Aghora* supply them with vegetables …"

"I remember."

"And I managed that renovation … a kind of middle man … you understand."

We were nothing more than translators, he said, someone else would have done it, or the Germans would have just gone ahead and grabbed what they needed – without paying for it.

"And now," he went on, "now they're calling me a *dhossiloghos*, a collaborator. Can you believe it? I, a collaborator, like those in the Quisling Government during the occupation? Those who persecuted our resistance fighters? I, a patriot, a wounded officer, a man who never stole or cheated or betrayed his country like some of the fat cats running around today?"

"Are they going to put you in jail?"

Unlikely, but there was talk of a big fine.

"It'll wipe us out, we'd have to sell the land in Ekali, the one for which you and I designed our dream house. You were only fourteen then, remember?"

Other memories come back.

> *I am entering the big market hall on Athenas Street. It's a warm day.*
> *I walk through the bustle and the hawkers' shouts on my way to the*
> *rear. There, in a corner, I see my mother sitting on a chair, the hem*
> *of a flowery summer frock raised above one crossed knee, jaunty hat*
> *on coiffed brown hair, gold earrings, a cigarette held between two long*
> *fingers. Her stylish elegance stands in jarring contrast to the crates of*
> *produce piled up behind her and the three beefy men next to her. I catch*
> *the word "Wholesalers" above the shop.*
> *"O yos mou," (my son) she tells the men, and we shake hands.*
> *"These kyrii are my business partners," she explains, smiling, and they nod.*
> *As we walk out I ask "Are these the people you write the letters for?"*

"I don't want you to talk to others about this. Pappi is nervous about it."
"But you write letters for him too."
"It's not what it looks like. We're in the middle between the Greeks and the Germans. Just helping out."

And a later picture …

My mother is sitting on the bed in the maid's room above the kitchen, the bed Kaiti and I tumbled on only a few years before. She is bent over a small object, a strand of hair crossing her forehead, her hands busy with a needle and thread embroidering a flower on what looks like a little purse with a zippered top, an etui, as she calls it. She has been selling several of these each month to her friend Lilli's husband, the owner of the fancy boutique on Voukourestiou. "I get pennies for these," she says and her lips quiver. "He sells them for a fortune to those war profiteers." The Germans were gone by then. Niko had escaped jailing but not a fine. "They took all our money," my mother says. "They almost took his pension away. We barely have enough to pay for your boat to America. All I can do right now is make these stupid little bags. He just sits around looking lost." She takes a handkerchief and blows her nose. "Please don't tell anyone about it, not even Thia Toula … I'm so ashamed."

After so many years, these snippets of memory haunt me. I ask myself today, where was I when all that was happening? I was old enough to understand what was going on. Yet I find no evidence of revulsion or protest. Quite the opposite. Deference and acquiescence would better describe my condition. Like other children, I had grown up under the authority of my father's strong convictions, their unbending sense of rightness that left little room for doubt. Compared to my father, school was a sideshow. He was my primary source of knowledge, information and belief; I, his faithful acolyte. Veneration, a love born of mutual dependency, tied us together. I was his obedient, trusting progeny and he the Pygmalion, eager to protect, nurture and cultivate his creation. It should have been possible for me, as a budding man, to exercise some form of moral judgment on my own. But I was brainwashed by love. I blithely allowed myself to be imbued with my father's ethos.

To a certain extent, my father was a victim of his time and place. Given other circumstances he might have lived a different life – but not very different. His nature and disposition limited his options. Niko, I see now, was haunted by fear of potential peril. True, he went to Berlin, married a foreigner against his mother's wishes, embarked on a new career less secure than the one he left behind, and, incredibly, *willed* himself to help me go to America. Those were extraordinary acts by somebody who was not a risk-taker. It's hard for me to reconcile these opposites in him. Throughout his life, he gave frequent evidence of indecision, a weakness motivated by a deep apprehension of what lay ahead. Witness his obsession with illness. Or his reluctance to buy and own a house, something his wife longed for and urged him to do. Or to be more aggressive in his pursuit of commissions, of professional recognition. He lacked cunning, had little sense of practicality. As the years went by and success eluded him, his energy seemed to wane. The war and occupation and the stigma of collaboration added to his helplessness and fed his bitterness. Bereft of entrepreneurial talent, he would unleash his contempt on business – industrialists, merchants and all those he called "wheeler-dealers, thieves, fat cats who thrive on dishonesty and manipulation, uncultured money grabbers, arrivistes." Similar attacks were hurled at most politicians. He took the high road, thought of himself as upright, cultured, above reproach - in contrast to those others. And his contempt went beyond the crass bourgeoisie - down to the lowly laboring classes. He would become indignant if a waiter addressed him in the familiar form. His face would twist in disgust at the sound of *rebetika* – songs of the urban underworld heard in neighborhood tavernas, or a bouncy country dance like *kalamatianos*.

Instead, Niko chose Europe. Although his habits and customs in many ways were "Greek," his aspirations went abroad. Along with many of his compatriots, he considered European products and culture to be superior, a sentiment translated into a debilitating sense of national inferiority. But here again is a paradox. Yes, Greece is seen as a "lowly, poor, worthless" country – called *Psoro Kostena* by Greeks themselves, in a self-derogatory, untranslatable expression. Greeks like to feel sorry for themselves saying *tina kanoume* (what can we do?) in a kind of helpless resignation. But Niko, a chauvinist, a patriot, went along with me in the parade, shouting *Meghali Elladha*, Great Greece, the jingoist cry of those who wanted to recapture territories lost to the Turks centuries before. No resignation, no sense of inferiority there.

As we have seen, and when Niko was still a boy, Greeks divided their favor between the Anglo-French democracies on one side, and the central, Germanic, monarchist powers on the other. Quite naturally, Niko, who liked the King and disliked the British and French for wrongs they had perpetrated on Greece, ended up embracing the militarist, authoritarian Germanic culture of the central European monarchies, even though, as a young man, he didn't speak a word of German and had chosen French as a second language, as most proper Athenian kids did. (French writers remained his preferred source of relaxation. He found German literature generally ponderous and didn't like the outmoded Gothic type some books were still printed in.)

My father liked to call himself an *Ethnikistis*, a Nationalist. Communists were internationalists, therefore contemptible. Their ideology, conceived by a bearded Jew in London - of all places! - and implemented by a cadre of Slavic revolutionaries in the steppes of western Asia, was alien, repugnant. Even so, his disdain for the thieving rich did drive Niko just a bit toward the left. He found the word Socialism attractive, (but for heavens' sake not the way the Communists use it!) Now, if that word were combined with the cozier, closer-to-home 'Nationalist'… The shift from Kaiser to Fuehrer, from King to Fascist dictator, came as easily to my father as it did for the Germans.

Writing these words today has exposed an altered image of my father – an image unaffected by my dependence on him, by sentimentality, the lack of maturity. Back then, as a child and early teenager and still within the range of his powerful influence, I was not quite ready to disagree, to doubt. Such sentiments rose slowly as I began to move out of his penumbra while still living with him. Once out of it, immersed in a new, quite different environment, the gap between us widened until, when we saw each other again twelve years later, our relationship had been recast. He was no longer the teacher, and now I, once his disciple, felt empowered to argue and disagree. What remained, however, and endures in me to this day, is the profound, almost irrational love that kept me in his thrall.

After Niko's death, Lotte bought a small apartment with a lovely terrace that she filled with potted plants. She lived there quite happily with her sister Grete for a decade, and alone for another, less happily, but still content. "Can you imagine," she would boast, "all those years, when you were a boy and later, until he died, I couldn't convince your father to buy and possess his own house - and now, I did it all by myself."

As far back as I can remember she had been in awe of him. "He is such an idealist – so honest, straight," she would say when I was still living with them, trying to justify him – more to herself than to me. "People always take advantage of him." She admired his nobility, had mounted him on the proverbial pedestal, a Greek demi-god.

In later years however, the image began to tarnish. She suspected infidelities, thought of herself as no longer attractive to him. After his death, criticism grew more explicit. Yes, he was honest but he was also weak, indecisive, timid. Had he been shrewd like some of his colleagues, more lucrative projects would have come his way. Had he been as strong and aggressive as those other pushy Greeks, he would be driving a Mercedes and own a villa in Ekali. "Can you believe," she would say, "in this day and age, he never learned to drive a car?" (And neither did you, *meine* Mutti. But then again, if you had the chance you probably would – and he probably wouldn't.)

From time to time I look through photographs of my mother – as a child, a teenager, a young woman in Berlin - alone, with her mother, with Grete, with various friends and later with my father. How alive she was, how pretty, how cheerful - a young girl, happy in love, her life before her. Her rosy cheeks, her red lips seem to shine through the worn black and white prints. Even today, I feel a tug of apprehension for the risk she took, swept up in her romantic pink cloud, leaving behind family, home, country, all that was familiar, comfortable, to travel into the Unknown, innocent in her trust of the exotic stranger who was taking her away.

Pictures of Lotte in Greece: She seems to have survived the trauma. By now a young matron, shown with or without baby, with or without maid or nanny, rarely with Niko, she looks poised, confident, even alluring. In only one or two pictures she allows herself to be seen in a bathrobe, disheveled, hair unkempt, probably in shock over the rural squalor of Maroussi. But mostly we see her well-dressed and coiffed, wearing fetching hats, high heels, gloves, scarves, holding on to chic pocketbooks, posing, aware of her good looks and the value of elegant clothes and accessories. She clearly loved to have her picture taken. It wasn't easy. Each time she had to engage the services of one of the itinerant photographers who roamed the parks, streets and tourist sites. He had to set up his large box of a camera on its tripod, put his head under a big black cloth, fiddle with the lens up in front, say smile and click the shutter. Then he would fuss with some chemicals in a tiny drawer on the side of the box under the hood, insert the paper, swoosh it around and finally produce the print with a flourish.

In my desk I still keep a number of snapshots taken in Athens in the thirties with Lotte prominent in a jolly crowd of well-dressed young men and women, posing on roof tops, balconies and gardens. Smiling or laughing, she seemed to be having a very good time - the center attraction in a gathering of up-and-coming youth most of whom must have spoken at least some German. And behind them all loomed the gentle landscape of Attiki bathed in the light of a Poussin painting. It seems, after all, that things didn't turn out so badly for little Lotte. Life in her new country looks good, better than it would have been in her own. It was worth having taken that risk.

Until my puberty or so, my mother and I were deeply in love with each other. This passion eventually abated and the son's love for the mother was redefined. Her love for me remained intense, although as the years went by, and especially after Niko's and later Grete's death, it could be described better as a need, a clawing need, with complex emotional undercurrents. But while I was a boy, mine was still a pure love, even though, now that I think of it, there, too, self-interest must have played a role. "Mutti," I would say to her, "*meine* Mutti," clutching at her skirt, holding onto her long fingers, caressing her rings, tugging at her bracelets. I wanted to be picked up, to be held against that soft welcoming bosom. With Niko next to her reading or sleeping, she would take me into bed. Lying side by side, facing her, I would reach out and run a hand across her mouth, tracing the labial contours, wanting to poke a finger between the fleshy pink folds and enter, past hostile teeth, into the dark, moist, purple interior.

Unlike my father, Lotte had no intellectual pretensions. She read a novel now and then and, regularly, her weekly German picture magazines. Although she communicated well in Greek, at a day-to-day utilitarian level, her reading and writing in her second language was less than adequate. Her knowledge of current affairs came to her mostly through her husband. A dutiful wife, she cooked well, supervised the maid, mended clothes, went shopping, cared for her child. But there was much more to Lotte. Later, when I could appreciate such things, I was impressed by her elegant, effortless German prose, mostly in personal letters, but also for business, when she wrote proposals to the German authorities during the occupation and after, when she was forced to take a job writing and typing letters in German for a textile import company. It was then that I began to recognize, alas from a distance, her boundless energy and get-up-and-go. This, while my father was nurturing his hypochondria, increasingly inventing reasons for inaction, for pulling back. I should have appreciated her talents earlier when, sitting at the large dining table in the Andhreou apartment, she corrected my German compositions and handwriting and even my arithmetic homework. Instead, I was upset by her toughness, her Teutonic insistence on correctness. Then and later, I looked to my father for proper guidance, for information, for superior knowledge. As did she, for that matter. Eventually however she came around to discover her worth, to gain enough confidence and compare herself favorably with him.

The last, and best, picture of the two of us together was taken toward the end of her life. She must have been about ninety. Our heads are turned toward each other, lovingly. She looks terrific. A wool scarf is wrapped around her neck. Her hair, now a graying brown, crowns a handsome profile graced by a strong nose and her familiar melancholy smile. A beautiful woman. But it's only a brief moment. Our love affair had long since come to an end.

She once told me, with a quiver in her voice, that on his death bed Niko had whispered, *"Lotte, ich hab' dich immer geliebt."* I have always loved you.

～

Niko and Lotte during their good days of the occupation.